Regional Aesthetics

Regional Aesthetics
Mapping UK Media Cultures

Edited by

Ieuan Franklin
Bournemouth University, UK

Hugh Chignell
Bournemouth University, UK

and

Kristin Skoog
Bournemouth University, UK

palgrave
macmillan

First published 2015 by
PALGRAVE MACMILLAN

Palgrave Macmillan in the UK is an imprint of Macmillan Publishers Limited,
registered in England, company number 785998, of Houndmills, Basingstoke,
Hampshire RG21 6XS.

Palgrave Macmillan in the US is a division of St Martin's Press LLC,
175 Fifth Avenue, New York, NY 10010.

Palgrave Macmillan is the global academic imprint of the above companies
and has companies and representatives throughout the world.

Palgrave® and Macmillan® are registered trademarks in the United States,
the United Kingdom, Europe and other countries.

ISBN: 978–1–137–53282–4

This book is printed on paper suitable for recycling and made from fully
managed and sustained forest sources. Logging, pulping and manufacturing
processes are expected to conform to the environmental regulations of the
country of origin.

A catalogue record for this book is available from the British Library.

Library of Congress Cataloging-in-Publication Data

Regional aesthetics : mapping UK media cultures / edited by Ieuan Franklin,
Bournemouth University, UK ; Hugh Chignell, Bournemouth University, UK ;
Kristin Skoog, Bournemouth University, UK.
pages cm
ISBN 978–1–137–53282–4 (hardback)
1. Local mass media – Great Britain. 2. Mass media and culture – Great
Britain. I. Franklin, Ieuan, 1980– editor. II. Chignell, Hugh, editor. III. Skoog,
Kristin, 1979– editor.

P96.l622G83 2015
302.230941—dc23   2015018875

Ieuan Franklin would like to dedicate this book to the memory of Derek Allsop (1968–2014) – Northern powerhouse

Contents

Part III   Broadcasting and Belonging

Part IV   Borders, Devolution and
Contested Histories

List of Figures

Foreword

In 2006, the European Network for Cinema and Media Studies (NECS) was inaugurated at the Historical Museum in Berlin. Three years later, I organised the third NECS conference, 'Locating Media', at Lund University, Sweden. The results had profound effects on the scholarly work in Lund, not least on the anthology *Regional Aesthetics: Locating Swedish Media* (2010), which gathered some of the NECS presentations about Sweden. Last year, I learnt that media historians at Bournemouth University had initiated a volume with similar perspectives on the British media. And after reading this exciting volume, I am now convinced that national perspectives on relations between space, place and media will continue to constitute a significant research area for many years to come. Our global and glocal ways of living have led to an increased general interest in the regional, local and individual.

In addition the inward-looking, almost centripetal, tendencies of domestic national media across the world have exposed the invariable need for historical and comparative perspectives on these matters across borders geographically, mentally and medially. As expected, however, there are of course risks connected to such research. Even though we never intended to publish a Swedish volume with nationalistic tendencies back in 2010, we soon realised that to some foreign readers our concentration on domestic vernacular media made the book seem stripped of critical perspectives on nationalism. Now, I am not in any way suggesting that the same is true with regard to the new British anthology – on the contrary. Rather, the point is that we should never underestimate the nationalistic aspects of regional and local media or, for that matter, of regional and local media studies. For these and several other reasons, *Regional Aesthetics: Mapping UK Media Cultures* constitutes a timely collection of sharp analyses that skilfully reveal the complex and entangled nature of regional and local media cultures in the UK. It offers new, thought-provoking insights into a century of British media culture with obvious domestic relevance, but which certainly also will prove useful for future research in many different areas, disciplines and nations.

Mats Jönsson
Lund University, 5 March 2015

Acknowledgements

First and foremost, we would like to thank all of the authors of this collection, some of whom we met for the first time when we invited them to deliver 'work in progress' papers at an 'authors' meeting' at Bournemouth University on 6 September 2013. This meeting was an opportunity not only to give feedback on each other's work, but also to discuss the project as a whole, and so our vision of the book was very much influenced by the thoughts of our authors. We would like to acknowledge the support of Mats Jönsson and Patrik Lundell of Lund University, who both encouraged us to write this book and provided the initial inspiration for it, in the form of the Swedish *Regional Aesthetics* collection (edited by Erik Hedling, Olof Hedling and Mats Jönsson). To this end we would also like to thank all the authors who contributed to that collection.

Many of the chapters in our collection are notable for their use of archival research, and we would like to thank various archives and their staff, and acknowledge the use of their materials, particularly: BBC Written Archives, BBC Northern Ireland Community Archive, the Media Archive for Central England (MACE) and Ulster Television (UTV).

Notes on Contributors

Peter Atkinson is Course Leader in Film and Media at the University of Central Lancashire. He has produced academic work on the role of broadcasting and the Beatles in the emergent myth of Liverpool 1958–1964, on Abbey Road Studios, tourists and Beatles' heritage, and on verse-film juxtaposition in TV documentary.

Hugh Chignell is Professor of Media History and Director of the Centre for Media History at Bournemouth University. He is a chair of the UK Radio Archives Advisory Committee. His published research is mainly on radio history, including news, current affairs and radio drama.

Kris Erickson is Lord Kelvin Adam Smith Research Fellow in Social Sciences at the University of Glasgow. He holds a PhD in Human Geography from the University of Washington in Seattle, where he studied online hacker communities. His current research investigates the intellectual property status of amateur cultural production, in particular recombinatory expressions such as parody, remix and fan work.

David Forrest is Lecturer in Film Studies at the School of English, University of Sheffield. His research focuses mainly on social realism in film and television, and his upcoming book (written with Sue Vice) is a study of South Yorkshire writer Barry Hines.

Ieuan Franklin is Lecturer in Film and Media at Wiltshire College, Salisbury and Bournemouth University. His PhD explored the relationship between oral history and radio broadcasting in the UK. Between 2010 and 2014 he worked as a research assistant on the AHRC-funded 'Channel 4 and British Film Culture' project at the University of Portsmouth.

Ken Griffin is a freelance postdoctoral media researcher who specialises in regional television, media historiography and archival silences. He is currently working with Ulster University on a project focused on preserving interstitial material, which is partly funded by the Broadcasting Authority of Ireland.

Mary Irwin is Lecturer in Media at Northumbria University. She specialises in television studies with particular interests in television history, television comedy and drama, and genre and gender. She has published widely in the areas of historical and contemporary television and is currently writing a monograph: *Love Wars: Television Romantic Comedy*.

Gloria Khamkar is a doctoral researcher at Bournemouth University, examining the 'Evolution of Asian Radio Broadcasting in England'. She works as a part-time radio lecturer at the University of West London, and presents a radio show at Southampton's Asian community radio station, Unity101.1FM.

Heather Norris Nicholson is a visiting research fellow at the Centre for Visual and Oral History Research at the University of Huddersfield. Her publications on identity, representation and amateur visual culture include *Amateur Film: Meaning and Practice, 1927–77* (2012), and she is currently co-writing a book on women amateur filmmakers.

Daryl Perrins is Senior Lecturer in Film Studies at the Cardiff School of Creative and Cultural Industries, University of South Wales. He is also a PhD candidate at Royal Holloway College, University of London. His post-graduate research centres on the representation of the Welsh working class in film and television.

Mandy Powell is Research Fellow in Media, Communications and Performing Arts at Queen Margaret University in Edinburgh. Previously she was a researcher at the University of London working on a three-year ESRC-funded project: Developing Media Literacy; she has published on media education and media literacy. Her current research interest is in practice communities with a specific focus on the production of educational film in the UK.

Simon Gwyn Roberts is Senior Lecturer in Journalism and Media at the University of Chester, and Deputy Head of the Media Department. His research interests include the relationship between the news media and political devolution, and the role of online media in the communication strategies of minorities.

Julie E. Robinson completed her PhD in Regional Television History at the University of Leicester in 2014. Her research project, funded by an AHRC Collaborative Doctoral Award, considered the history of ITV regional programming in the Midlands based on the ATV/Central Independent Television collection held at the Media Archive for Central England. She is currently working in academic services development for the University of Warwick Library.

Dafydd Sills-Jones is Lecturer in Media Production Cultures at Aberystwyth University. His research interests include media production studies, including television documentary in the UK and Scandinavian cinematic documentary. Before becoming an academic he worked in the media-production industries for ten years.

Kristin Skoog is Lecturer in Media Theory at Bournemouth University, where she is also Assistant Director of the Centre for Media History. Her research focus is centred around twentieth-century radio and media history and, in particular, women's radio and reconstruction in post-war Britain and Europe.

Sue Vice is Professor of English Literature at the University of Sheffield. She has written on such topics as the work of Jack Rosenthal and Claude Lanzmann, and her most recent book is *Textual Deceptions* (2014), a study of literary hoaxes and false memoirs.

Introduction

Ieuan Franklin

In recent years there has been evidence across the humanities disciplines of a growing awareness of the relevance of space and geography, often referred to as a 'spatial turn'. This has been assisted by new geo-mapping technologies and the productive relationships between locative media and local narrative or testimony (for instance, oral, urban and social history), that have received some attention from scholars of new media. In recent years a fertile set of dialogues have also emerged between literary studies and cultural geography, 'in which the valences of space and place are open to processes of contestation and reimagining' (book description, in Alexander and Cooper, 2013).

The relevance of space and geography in relation to UK media, and particularly UK media history, has hitherto (and by comparison) remained largely unexplored, due in part to the prevailing interest in the discursive formation or ideological mediation of national and globalised – rather than regional – identity through the (typically centralised) mass media. Arguably, such work has also been subject to a historicism that privileges time over space. Broadly speaking, there is a need for a historically *and* spatially based approach to the chronicling of the interactions amongst media producers, 'users' (or viewers and listeners) and places, equivalent to such developments mentioned above. Current work on locative media and the network society risks overlooking historical precursors – forms of 'vernacular' media that explore and exemplify the interrelationships between media, culture and locale. Tina Askanius has remarked:

> The insistent focus in contemporary social theory on concepts such as mobility, de-territorialization, networks, flow and the abstraction of space brought about by digital information and communication technology shouldn't make us lose sight of the continued importance

of place-based practices and discourses for the production of culture. (Askanius, 2010: 342)

The edited collection *Regional Aesthetics: Locating Swedish Media* (see foreword), in which Askanius's remarks appear, has made a modest but significant contribution to the 'spatial turn'. The brief, but highly descriptive, chapters in this Swedish anthology deal with a diversity of forms of media (film, television, print media, travel writing and new media, amongst others) and 'navigate us through a variety of media landscapes' (Hedling et al., 2010: 9). This collection is conscious of both geography and history and provides a kaleidoscopic view of Swedish culture. Our own edited collection is partly inspired by the example set by this book, and aims to map out, through detailed but accessible and concise case studies, some key historical representations of 'regional aesthetics' by the UK media, thus providing a set of coordinates for learning and for future research.

Another Swedish influence was the geographer Torsten Hägerstrand, who in the 1950s and 1960s pioneered the study of spatial diffusion – the movement of new ideas, products and services over time and throughout geographic space. In a world connected by instant communications and integrated into an international economy, 'one's sense of place might seem to matter less than ever before..., in terms of ideas, news, and the production and exchange of goods and services' (Mahoney and Katz, 2008: x). Yet, as the chapters in this book attest, region and place have come to be even more intrinsic to people's sense of self due to the disorienting and dislocating effects of this rapid cultural diffusion. It is then only a small step to the disavowal of the '*discourse* of globalization and the narratives it dictates' (Askanius, 2010, emphasis in original) to which local identities are being subjected, and/or the reinforcement or development of a regionalist ethos; 'a cultural effort which attempts to endow a specific region with all that is unconsciously its own' (E. W. Martin, quoted in Baker, 1950: 19). Our sense is that Hägerstrand had an early understanding of this, particularly apparent in an article he published in 1986 titled 'Decentralization and radio broadcasting: on the "possibility space" of a communication technology', which is a useful text for any scholar concerned with local, regional or vernacular forms of media. In the article, Hägerstrand distinguishes between two key principles of human integration and sociability: the *territorial* and the *functional* modes.

> In the territorial mode of integration *nearness* is the supreme category and therefore thinking, loyalty and acting become highly

place-bound. Conflicts arise across geographical boundaries between neighbouring groups. In the functional mode of integration, on the other hand, similarity is the supreme category. Thinking, loyalty and action become of a 'non-place' kind and unite what is similar in function over wide geographical areas. Critical boundaries emerge between interest groups, whether these are made of up of subsets of the population or of professionals in competing sectors. (Hägerstrand, 1986: 8)

Hägerstrand goes on to outline how, until the advent of rapid industrialisation in the second half of the twentieth century, Sweden had been a largely agrarian and *territorial* society based around face-to-face communication. Since 1945, Hägerstrand argues, the *functional* mode of organisation developed globally, but to an exceptionally high degree in Sweden (10). Although Hägerstrand acknowledges that no one mode is ever completely predominant in any given society (there is a balance), he notes that the electronic media (in comparison, e.g., to local and regional newspapers in the Swedish example) have a heavy bias towards the functional.

More broadly, Hägerstrand's article can be seen as a call for the reassertion of territorial integration into a society predominantly organised along functional lines, through the development and cultivation of local and regional media. This is by no means easily achieved, given the concentration of media ownership, the unidirectional and centrifugal flows of broadcasting and their restriction to what he terms 'a limited class of communication leaders'. But several suggestions are made by Hägerstrand at the level of broadcast content, including the possibility of the integration of oral history and regional broadcasting, which 'offers a great opportunity to establish a widespread tradition of collecting (and preserving) accounts about times past' (25). Hägerstrand advocates not a reactionary or nostalgic 'withdrawal to the museum realm', but a strengthening of the role of the media in balancing old and new cultural elements and 'increasing consciousness of place' (25).

All of the chapters in this collection likewise display keen attention to the ways in which media (particularly local, regional and grass-roots forms) can increase consciousness of place, whether this means film (feature films, amateur film and educational film); novels; television (drama, comedy, documentary and educational series); music, radio and digital media. Collectively, these chapters build up a concept of regional aesthetics, interrogating the 'relationships between the immanent qualities of certain representations and the locations they were either received in, produced at, or depict' (Hedling et al., 2010: 13).

The structure and content of the book

All the chapters in this collection are interested in the idea of self-identification or self-definition through regional aesthetics, and they pay close attention to the generation of meaning and identity through localised cultural processes that operate in spite of, or in resistance to, globalisation. As Heather Norris Nicholson writes in her chapter about amateur film and other 'vernacular media' in Yorkshire, which opens this collection, '[if] globalisation erodes local culture and produces more homogenised spaces and lives (Cresswell, 2006: 8), the particularities of place and individual experience offer reassurance and direction' (18). The book's first section, in which Nicholson's chapter appears, is entitled *Living on Location,* and concerns the way in which filmic and narrative imagery can document, shape and mediate the meanings and perceptions of place over time.

Predominantly concerning roots, memory, class, mediation and a regional 'poetics', this section covers a wide range of creative forms, including art, theatre, radio, literature, film (amateur, feature and documentary) and television. The first chapter starts with a local film night at the Holmfirth Film Festival, in the Pennine hills of Yorkshire, where Heather Norris Nicholson considers how different representations of the area contribute to a local aesthetic. The chapter includes analysis of the BBC comedy series *Last of the Summer Wine,* the early films of James Bamforth and the extraordinary output of Wylbert Kemp; barber, writer, poet, playwright and painter, amongst other things. Norris Nicholson convincingly argues for the place of the amateur producer in our understanding of a unique and rich local culture.

Daryl Perrins examines three competing versions of Wales: Welsh Wales, English Wales, and American Wales. Various films have provided very different representations of Wales, including, most famously, John Ford's *How Green Was My Valley* (1941), but also the first Welsh language 'talkie', *Y Chwarelwr/The Quarryman* (1935), and Paul Rotha's documentary, *Eastern Valley* (1937). In these films, industrialisation, especially coal mining, is depicted either as dystopian and inhuman, or tied to a more positive expression of Welsh radicalism, chiefly depending on whether the Welsh community is represented and defined as *y gwerin* (the folk), or as working class. Darryl Perrins' chapter is concerned with the way in which 'outsiders' have constructed a version of Wales influenced by external beliefs and ideology, often as a rural 'Arcadia' despoiled by industrialisation. In exploring what he terms landscape as 'national redoubt' (42), Perrins provides an excellent survey of cinematic representations of the Welsh valleys, influenced by art history and cultural geography. Through the incorporation of the indigenous *Y Chwarelwr/ The Quarryman* and left-leaning 'outsider' documentaries like *Today We Live* and *Eastern Valley* (both 1937), Perrins makes a convincing case that the tension between the pastoral and the industrial (characterising Wales as a place of contradictions), which has frequently been a central motif in cinematic representations of the valleys, long precedes the 'watershed moment' of *How Green Was My Valley*.

The chapter by David Forrest and Sue Vice is also concerned with coal mining communities and the tension, not just between pastoral and industrial, but also between the working and middle classes. Their chapter explores two pairings of texts; two television plays known collectively as *The Price of Coal* (1977) directed by Ken Loach and written by Barry Hines, and the novels *A Northern Clemency* (Philip Hensher, 2008) and *GB84* (David Peace, 2004), all of which build up, in their careful attention to the social texture of life in the South Yorkshire region in the 1980s, what they term a 'poetics of the North'. Forrest and Vice here employ Bakhtin's notion of the 'chronotope', which can be described as a unit of analysis for assessing the aesthetic construction of space in literary texts via 'spatial and temporal indicators' (55).

The decision by Vice and Forrest to employ a cross-media approach is reinforced by the way in which the chosen texts, themselves, blur the boundaries between visual and literary media and their supposedly medium-specific tropes. In the case of the Barry Hines television plays, this is largely due to the intertwining of visual and verbal effects. The plays cleverly incorporate symbolic motifs into the vernacular language of their characters, all related to the imminence of danger and concerning the attenuated nature of light, sight, foresight and future prospects, both in relation to mining as an industry and to the pit itself. In the case of the pair of novels about the 1984–1985 miners' strike, there is another kind of intertwining: with the inclusion of both direct (from the perspective of a lead character) and mediated witnessing (e.g., descriptions of television news), the strike is presented as a series of images and media fragments that are constructed and narrated within both a national and regional iconography.

The next section, entitled 'Urban Subcultures and Structures of Feeling' examines the city as a depository of memory and experience, exploring aspects of everyday life and popular culture in Manchester, Glasgow and

London. Several chapters make use of Raymond Williams's concept of the 'structure of feeling' to uncover and describe the lived experience of a particular time and place. It begins with Peter Atkinson's chapter on Manchester and The Smiths, which explores the iconic status of the 1980s indie band through a historical prism that sheds light on Manchester as a site of artistic independence and radical cultural production, particularly in theatre, radio and music. In doing so, Atkinson establishes a surprising, original and productive connection between Morrissey, lead singer of The Smiths, and Ewan MacColl, the folk singer whose talents encompassed activity in all of the fields of cultural production referred to above. Both men aligned themselves at key junctures in their musical careers with a distinctive regional aesthetic, and were strongly influenced by female artists active in reflecting this aesthetic via radical strands of theatre, radio, film and music: Joan Littlewood and Peggy Seeger in the case of MacColl, who was married to both; and Shelagh Delaney (who sent Littlewood her first play, *A Taste of Honey*, which was first produced by Theatre Workshop in 1958) and Kirsty MacColl (Ewan's daughter), in the case of Morrissey. Both outspoken singers grew up in Salford as working class autodidacts, and quickly developed left-wing political sympathies. As Atkinson suggests, especially in the context of the politically charged and polarised eras in which they produced their first work (MacColl in the 1930s, Morrissey in the 1980s), both songsmiths can be regarded as highly individual pioneers and exemplars of what Mark E. Smith (leader of the Mancunian post-punk group, The Fall) has coined 'prole art threat'.

Mary Irwin's chapter centres on televisual representations of Glasgow, a city that like Manchester is also often noted for its 'edginess', dialect, music and humour. Unfortunately, as Irwin observes, Glasgow remains 'consistently poorly served and little understood by national broadcasters', meaning that the city is 'frequently and lazily deployed as cultural shorthand for the most violent and deprived of UK communities' (93). In other words, the cultural shorthand determines that edginess equates to violence, and dialect equates to 'belligerent incomprehensibility' (93). Irwin's chapter is concerned with a BBC Scotland comedy series that, by contrast, presents a racy but nuanced and affectionate view of the city. *Still Game* (broadcast between 2002 and 2007) was set on the fictional Craiglang housing estate on the outskirts of Glasgow, and it revolved around pensioners Jack Jarvis and Victor McDade and their friends and enemies on the estate. As Irwin observes, the cast and writers' own specific social, cultural and *familial* heritage as post-war working class Glaswegians is 'reanimated' through this series, which combines mischievous humour with genuine nostalgia and affection for the places, icons and tight-knit communities of Glasgow – communities that have been lost or irrevocably altered with the dislocating and disorienting social changes of the post-war era. At the same time the series is not merely nostalgic; it presents a modern-day Glasgow distinct from the 'edgy' or 'grimy' Glasgow we have seen in many film and television representations; Glasgow here is full of green spaces and is 'refashioning a post-industrial future from the industrial past' (100).

It is perhaps Kris Erickson's chapter in this collection that best embodies Massey's concept of 'places as processes', composed of social relations (Massey, 1991). Influenced by situationist theory, the chapter examines the affordances of certain London-themed mobile apps in mapping out new topographies or virtual depictions of present-day London. In doing so Erickson devises a highly original methodology for analysing mobile apps, influenced by situationist Attila Kotányi's quasi-empirical idea of assessing societies on the basis of their capacity to generate new encounters. For the situationists, the encounter encapsulates 'authentic connections between individuals as well as their surroundings, in opposition to the routinised interactions that characterised most of life in the modern city' (114). Erickson's methodology, applied to several case studies of mobile apps, points the way towards future potential research directions, as does the concept of 'anonymised geolocative matchmaking' (113) via mobile apps. Exploring the 'politics of technologically mediated urban mobility' (106), Erickson's chapter is characterised by a vital concern about how every aspect of our lives is influenced and surveilled by an information economy and a physical architecture that have authoritarian, hierarchical and repressive structures, implications and effects. In this context, situationist strategies based on psychogeography and the unplanned encounter offer a potential means of resistance, and Erickson implies that pursuing such strategies through geolocative mobile technologies (whether consciously or unconsciously) offers political opportunities to transform, in the words of the artist Stephen Willats, 'the object-based determinism of our contemporary culture [into] a counter consciousness of self-organisation based on people' (quoted in Kelly, 1997).

The third section, entitled 'Broadcasting and Belonging in an Era of Media Scarcity', focuses on attempts to give representation in British broadcasting to places and communities of various kinds, whether local, regional or sub-regional groupings (e.g., Bodmin in Cornwall; the Black Country of the Midlands); an ethnicity or diaspora (in the case of local radio services for the Asian community in Leicester), or a small nation (in the case of the 'national region' of Wales). The section is organised in chronological fashion, with each chapter dealing with a different time period and with a different media organisation or sector, from BBC West Region radio in the immediate post-war era (Franklin), to ITV programming about the Black Country between the 1960s and the 1980s (Robinson), to BBC Local Radio in Leicester in the 1960s and 1970s (Khamkar), and finally to the work of Welsh independent production company Teleiesyn for the Welsh Fourth Channel S4C in the 1980s and 1990s (Sills-Jones).

Franklin's chapter explores the post-war output of the BBC West Region, which, aside from its renowned status as founder of the BBC's acclaimed Natural History Unit, has received surprisingly scant attention from historians and scholars, despite having also pioneered hugely successful and long-running programmes, such as *Any Questions* (1948–) and *The Archers* (1951–). Indeed, Franklin notes that there has also been a neglect of the post-war period of BBC regional broadcasting, as compared to broadcasting in the inter-war period. Franklin's particular focus is on the early work of the radio producer, Brandon Acton-Bond, best known for producing the fondly remembered serial, *At the Luscombes*, and for his radio and television adaptations of Thomas Hardy. Acton-Bond's early work included several radio features that featured extensive use of voices and sounds captured on disc-cutting machines at a time when recording and editing such 'actuality' was a difficult and time-consuming business. These features were longitudinal studies of a tiny community (Bodmin Moor, in Cornwall) and relied on close cooperation with that community. Franklin contends that through incorporation of commonplace social rituals in these geographically pinpointed programmes, Acton-Bond was endeavouring to create both a microcosm of the West Country region, and what might be termed a parochial 'calendar in sound'.

All chapters deal to some extent with the incorporation of vernacular culture in media; particularly Julie Robinson's, which takes us to the English Black Country, an area of the Midlands lying immediately to the west of Birmingham. This industrial region is associated with heavy industries like chain- and nail-making, and is a place where a unique and colourful culture has developed. Black Country pursuits included dog breeding and dog fighting, its dialect and humour long distinctive and vital. The representation of the Black Country on ITV programmes from the 1960s to the 1980s, most notably *Gi It Some 'Ommer*, embraced a rich and distinctive cultural heritage in an unusually performative style of documentary.

The chapters in this section are, to varying extents, also concerned with efforts to overcome 'democratic deficits' in media networks and media representation; to increase diversity, or to, in Raymond Williams' words, 'disperse the control of communications, and truly open the channels of participation' (1989: 30). This is especially true of Gloria Khamkar's chapter, which uses interviews and archival material to build a history of the development of BBC Local Radio programming for the Asian community in Leicester, in the East Midlands. The patterns of migration and settlement in Britain during the 1960s and 1970s had an impact on both the local and the media landscape of this area (and of Britain as a whole). In fact, Khamkar provides a useful account of the transition from programming *for* the Asian community to programming *by* the Asian community, and also the augmentation of what in this context is sometimes known as the *orientation function* of broadcasting (providing information about local services, etc.) with indigenous entertainment (e.g., Bollywood and Bhangra music) and the *connective function* of broadcasting – connecting immigrants to news and events in their home country (for an example of the use of these terms, see Matsaganis et al., 2010: 58).

The narrative of regional revival is then concluded by Dafydd Sills-Jones; his chapter looks at the launch of Channel 4 and S4C (in 1981–1982), and the attendant growth of small independent production companies and film and video workshops, developments which, in the words of David Morley and Kevin Robins, 'succoured real hopes and anticipations for the deconcentration, decentralisation and democratisation of the audiovisual industries' (1999: 343). Unfortunately these hopes were largely dashed for reasons that Dafydd Sills-Jones systematically explores and explains in his chapter. Sills-Jones tells the story of the acclaimed Welsh independent production company, Teliesyn, which – between 1981 and 2002 – produced work for S4C, BBC Wales and HTV (the Independent Television franchise area in Wales and the West of England, now known as ITV Wales and West). Teliesyn were run as a cooperative and had a 'horizontal' management structure that encouraged maximum participation, both in terms of the running of the cooperative and the germination of programme ideas. Sills-Jones's chapter adeptly captures the changes in the television industry landscape in the 'post-classical' era following the launch of Channel 4 (in 1982); from the somewhat anarchic growth of small independent companies and workshops, to a more commercially driven consolidated and transnational independent broadcast media sector in which the smaller companies died out or were absorbed by 'super-indies'. Teliesyn shared the cooperative structure and radical ethos of the film and video workshops, but it was staffed by programme-makers who had experience working in public service and commercial television: for a significant period of time it was able to successfully 'weather the storm' of these changes. As Sills-Jones explains, this was largely due to their imaginative and innovative output, which was regionally specific and informed by the feminist movement and the grassroots 'history from below' approach associated with scholars like E. P. Thompson.

The final section of the book is entitled 'Borders, Devolution and Contested Histories'. The opening chapter of this section, by Chignell, develops some of the issues raised around the relationship between regional broadcasting, vernacular culture and democratisation in the previous section; and it also introduces the final section's engagement with borders and with contested histories. In the chapter, Chignell chronicles the key political, thematic and creative tendencies and preoccupations of Sam Hanna Bell's prolific radio career at the BBC Belfast. Bell, a novelist, short story writer and playwright, as well as a radio producer and broadcaster, was a man of many talents and of socialist convictions. In retrospect it is surprising that Bell gained employment and sustained such a long career at the BBC Northern Ireland, which was conservative in its tendencies, had very close ties with the Stormont government, and was extremely wary of provoking the ire of the unionist majority. One key factor that played in Bell's favour was that regionalism became something of an 'officially sanctioned ideology' under Andrew Stewart, who arrived at the station in 1948. Bell was empowered to pursue his belief in the need to document rural dialects, folklore, folk song and other forms of vernacular culture, the broadcasting of which Bell clearly hoped would circumvent religious and political animosities in the focus on shared heritage. However, Chignell also takes a critical view by pointing out that whilst Bell's programmes were subversive insofar as they refused to divorce Ulster from its history as a Gaelic province, and refused to distinguish between people on the basis of creed, ethnicity and class, they stopped short of criticising (or even acknowledging) the partition of Ireland and thus challenging the status quo.

Sam Hanna Bell was a regular contributor to BBC schools broadcasting in Northern Ireland, often writing and narrating radio scripts that were influenced by his own Ulster Scots heritage. To this end, for teachers and pupils alike, Bell's input in schools broadcasting (and that of the poets and writers whose careers he fostered) perhaps helped to bring history to life while playing a small part in mitigating the religious and social divisions in the province – divisions that were reflected in, and exacerbated by, the divided school system. The state, under the control of the pro-British Protestant majority, funded schools for Protestants, while Catholics had to make do with voluntary, largely unfunded education. The historical 'narratives' taught in schools were directly affected by this polarisation, with Northern Ireland's Ministry for Education seeking to promote the region's identity as part of the United Kingdom, and discouraging any references within the classroom to long-standing historical and cultural ties between Northern Ireland and the rest of the island (198). Ken Griffin's chapter describes the early work of the pioneering educator and broadcaster, Rex Cathcart, in commercial television in Northern Ireland, and his attempts to ameliorate this situation in a more pragmatic and organised manner as compared to Bell, with his poetic and somewhat idealistic approach. From the late 1960s Cathcart made programmes that were distinctive in their attempts to combine geography and history and to correct or avoid the omissions and distortions that had often characterised previous programming made in alignment with a Unionist view of Northern Ireland. Cathcart used schools programmes to present 'Ulster' as part of the whole island of Ireland and not just a British outpost.

Mandy Powell also focuses on the use of media in education; in this case the use of the educational film in Scotland. In charting the considerable policy networks that developed in Scotland to promote the use of the 'educational film'– particularly between the 1930s and 1950s – Mandy Powell's chapter makes a complex and incisive argument about the contribution made by educationalists, filmmakers and policymakers to administrative devolution in Scotland. Powell's painstaking archival research uncovers the considerable linkages between education policy and film policy in regards to the exposure of young people to forms of cinema in Scotland; Powell charts the confluence between 'jurisdictions, national institutions, local networks and policy arenas in a converged media environment' (224) many decades before the idea of 'media convergence' was even conceptualised. The considerable body of practice and evidence built up around the use of the educational films in schools became an area of cultural policy in which Scotland could assert its distinctiveness and particularity. Therefore, according to Powell, it represented a cultural precipitant for political devolution. Such conjunctures underline the lack of historical awareness in the separation of oversight of media and communications (oversight of which remained with Westminster) and of culture (which was devolved to the Scottish Parliament), following the 1998 devolution settlement. Of course, this is a highly topical issue given the 2014 independence referendum and current possibilities and uncertainties surrounding the future regulatory framework for the media in Scotland.

Simon Gwyn Roberts's chapter provides a useful point of comparison between the Scottish and Welsh media post-devolution landscapes, with particular attention to newspapers. Although Scottish newspaper sales have suffered in the downturn, Welsh newspapers face a more existential state of crisis, as, according to Roberts, there is 'no real tradition of a Welsh national press to draw on and the majority of newspaper readers [are] dependent on London-based publications' (230–231). The uneven nature of the media ecology in Wales, and the uneven spread of Welsh language acquisition and use, have led to the exclusion of some areas of Wales in terms of, for example, journalistic coverage and fictional or documentary representations on television. Whilst S4C has a decentralist approach, it predominantly serves Welsh-speaking communities and, tellingly, there is not one independent television production company in the (predominantly English-speaking) north-east of Wales. Roberts deploys a cross-media approach (examining long-established local newspapers from Wales' north-eastern border with northern England, and a short-lived Welsh S4C TV comedy) to demonstrate the significant omissions and compromises that have characterised representations of the north-eastern Welsh county of Flintshire. Roberts identifies this county as being not just geographically, but also culturally and politically, peripheral and marginal, given its lack of attention from the Welsh media. The attempt of the S4C television programme *Mostyn Fflint n'aye* to depict the county and its culture through the medium of the Welsh language and the dialect of Flintshire was a rare and innovative exception, but, in fact, the series was produced by a Cardiff-based company and did not run to a second series.

Roberts' historical case study of the newspaper coverage of the Mold riots in the 1860s (from archives of the *Flintshire Observer* and the *Chester Chronicle*) perfectly exemplifies the tensions and negotiation involved in simultaneously upholding a political ideology and attempting to cater to a specific local or regional audience. In turning his attention to their current-day descendants, Roberts identifies a tendency to avoid engaging either fully or meaningfully with either regional specificity or with how the region has adapted to the new devolutionary political realities. Roberts suggests that, were they were to 'grasp the nettle' in this manner, such newspapers could potentially foster an interest in political issues amongst their readership whilst asserting their own distinctiveness – something of a 'survival strategy' in a competitive marketplace in which the future of local and regional newspapers is threatened by the Internet.

Roberts and Powell both appear to agree that the major constitutional changes achieved through the gradual processes of devolution in Scotland and Wales have not been matched by a realignment of the UK media. This provides a suitably topical note on which to conclude this introduction, as well as an opportunity to underline the fact that – to paraphrase the Swedish *Regional Aesthetics* collection (Hedling et al., 2010: 11) – although predominantly historical in outlook, all these chapters have been exclusively written and revised with the themes and concerns of the present collection in mind, and therefore have been conceived during a period in British history marked by major debates and shifts in geopolitical affiliation.

References

Alexander, N. and Cooper, D. (eds.) (2013) *Poetry and Geography: Space and Place in Post-war Poetry*. 1st edition (Liverpool: Liverpool University Press).

Askanius, T. (2010) Video Activism 2.0: Space, Place and Audiovisual Imagery. In E. Hedling, O. Hedling, and M. Jönsson (eds) *Regional Aesthetics: Locating Swedish Media* (Stockholm: National Library of Sweden), 337–358.

Baker, D. V. (1950) *Britain Discovers Herself* (London: C. Johnson).

Cresswell, T. (2006) *Place: A Short Introduction* (Oxford: Blackwell).

Hägerstrand, T. (1986) 'Decentralization and Radio Broadcasting: On the 'Possibility Space' of a Communication Technology', *European Journal of Communication*, Vol. 1, No. 1, 7–26.

Hedling, E., Hedling, O. and Jönsson, M. (2010) Mapping the Regional: An Introductory Note. In O. Hedling, E. Hedling, and M. Jönsson (eds) *Regional Aesthetics: Locating Swedish Media* (Stockholm: National Library of Sweden), 9–19.

Kelly, J. (1997) Stephen Willats: Art, Ethnography and Social Change. *Variant*, (4). Available at: http://www.variant.org.uk/4texts/Jane_Kelly.html (Accessed 18 March 2015).

Lee, M. (1997) Relocating Location: Cultural Geography, the Specificity of Place and the City Habitus. In J. McGuigan (ed.) *Cultural Methodologies* (London: SAGE Publications Ltd), 126–142.

Mahoney, T. R. and Katz, W. J. (2008) *Regionalism and the Humanities* (Lincoln: University of Nebraska Press).

Massey, D. B. (1991) 'A Global Sense of Place', *Marxism Today*, Vol. 35, No. 6, 24–29.

Matsaganis, M. D., Katz, V. S. and Ball-Rokeach, S. J. (2010) *Understanding Ethnic Media: Producers, Consumers, and Societies* (California: SAGE).

Morley, D. and Robins, K. (1999) Reimagined Communities? New Media, New Possibilities. In H. Mackay and T. O'Sullivan (eds) *The Media Reader: Continuity and Transformation* (London: SAGE), 336–352.

Williams, R. (1989) *Resources of Hope: Culture, Democracy, Socialism* (London: Verso).

Part I
Living on Location

1

Living on Location: Amateur Creativity and Negotiating a Sense of Place in Yorkshire

Heather Norris Nicholson

Introduction

Fenella the Tiger launched the local film night at Holmfirth Film Festival in 2013. At the outbreak of World War II, a circus family returned to the South Pennine market town from their South African tour with a tiger cub that became a household pet and familiar sight on its daily walks. Memories of Fenella sparked various collaborative creative projects, including work by an arts-reminiscence group, Sharing Memories, and a local musician, which culminated in archive footage accompanied by a children's performance of music and songs at the film's showing.[1] An audience member later wrote, 'What a good idea to have the children's song in the same programme as the old films – you would be reaching their parents and ensuring the history of the area is passed on to future generations'.[2] The comment highlights the value of narrative within local culture and how, 'stories retold keep a place and its community in touch with its past' (Clifford, 2011: 1).

As Fenella's exotic tale – and taking part in its retelling – engages another generation, these memories become embedded fragments of shared experience and local lore that connect individual lives to a particular place. For Holmfirth – long associated with the television comedy series *Last of the Summer Wine* and the even-earlier production of Bamforth's saucy postcards with their dated risky innuendos and clichéd images – local film nights open ways to reclaim other aspects of the valley's history and character. Framed by the local film night, this chapter charts how connecting festival viewers with imagery opens fresh ways to explore and understand how a locality's changing identity has contemporary relevance.

Apart from *Fenella*, the May evening programme comprised other archive discoveries sourced from a distant regional film archive, including *Market Day* by Wylbert Kemp (1904–1990), one of the valley's earliest amateur film-makers, who immersed himself in capturing local life, as is discussed later. Additional, informally acquired, footage was screened, too, reflecting the festival's wide perspective and its reliance upon imagination and individual effort. The format was well-practised: humorous and familiar scenes by cine-enthusiasts, interspersed with YouTube downloads, and the previous year's best entries to the young filmmakers' competition.

Such events typify the localism sustained and encouraged by small-town film festivals and seem far removed from the British Film Institute's (BFI) wish to bring quality films and build cinema audiences in under-served areas.[3] Other programmed festival events often fulfil those goals and excel in bringing international releases, little-known gems of different genres, and opportunities for large-screen watching of classics. Interspersed between 'hands off' local issue films that oppose corporate greed and development threats, overall film content mirrors the complexities, overlaps and messiness of the global cultural economy. It reflects how the flows and influences of mass-mediated images, ideas, values, life styles and goods intersect with our own daily lives, as discussed by Appadurai (2000) and Marijke de Valck (2007). Local film nights, in contrast, sustain their appeal via their narrower focus on sharing visual material that has significance through immediacy. However mundane and ordinary, local content's familiarity and recognisability has value, especially when watched publicly. This is not comforting nostalgic time-travel; rather, these occasions help to bind the instabilities of change and impermanence into longer historical narratives that compensate for, and validate, the brevity of individual lives. As globalisation erodes local culture and produces more homogenised spaces and lives (Cresswell, 2006: 8), the particularities of place and individual experience offer reassurance and direction. In exploring what Lippard (1997: 6) calls the 'lure of the local', we discover subjectivities and attachments that are concerned with belonging, stability and identity. These affective qualities are relevant in understanding how local film nights foster regional aesthetic sensibilities through linking audiences with specific kinds of visual heritage. With detailed reference to the amateur output of Wylbert Kemp and the wider portrayal of the Holme Valley in early cinema history and *Last of the Summer Wine*, this chapter explores how culture, history and identity contribute to the dynamics of mediating local distinctiveness and intermesh with wider narratives of change.

Defining place

Holmfirth, a small market town in West Yorkshire, is the quintessential valley-bottom settlement of the Southern Pennines. It typifies what regional tourism promoters call Pennine Yorkshire: a riverside cluster of buildings, still predominately in the local slate and grit stone – with some later additions in brick and contemporary materials – that gives way to a vast enclosure landscape of fields, drystone walls and outlying hamlets interspersed with plunging ravines cloaked in deciduous woodland. Scattered farms dot marginal grazing lands that open to moorlands, reservoirs and communication masts. Undeniably wild at its margins, its core settlement and the intermingling of mill conversions, semi-derelict industrial sites and commuter homes along the valley floor, all point to the locality's shift from its former woollen traditions and textile heritage. This hybrid urban/rural character is pervasive: sheepdog trials, a mountain-rescue group and beagle hunt coexist with civic, cultural, sport and other activities.

Plurality permeates administrative classification, too; in drawing up landscape-character area profiles – essentially, an assessment tool for planning and land-management decisions – Natural England, the advisory body for the government's Department for Environment, Food and Rural Affairs, uses three designations to cover natural and cultural landscapes in the Holme Valley.[4] Indicators used to assess the tranquillity of the English countryside, currently being undertaken by the Campaign to Protect Rural England, also identify the valley's apparent contradictions: nine out of ten key qualities associated with tranquil places feature along with eight factors that detract from that sense of peace and well-being.[5]

Reliant mainly on visual distinctiveness, such objective exercises omit the depth and shifting nature of mediated meaning over time and disallow the coexistence of multiple perspectives. Common Ground, an environmental campaign group, encourages more intimate responses in identifying what is special about a place (Clifford, 2011: 24). Its 'ABC approach' reveals a locality's unique fingerprint through an alphabetical assemblage of word associations that 'levels and reshuffles everything' as it juxtaposes different place attributes and personal meanings (Clifford and King, 2006, cited in Schofield et al., 2011: 24–25). Attachment, memory, emotion, history and story interplay with other sensory responses and articulate a 'genius locii' rooted in agency and authorship. Such subjective 'situated knowledge' shaped by local understanding and experience (Haraway, 1988) transcends definitions that may neutralise, sanitise or oversimplify and de-politicise place identity. Identities of places, like people, are composite, unevenly shaped by different processes; relational, dynamic and contingent. The valley, like any other locality, is simultaneously different places – real, imagined and invented; like the communities of interest groups within it, the valley is experienced, constructed, maintained, negotiated and revised endlessly. The annual kaleidoscopic representation of daily routines and familiar scenes and themes via local film nights unashamedly celebrates that particularity and rebuts standardisation. These eclectic programmes offer alternative ways of seeing. They offer a place and an occasion in which local people and visitors may claim, reappraise or simply encounter earlier – and arguably more interesting – identities.

As with many regional identities, scenery, weather, dialect, humour and food probably inform many people's sense of Yorkshire when the region is seen from a distance. Such attributes construct a regional aesthetic and reputation that oversimplifies and stereotypes, yet remains recognisable in its mix of pride, resilience and playful self-deprecation. For over 35 years (1973–2010), the BBC comedy, *Last of the Summer Wine*, helped to brand an English region using landscapes and lives that focused on Holmfirth and the Holme Valley (Betton, 2005: 22, 153). Claimed to be Britain's longest-running comedy programme, and generating its own critical and popular press, its central duo of characters, together with their relationships with other local valley 'folk', brought generic notions of Yorkshire identity and northernness to viewers worldwide (Jenkins and Pigram, 2004: 242; Chaplin, 1994: 128).

As the series' audiences changed over time, it spawned other productions that were set and filmed nearby and elsewhere in Yorkshire for which popular success also relied upon the distinctive textures of scenery and clichés of local life. A media-based tourism emerged that helped to offset the valley's economic decline during the seventies and eighties, and as production teams sought different locations, paid opportunities emerged for locals, including playing extras and offering domestic interiors or parking. Acceptance, expediency and complicity occurred, but novelty prompted local interest and brought enjoyment, too. Despite some ambivalence about receiving such attention and rebranding, the residents of Holmfirth and the surrounding villages seemed to accommodate the media presence and share ownership of an imposed identity. Places named after key settings in the series – Sid's Cafe, Nora Batty's House and Compo's Fish and Chip Shop – still remain part of the local townscape, even though the sitcom-inspired tourism has lessened. Indeed, the altered geographies of media production employ more transferable notions of time and place. Tropes of windswept ruggedness in the valley's recent uses as a film location include the BBC's 'visceral and authentic' 2014 remake of Daphne du Maurier's Cornish tale, *Jamaica Inn* (1936) as well as the 2014 mini-series, *Remember Me.*[6]

Holmfirth, not Hollywood?

Comic characters, broad Yorkshire dialects and tall tales are deep-rooted elements of the valley's identity. While the rapid expansion of popular print media during the nineteenth century is often associated with the nationalisation of English culture, its promotion of regional distinctiveness – via newspapers, almanacs, regional writing and printed ephemera – reinforced notions of local pride and self-promotion (Marshall, 2011). The exceptionalism and self-perpetuation of Yorkshireness found its county equivalents in other places (as discussed elsewhere in this volume). Since Holmfirth was at the forefront of pioneering visual media activity during the formative years between about 1895 and 1908, it is not surprising to find that notions of local character also foregrounded in early cinematic activity. Established tropes of local humour and identity combined with new media novelty in two brief intense periods of locally focused film production.

James Bamforth (1842–1911) started his photographic portrait studio in Holmfirth ca.1870 and expanded into lucrative lantern-slide production during the next decade, then into postcard design. In the late 1890s, Bamforth and Company made an experimental shift into film (Brown, 2005: 256). Established skills in set design, camera work, and using 'life models' were transferred, first from making magic-lantern slides, to making scenic romantic postcards with accompanying verses of popular sentimental songs.[7]

Bamforth's move into producing short comic melodramas on film with musical accompaniment was a key development within the music-hall tradition of northern slapstick comedy (Toulmin et al., 2004). The company offered an employment alternative to the valley's mills, and local people already familiar with work as models found fresh opportunities to feature in Bamforth's earliest films, shot using local places and landscapes.[8]

Seeing the familiar, and the visibility of the working class, were part of early cinema's novelty (Gunning, 2004: 53). Recognising Holmfirth's neighbours and locations and playing extras were variants of the 'see yourself' audience appeal of the urban factory-gate, park and crowded

Figure 1 'My Irish Molly! O!' No. 2, from the 1905–1906 season series of illustrated 'life model' postcards based on popular pantomime songs, produced by Bamforth and Co., Holmfirth

Source: Reproduced from *The Caxton Magazine/The British Stationer*, January 1906, p. 11. Courtesy of Kirklees Museums and Galleries.

street scenes being made by Mitchell and Kenyon and other contemporaries (Toulmin and Loiperdinger, 2005: 7).

According to Doel (2008: 91) some early commentators on film lamented the absence of landscape. Bamforth's sense of place is evident even where action focuses on a park bench, a fence or a train; background fields and stone walls feature in *Catching the Milk Thief* (1899) and *Boys Sliding* (1900).[9]

The company's later film production phase (1913–1918) coincided with the opening of Holmfirth's first purpose-built cinema building

Figure 2 'How the "life models" are taken'

Source: Original caption from *The Caxton Magazine/The British Stationer*, January 1906, p. 7. Courtesy of Kirklees Museums and Galleries. (Bamforth and Co.'s extensive studios were a few minutes' walk from the Kemp's home and family business in the centre of Holmfirth and ideally placed for Wylbert Kemp's first job after leaving school.)

in 1913 (Riley, 2006: 19), and local people increasingly worked with diverse professional performers.[10] Film locations included parks and local beauty spots now submerged by the creation of reservoirs. A long-time resident recalled how, at Hope Bank Pleasure Grounds and Gardens (now an informal community arts venue), Freddie Bullock and Shiner, two local stars, had to stand up in a boat and have a fight. The boat rocked dangerously, and Freddie called out: 'Howd on Shiner, yo' gret fooil. Thar're going to have me in t'watter'.[11]

As both stars had instructions to push the other out of the boat, the resultant struggle that landed both men in the lake was precisely the visual effect sought by the film director.[12] For valley residents, such tales about known people probably added to audience enjoyment and helped to bind silent film production with local lore. Spectacle and surprise were plentiful, but in this 'cinema of attraction' (Gunning, 1998: 266), viewers' interest went beyond evocations of urban modernity. Cinema had its origins in urban centres, but some audiences (and participants) came from areas like the Holme Valley, where a rural lifestyle and

Figure 3   James Bamforth demonstrating 'I only want an hour's notice to illustrate any song on the market' to magazine representative (with notebook), cited in *The Caxton Magazine/The British Stationer*, January 1906, p. 3

Source: Courtesy of Kirklees Museums and Galleries. The propped-up sign suggests the company's recent move into new premises that expanded space for painting backdrops and storing props.

economy persisted. Bamforth's productions, like the variety formats in which they were often exhibited, illustrate how early film-makers and exhibitors found ingenious ways to 'stitch themselves' into 'the fabric of everyday life' (Kember, 2009: 213–214; see also Fullerton, 2005: 3). Place-recognition (Johnson, 2010: 24) and Holmfirth's rural–urban mix, itself, seem to be part of the visual appeal. Symbols of rural life (*The Would-Be Conjuror*, 1900) occur among more caricatured and less place-specific characters borrowed freely from other films and sources: young lovers, gossiping neighbours, as well as a policeman, nurse or tramp.[13] Bamforth's work thus highlights early cinema's capacity for comic pastiche that could engage viewers via big themes and grand gestures coupled with localism.

Myth-making recurs in popular explanations for the end of local film production: '[B]ut for the 1914–18 war, Holmfirth might have become a second Hollywood' (Williams, 1975: 174). Plausible reasons for Bamforth's decline include wartime shortages in materials; a reduced labour supply as the war continued and casualties grew in number; and an expansion of postcard production that continued as peacetime travel opportunities grew. Later scholarship points to the fickle nature of public interest in early moving images and how, as its novelty lessened, film 'slipped down the order of attractions and disappeared entirely in some places' (Bottomore, 1996, cited in Doel, 2008: 90). However, in a characteristically jokey acceptance of missed opportunities and 'making do', poor local weather and having 'too little sun' finds wide acceptance as the cause for Holmfirth's cinematic eclipse.[14] Like the films and their characters, such tales are recycled and embellished over time.

Retelling stories about Bamforth's place in local and media history reinforces rootedness, particularly when a shared public past interweaves with more private memories, as when someone identifies a Victorian-era boy throwing snowballs on film at his grandfather.[15] Vernacular creativity thrives on such processes, which help to sustain, enact and even revitalise local culture and identity. Thus Bamforth's visible legacy is a single blue wall plaque, but an invisible network of personal links bind past and present into longer narratives that maintain a strong sense of regional aesthetic, cultural production and local affiliation. The shaping of that collective 'social imaginary' (Noyes, 1995: 471) via local residents' memories evokes a sense of 'topophilia' (Yi-Fi Tuan, 1974) that is based on the affective link between place and people. An 'inhabited community' rather than Benedict Anderson's 'imagined community' (1991) is traceable through the valley's media history and identity formation, and the life of Wylbert Kemp, a former valley resident, exemplifies how amateur creativity further negotiates local place identity through later modernity.

A man of the valley

Like others of his generation, Wylbert Kemp found Bamforth's an exciting alternative to mill work or entering a family business. Leaving school at 13 with an art prize, his apprenticeship seemed ideal but, within two years, Kemp had joined his father in the family's barber shop and, apart from service in the RAF during World War II, he remained a barber until retirement. He became a member of the Holmfirth Board of Trade, the Rotary Club, organised a town shopping festival and expanded the family hairdressing business after his father died. Repairing umbrellas and informal chiropody work in pre-National Health Service days were sidelines as Kemp involved himself increasingly in local commercial and civic life. Listening to people as he worked, however, sustained his imagination and sparked his wish to record local voices and stories.[16]

For over 40 years, Kemp captured facets of valley life in prose, poetry and plays. The vibrant amateur dramatic culture of the interwar period meant there were many performers, audiences and small publishers willing to encourage local performances and drama festivals. Over the years, Kemp brought together enthusiastic amateur actors under many different names, sometimes just for a single production. One of his early plays, dating to 1933, was performed by the Wylbert Kemp Players in a travelling-wagon format, using a box set built on the back of a small truck and presented to standing audiences at different venues in the valley. After writing the dialect comedies, *Old Broth, A Tooth for a Tooth* and *Joe Badger's Een*, Kemp had another of his early one-act plays, *Comfortable Like*, aired on BBC North Region in March 1936. It was produced by James Gregson, a fellow local playwright and theatre enthusiast, who went on to become a leading figure in the development of the BBC Leeds Studio.[17] A post-war upsurge of academic interest in folklore and dialect studies at the University of Leeds,[18] and the university's proximity to the studios, provided Kemp with other opportunities to give talks and recite his poetry in *The North Countryman* series in the early 1960s.[19] More of Kemp's work featured during the 1970s on *Local Colour*, a series dedicated to local stories and poetry. He gave his final Leeds radio interview in 1987. Kemp's involvement may be seen as part of Gregson's wider BBC legacy in developing distinctive regional broadcasting output.[20]

Kemp's ear for local anecdote and his self-taught interest in history sustained his own involvement in amateur theatre. Like other writers promoted by small, independent publishing houses, Kemp perpetuated the dialect play, a distinctive genre of nineteenth-century regional expression that was still widely in repertoire in the mid-twentieth century. Writing about *Smoke in the Valley*, Kemp's three-act 'drama of the Industrial Revolution' broadcast on World Radio Theatre Australia in 1949,[21] one critic in *The Stage* wrote: 'The characters are allowed to speak with native wit and shrewdness that makes for very good comedy'.[22] Addressing a regional audience, the *Yorkshire Post* proudly claimed that the play 'must rank with the best plays yet written about the grim but romantic story of how the West Riding came to clothe the world'.[23]

In the early 1960s, a professional production at the Oldham Coliseum of *Bill o' Jacks*, a play based on an unresolved murder set on the local moors in 1832, attracted the Lord Chamberlain's censure.[24] Public performance was licensed subject to amendments negotiated with the theatre manager: the milder dialect phrases 'you', 'und' and 't' tail-end' replaced Kemp's use of the word 'arse' but retained its comic effect. One critic wrote: 'The dialogue which is lively and colourful with the feel of the people is also occasionally Rabelaisian but honest and packed with historical detail made theatrically stimulating'. The first amateur and professional productions coincided with early press coverage of the Moors murders (committed by Myra Hindley and Ian Brady), which were later investigated in the nearby uplands. Kemp took the cast by coach to shoot atmospheric publicity photographs at the desolate sites associated with the lonely inn where his play's brutal killings occurred. An amateur revival of the play was staged when the 'Yorkshire Ripper' serial murders again brought regional notoriety and public disquiet about the moors beyond Kemp's beloved valley. Crime writers in any genre know the close link between community and mystery. This was (and is) no easy place to love: seeking out the significance of localities discloses not just dismal weather and grim grit-stone landscapes but also the deaths and hardships that recur throughout the wider region's history.

As scriptwriter, set designer, sound engineer (using reel-to-reel equipment to create sound effects, record music and make audio recordings of different works), director and occasional performer Kemp was involved in local amateur theatre for decades. He welcomed 'incomers' to the valley who recall that getting the dialect right was an important aspect of Kemp's sense of authenticity.[25] He encouraged school leavers to join the local drama group, bridged gaps between older and younger members and championed productions and fellow writing enthusiasts by setting up his own small publishing business. The impact of earlier industrial change ('and the inevitable repercussions between master and worker'),[26] and the juxtaposition of rural and urban influences (as seen in set, plot, character details and language) provided material for much of his writing.

Kemp's role as custodian of local knowledge grew after retirement. Writing to Huddersfield Library, he recalled that Bamforth's indoor filming occurred 'in the top storey of their works in a glazed room known as the model room...(so-called)...because the photographs of the actors (models) were taken there and later in the art department, were superimposed on the setting whatever it might be'.[27] He remembered outdoor shooting, too: 'in the village street, woods and field, using local characters who were always prepared to "star" for a pint or two. The local band was often called in, and as they were a thirsty lot, production expenses mounted'. Kemp's radio broadcasts gave further impetus to preserve 'local legends and stories of local characters who in the early days of this century – made up the rich patterns of our village life'; and his illustrated anthology of prose and verse was published locally in 1987. As with *Pratty Flowers*, a large-scale community pageant in 1980, Kemp's commitment to documenting the vernacular and ordinariness of valley life intensified as wider social, economic and cultural changes occurred. As he sought to record such expressive culture for future generations, and visited local care homes for the elderly with his recorded stories, Kemp seemed to recognise the impending loss of a distinctive regional aesthetic. He also noted with gentle irony that broadcast media had renewed interest in regional accents even as 'dialect ha(d) almost been eliminated by the BBC'.

Attempts to capture the valley's ambivalent visual character in painting and sketches started after Kemp's retirement. For fifteen years, he explored topography, scenic views and built form in line drawings and water colours, and he produced many miniatures painted painstakingly on ivory piano keys or inside glass bottles. Mills, chimneys, cottage rooftops and washing lines, as well as distant skylines and landmarks recur in these tiny cameos. Kemp also painted outside, inspired in his use of watercolours and handling of light by Ashley Jackson, a professional artist who came to live and teach in the valley. Kemp's hand-tinted ink sketches on gift cards, postcards, programmes and local publications reinforced the memory of disappearing familiar scenes. His pictorialism framed remnants of the valley's built heritage and reproduced townscape views recalled from his own infancy. Kemp's prints and originals sold readily at local art festivals and elsewhere: inadvertently, his own mix of rustic and industrial nostalgia, local knowledge and sense of the picturesque helped to define and refine a place identity and valley aesthetic that suited both the urban professionals opting for commutable semi-rural and country living, and the tourism and heritage industries of later twentieth-century Britain.

As Kemp's involvement in local business and civic life grew, he purchased a car, a typewriter and also a single-lens Dekko cine camera. During the 1930s, he and a local doctor became active amateur filmmakers within the valley and for over 20 years, Kemp made films for himself and his family. Although Kemp later used Standard 8mm for recording holidays and chronicling aspects of the valley's life in colour, attention here focuses on *Market Day*, one of his earliest films. *Market Day* won the first annual club trophy at the newly set up Holmfirth Camera Club although, due to Kemp's RAF military service, the cup stayed within the family home until 1945. Shot in different locations and exhibiting the simple visual tricks with light, titling and subject matter that were then popular with cine enthusiasts (Norris Nicholson, 2012), this 9.5 mm film exemplifies the early amateur's love of local subject matter. It also highlights how amateur film invokes different meanings when brought out of archival obscurity and exhibited to a socially diverse audience.

Inscribing meaning

Market Day passed into archival care when Wylbert Kemp died in 1990. The film's transfer for public viewing at Holmfirth Film Festival brings this discussion full circle, and this final section considers some of its implications for understanding how regional aesthetics evolve and retain significance. For Kemp's relations, the night spent with locals watching the grainy imagery projected on a large screen was a public reconnection with private material that had not been seen since the family projector had ceased to work many decades earlier. For his grand-children and other audience members, its interest was more historical curiosity. Filmed possibly with his firstborn son in mind, the opening scenes record haymaking and other seasonal outdoor activities in upland settings. A trick sequence, which prompted much audience laughter, shows one cow repeatedly entering and leaving two cottage doorways. The film traces the journey to market, how animals misbehave, the auction and clearing up at the end of the day. Kemp records the hill farmers and homesteaders as they manage their unruly livestock, nego-tiate business deals and leave with new purchases or unsold animals. Close-ups capture expressions, and the dress codes of onlookers, dealers and other participants. Captions identity some people – including the auctioneer – while names on vehicles and adjacent buildings offer local connections.

Accompanied by recorded sounds of cine projection, modern festival viewing of archive material is rarely silent. *Market Day's* screening was no exception. Audience members were attentive, predisposed to laugh, perhaps due to popular television's treatment of home movies. People responded to the evidential appeal of early amateur cinema and the cine enthusiast's self-appointed role as visual story-teller (Norris Nicholson, 2012). Audible whispers of 'I remember that', occurred as older viewers spotted clues to continuity and change. They located buildings lost to severe floods in 1944 and where a runaway bus tragedy occurred among other sites that have become part of Holmfirth's history of wartime loss and struggle. Period vehicles, clothes and shopfronts also provoked comments. For younger viewers, recognising the past in the present tended to be more private, if recognition occurred at all. Afterwards, an informal exit poll, email comments and follow up interviews elicited further responses about the film and its maker.

Showing *Market Day*, like *Fenella the Tiger* and other archive films of local interest, enabled newcomers and festival visitors to learn about past lives and landscapes. If attending this community screening might itself become a point of reference for future memories, and arouse curiosity about a place's uniqueness, the public appreciation also highlights that localism remains significant within a globalised world. Audience reception reveals that emotional engagement with place is multilayered. Knowing a place or landscape is relative: familiarity over hours or days differs from the rootedness of generations but, as tourism operators know, may still offer a meaningful encounter. Screening local footage enables festival goers, like valley residents, to engage even briefly in a social act of belonging and being in a place.

As Cecilia Morner (2010) shows in her discussion of how official local place identity is constructed, with reference to the Swedish town of Falun, this chapter considers how local identity is lived, experienced and reproduced through representations that affect, and draw upon differently, the everyday lives of a particular community. Wylbert Kemp's personal history, lifestyle and interests bridge almost a century in which early film-making and later media interest in regionally based popular domestic comedies brought wider recognition to the South Pennines. Like the distinctive identities shaped by Bamforth's lantern slides and film productions, and the clichés of the later sitcom, Kemp's prolific work on the valley he loved and knew, was incomplete, selective and yet responsive to wider changes. Bamforth's films are part of a wider cinematic narrative and commercially driven visual practice. The valley's *Last of the Summer Wine* associations also sit comfortably within the expansion of later twentieth-century popular visual culture and the commodification of an appropriated local identity. Although Kemp's explorations of local place identity through written, visual and dramatic forms reflect altering needs and circumstances during decades of socio-economic, physical and cultural transformation, his actions were often prompted by generosity rather than self-gain.

Alternative versions of valley life exist away from the exaggerated personalities and places found within these professional and amateur representations. Food and drink, sport (especially cricket and rugby), church and chapel, and the rich musical traditions of choral singing, brass bands and other instrumental ensembles are virtually absent from Kemp's valley view. Similarly, local political affiliations, whether via electoral representation or trade unions remain largely outside the world he evokes, unless distanced to years of early industrial unrest. Such absences highlight how local social life and culture develop unofficially over time via particular interest groups and networks that help ideas, meanings and values to circulate. Kemp played a major part in developing local cultural and artistic capital and interacted with others who shared his enthusiasms, during decades when people, of diverse backgrounds took their leisure time seriously and often found fulfilment outside their employment. Yet, recording memories of a real place, and thereby capturing the local vernacular and aesthetic identity through creative means, is neither unique nor intended to privilege one place over another because localities gain their distinction and reputations differently. Kemp's versatility offers one way of delving into processes that confer a shared identity and reference points – and also tempting analogies with how digital technologies might play more contemporary roles in shaping individual and shared notions of place identity.

This discussion identifies how communities of interest and fluid associative links enabled one self-educated man to contribute to a distinctive sense of time and place that was sustained by regular interaction, overlapping common frames of reference and willing involvement by different groups at different times. Well-connected through developing the valley's first centrally heated barber shop, Kemp established himself as a key point of social contact around whom stories circulated. As a gatherer and teller of tales, Wylbert Kemp became a story too: screening *Market Day* aroused fresh curiosity about individual contributions and connections to the valley's past. Film festivals open spaces where dialogues on negotiating place meaning and memory may occur. This chapter has sought to be what one filmmaker calls 'an archaeological dip into memories and understanding' that dredges up, heightens and alters both the understanding and the memories themselves (Kennedy, 2008: 190). As we explore the nature and function of regional aesthetics it seems that media history, archive film and changing forms of amateur creativity have relevance in understanding how film-festival programming may contribute to wider conversations about regional culture and identity in post-modernity.

Notes

1. 'Holmfirth tiger Fenella to be immortalised in folk song', *Huddersfield Examiner*, 4 May 2014, http://www.examiner.co.uk/news/west-yorkshire-news/holm-firth-tiger-fenella-immortalised-folk-4951491, accessed 1 November 2014.

2. Email from WS to author, 23 May 2013.
3. What is BFI neighbourhood cinema? http://www.bfi.org.uk/sites/bfi.org.uk/ files/downloads/bfi-neighbourhood-cinema-2014-08.pdf, accessed 5 January 2015.
4. See, for example, *National Character Area (NCA) Profile: 36 Southern Pennines* (NE323), http://publications.naturalengland.org.uk/publication/511867; *NCA Profile: 51 Dark Peak* (NE378), http://publications.naturalengland.org.uk/ publication/3684793; *NCA Profile: 37 Yorkshire Southern Pennine Fringe* (NE490), http://publications.naturalengland.org.uk/publication/5459581769613312, all accessed 1 November 2014.
5. Campaign to Protect Rural England (CPRE), 'How we mapped tranquillity', http://www.cpre.org.uk/what-we-do/countryside/tranquil-places/in-depth/ item/1688-how-we-mapped-tranquillity, accessed 19 November 2014.
6. 'BBC's Easter blockbuster *Jamaica Inn* filmed in Huddersfield', *Huddersfield Examiner*, 15 April 2014, http://www.examiner.co.uk/news/west-yorkshire- news/bbcs-easter-blockbuster-jamaica-inn-6990488, accessed 19 December 2014; 'Jamaica comes to Yorkshire', http://www.brookesmill.co.uk/news- events/ (posted 7 May 2014), accessed 19 December 2014; '*Remember Me*, BBC1 – TV review: Nice scenery but shame about the script', *The Independent*, 30 November 2014, http://www.independent.co.uk/arts-entertainment/tv/ reviews/remember-me-bbc1--tv-review-nice-scenery-shame-about-the-script- 9893882.html, accessed 5 January 2015.
7. KB interview with author, Tolson Museum, Huddersfield, 5 November 2014; see also *Who's Who of Victorian Cinema*, James Bamforth, http://www.victori- an-cinema.net/bamforth, accessed 6 January 2015.
8. RK interview with author, 10 December 2014; CB and EB interviews with author, 1 December 2014.
9. *Boys Sliding* (Bamforth Company, 1900), http://www.screenonline.org.uk/ film/id/574926/index.html; *Catching the Milk Thief* (Bamforth Company, 1899), http://www.screenonline.org.uk/film/id/532518/index.html, accessed 1 November 2014.
10. Peter Riley (2006) *Holmfirth. A Bygone Era* (Bridgeway East, Cheshire), http:// www.screenonline.org.uk/people/id/532480/, accessed 5 January 2015.
11. Sound recording of Wylbert Kemp. Played during BK interview with author, 18 December 2014. Also in published version in Wylbert Kemp (1987) *Holmfirth by Lamplight* (Toll House Reprints, Holmfirth), pp. 36–37.
12. Wylbert Kemp, *Holmfirth by Lamplight*, pp. 37.
13. *The Would-Be Conjuror* (Bamforth Company, 1900), http://www.screenon- line.org.uk/film/id/574903/index.html, accessed 19 December 2014; See also Bamforth and Co., http://www.screenonline.org.uk/film/id/449654/index. html, accessed 19 December 2014.
14. JB and HB interviews with author, 28 November 2014; See also 'Filmmaking in Yorkshire', *BBC Inside Out – Yorkshire and Lincolnshire*, 17 February 2003, http://www.bbc.co.uk/insideout/yorkslincs/series2/films_movies_history_ early_bradford_holmfirth_bamforth_james_amateur.shtml, accessed 30 November 2014.
15. CB interview with author, 1 December 2014.
16. 'Ovation for hairdresser's play', *Yorkshire Post and Leeds Intelligencer*, 31 May 1949. Information also derives from many interviews conducted in

the Holme Valley and elsewhere during 2014–2015 as part of continuing research on Wylbert Kemp and his contribution to local and regional culture. Special thanks are owed to his sons for their willingness to share family memorabilia.

17. CV interview with author, 2 December 2014.
18. Yorkshire Dialect Society, http://www.yorkshiredialectsociety.org.uk/; Special Collections University Library, Leeds Archive of Vernacular Culture, http://library.leeds.ac.uk/special-collections/collection/61/the_leeds_archive_of_vernacular_culture/62/what_is_the_leeds_archive_of_vernacular_culture, both accessed 19 December 2014.
19. Letter to Wylbert Kemp from Dorothy Smith, secretary to the editor of *The North Countryman*, BBC Radio North (Manchester), 5 January 1960.
20. Email correspondence with Peter Hawkin, former producer of *Local Colour* at Radio Leeds, 22 January 2015.
21. Wylbert Kemp: Letter to R.K. Aldridge, Huddersfield Library, 5 July 1965, Bamforth Collection, Tolson Museum, Huddersfield.
22. Wylbert Kemp (1949), *Smoke in the Valley*, Proscenium Press, Holmfirth (cited on inside cover).
23. Wylbert Kemp, *Smoke in the Valley*.
24. JK interview with author, 12 December 2014.
25. AH and BH interviews with author, 4 November 2014.
26. Kemp, Wylbert, *Smoke in the Valley* (inside cover).
27. See note 21.

References

Appadurai, A. (2001) Grassroots Globalisation and the Research Imagination. In A. Appadurai (ed.) *Globalisation* (Durham and London: Duke University Press), 1–21.

Beal Kennedy, C. (2008) Living with Film: An Autobiographical Approach. In C. Lukinbeal and S. Zimmerman (eds) *The Geography of Cinema – A Cinematic World*, (Stuttgart: Steiner Verlag), 187–203.

Betton, S. (2005) *Film-Induced Tourism* (Bristol: Channel View Publications).

Bottomore, S. (1996) 'Nine Days' Wonder': Early Cinema and Its Sceptics. In C. Williams (ed.) *Cinema. The Beginnings and the Future. Essays Marking the Centenary of the First Film Show Projected to a Paying Audience in Britain*, (London: Routledge), 135–149.

Brown, R. (2005) Film and Postcards – Cross Media Symbiosis in Early Bamforth Films. In V. Toulmin and S. Popple (eds) *Visual Delights Two: Exhibition and Reception* (Eastleigh: John Libbey), 236–256.

Chaplin, E. (1994) *Sociology and Visual Representation* (London: Routledge).

Clifford, S. (2011) Local Distinctiveness. Everyday Places and How to Find Them. In J. Schofield and R. Szymanski (eds) *Local Heritage, Global Context. Cultural Perspectives on Sense of Place* (London: Routledge), 13–32.

Clifford, S. and King, A. (2006) *England in Particular. A Celebration of the Common Place, the Local, the Vernacular and the Distinctive* (London: Hodder and Stoughton).

Cresswell, T. (2006) *Place. A Short Introduction* (Oxford: Blackwell).

Doel, M. (2008) From Animated Photography to Film: The Formation of Vernacular Creativity in Early English Films, 1895–1908. In C. Lukinbeal and S. Zimmerman (eds) *The Geography of Cinema. A Cinematic World* (Stuttgart: Franz Steiner Verlag), 87–99.

Fullerton, J. (2005) 'Introduction: Local Film', *Film History*, Vol. 17, No. 1, 3–6.

Gunning, T. (1986), 'The Cinema of Attractions: Early Film, Its Spectator and the Avant-Garde', *Wide Angle*, Vol. 8, No. 3/4, 63–70. Reprinted in T. Elsaesser (ed.) 1990, *Early Cinema: Space, Frame, Narrative* (London: BFI Publishing), 56–61.

Gunning, T. (2004) Pictures of Crowd Splendour: The Mitchell and Kenyon Factory Gate Films. In V. Toulmin, S. Popple and P. Russell (eds) *The Lost World of Mitchell & Kenyon: Edwardian Britain on Film*, (London: British Film Institute), 49–58.

Haraway, D. (1988) 'Situated Knowledges: The Science Question in Feminism and the Privilege of Partial Perspective', *Feminist Studies*, Vol. 14, No. 3, 575–599.

Jenkins, J. and Pigram, J. (2003) *Encyclopaedia of Leisure and Outdoor Recreation* (London: Routledge).

Johnson, M. J. (2010) 'The Places You'll Know: From Self-Recognition to Place Recognition in the Local Film', *The Moving Image*, Vol. 10, No. 1, 24–50.

Kember, J. (2009) *Marketing Modernity. Victorian Popular Shows and Early Cinema* (Exeter: University of Exeter Press).

Kemp, W. (1987) *Holmfirth by Lamplight* (Holmfirth: Toll House Reprints).

Lippard, L. (1997) *The Lure of the Local. Sense of Place in a Multicultural Society* (New York: The New Press).

Marshall, W. (2011) *The Creation of Yorkshireness: Cultural Identities in Yorkshire c.1850–1918.* Doctoral thesis, University of Huddersfield. Available at http://eprints.hud.ac.uk/12302/.

Morner, C. (2010) Film in Falun – Falun on Film: The Construction of an Official Local Place Identity. In E. Hedling, O. Hedling and M. Jönsson (eds) *Regional Aesthetics: Locating Swedish Media* (Stockholm: National Library of Sweden), 153–168.

Norris Nicholson, H. (2012) *Amateur Film. Meaning and Practice* (Manchester: Manchester University Press).

Noyes, D. (1995) 'Common Ground: Keywords for the Study of Expressive Culture', *The Journal of American Folklore*, Vol. 108, No. 430, 449–478.

Riley, P. (2006) *Holmfirth. A Bygone Era* (Bridgeway East, Cheshire: P. & D. Riley).

Toulmin, V. and Loiperdinger, M. (2005) 'Is It You? Recognition, Representation and Response in Relation to the Local Film', *Film History*, Vol. 17, No. 1, 7–18.

Toulmin, V., Popple, S. and Russell, P. (eds) (2004) *The Lost World of Mitchell & Kenyon: Edwardian Britain on Film* (London: British Film Institute).

Tuan, Y. F. (1974) *Topophilia: A Study of Environmental Perception, Attitudes, and Values* (Englewood Cliffs, NJ: Prentice-Hall).

Valck, M. de (2007) *Film Festivals: From European Geopolitics to Global Cinephilia* (Amsterdam: Amsterdam University Press).

Williams, E. (1975) *Holmfirth from Forest to Township* (Huddersfield: The Advertiser Press).

2
Arcadia in Absentia: Cinema, the Great Depression and the Problem of Industrial Wales

Daryl Perrins

> The Welsh Folk museum: a lovely place. But what happens to a
> people when it calls itself, even temporarily, a folk? That hard
> German sound is softened and distanced in English, and it is
> in the softening and distancing that you select your memo-
> ries. For it is significant isn't it, where that Folk Museum stops.
> Just before, precisely before, the Industrial Revolution. You
> look among all those places and instruments of work and you
> remember, up the road, industrial South Wales: coal and steel
> and their depravities; the thickly populated valleys, the terraces,
> the slagheaps; the place of life and work of the majority of the
> Welsh.[1]

It is really no surprise that The Welsh Folk Museum, which opened
in St Fagans near Cardiff in 1948, omitted industrialised Wales, for it
was founded by the Welsh nationalist poet and scholar who was also
its curate: Iorwerth C. Peate. Peate saw a rural and pre-industrial arti-
sanal based and monoglot Welsh-speaking culture as the only way to
preserve Welsh identity. It is indicative of a fortress nationalism that
has deep roots in Wales, a nation that has been perpetually under
threat from extinction by invaders. The locus of this 'fortress Wales'
was not, however, to be found in the anglicised south at all but in
the Welsh speaking West and North. In particular, it was traditionally found in Gwynedd (formerly a kingdom centred in what would
become Caernarvonshire, which at its height – roughly between 1063
and 1081 – stretched across all of North Wales to the border), heartland
of the language, and home of the medieval Welsh princes and thus the
landscape of national autonomy. Image makers have long been drawn

to this defiant landscape. In the age of romantic nationalism that swept across Europe in the eighteenth century, the connection between landscape and national identity was made flesh by artists through the figure of the defiant bard set in the sublime and stormy mountain-scapes of Gwynedd, which came under attack from Roman and Saxon alike (see Thomas Jones's *The Bard*, 1774, and John Martin's *The Bard*, 1817). The bard became an icon of the durability of a pure pre-Roman Wales, forged in antiquity, and was given 'official' national status via the first Gorsedd of the Bards on Primrose Hill, London, in 1792. As Donald Moore (1979: 144) suggests, during the romantic period Wales drew in tourists, writers and, in particular landscape painters, because it possessed all three landscape classifications recognised at the time: the sublime, the beautiful and the picturesque. However it was the North Wales of Richard Wilson, Machynlleth-born and 'father of British land-scape painting', that would emerge as *the* national image of Wales. *Snowden from Llyn Nantile* (c.1765–1767), with its elevated perspective of proportional peaks and water features framed by clumps of trees, among which the simple people of the land fish the lake and frolic, created an idealised and orderly Wales under a clear blue sky that was both sublime but also classically Italianate. Nature was tamed in the service of man. This was Wales as Arcadia: 'a land of eternal summer' (Moore, 1979: 135). It was only much later in the nineteenth century that the bards and the yokels were replaced by artists 'in favour of presenting the Welsh as a pious rural folk, facilitating the construct of *y Werin Gymreig* [the Welsh Folk].........., a myth which dominated self perceptions among romantic nationalists well into the twentieth century' (Lord, 2000: 11).

It should be noted, however, that since Raymond Williams in 1975 wrote the words above on the omission of industrial Wales, the past, to paraphrase Robert Hewison (1987: 83), has got a lot closer. The newly renamed 'St Fagans National Museum', while still remaining *Amgueddfa Werin Cymru* (Welsh Folk Museum) in Welsh, now acknowledges 'the majority of the Welsh'. And so, now in 2014 the showgrounds hold a terrace of ironworkers' houses, a workmen's institute and even a post-war prefab alongside the whitewashed and/ or timber-framed pre-industrial vernacular buildings. Two traditions and two social mythologies held together on a single national stage, the cleansing glow of nostalgia stripping the scene of any possible contradiction. The pre- and post-industrial buildings of St Fagans are, however, far more than 'the way we were'. They are signifiers of distinct and sometimes conflicting methods of defining the common people of Wales, those who inhabit that landscape. And these have historically reflected nationalist and socialist traditions in Wales. As Gwyn Alf Williams wrote (1985: 237), these types have, historically, been influential and persuasive:

> Public perception of a people in Wales for a century and a half has been expressed in two archetypal myths; both were powerful abstractions derived from reality and both became increasingly unreal; the *gwerin* [folk] and the *working class*.

This idea of a contested national space, only hinted at in St Fagans, has been, I will argue, adopted by cinema as an often-partisan central motif of human conflict expressed through a collision between modernity and tradition. I want to suggest, therefore, that the industrialisation of a previously romantic and often sublime Wales creates a problem when compared to the bespoke representation of the other Celtic nations in the cinema during the period under review. In Ireland, for example, as Martin McLoone (2000: 33) has argued, a primitivist image located in the haunted landscapes of the West of Ireland prevailed. And, while it was created by outsiders, it was embraced by natives (in particular nationalists) as a bastion against Anglo-Saxon urbanity. In Scotland, meanwhile, the classic tropes of Scottish representation on screen, according to Colin McArthur's groundbreaking essay of 1982, largely resided either in Tartanry and Kailyard, which was located in the Jacobite-themed, biscuit-tin-framed Highlands, or to a lesser extent in a 'Clydesidcism' located in the masculine working class environment of the heavily populated and industrialised Central Belt epitomised by the 'second city of the empire', Glasgow. Thus, in the cinematic representation of Ireland and Scotland, the lines between the rural and the urban – and indeed around the national – were clearly drawn. Wales, however, is much more a nation of contradictions, and the lines between urban and rural appear, to outsiders especially, to be blurred, as in the tightly packed showgrounds of St Fagans.

Wales, of course, as we are constantly told, is an ancient culture with an ancient language, but in ways, unlike Ireland and even Scotland, it is also importantly a very young culture. For example, as the historian Gareth Elwyn Jones notes, in the latter stages of the nineteenth century 'labour was being drawn into the South Wales coalfield at a rate exceeded only by immigration into the USA', and by the beginning of the twentieth century 80% of the population lived in industrial areas (1994: 152). This, according to Alfred Zimmern, led to a 'lop-sided development', where 'South Wales and the rest of Wales have fallen hopelessly out of step in their onward march' (1921: 28). Indeed, in a 1921 lecture he gave to the Cambrian Society at Oxford University, entitled 'My Impressions of Wales', Zimmern offered up a tripartite regional ethnography of Wales that would form the template for recognised cultural difference within the principality. For Zimmern the Wales of the inter-war period was anything but unified:

> There is not one Wales; there are three Wales. There is Welsh Wales; there is industrial, or as I sometimes think of it American Wales; and there is upper-class or English Wales. These three represent different traditions. They are moving in different directions, and if they all survive, they are not likely to re-unite. (1921: 29)

This schema, however, would not be fully realised until political analyst Dennis Balsom's highly influential 'Three Wales Model' of 1985. This used the 1979 election results – together with a survey that asked if people thought they were 'Welsh', 'English' or 'British'– to essentially qualify Zimmern's earlier polemic and divide Wales into three distinct regions that overwhelmingly voted either for Plaid Cymru, Labour or a mix of Liberal and Conservative. Recognising both the 'New World' demographics and the increasingly internationalist working class culture of the southern valleys, Zimmern labelled an area we can confidently surmise as containing all of the coalfields of the south (except for the Welsh speaking anthracite belt in Eastern Carmarthenshire), located in upland Glamorgan and western Monmouthshire and including where the coalfield meets the sea at Swansea and in the Neath Valley area: 'Industrial/American Wales'. Its strongholds were in the townships and ribbon development that snaked northwards from the ports on the Bristol Channel. And these lines of urban encroachment created, as in America during its rush to the West, a frontier culture in miniature. 'Welsh Wales' on the other hand would be represented by the historic counties of the North and West; Anglesey, Caernarvonshire, Denbighshire, Merionethshire, Cardiganshire and Carmarthenshire. In all these counties, Welsh was, at the time Zimmern was writing (in 1921), still the dominant language, and the nonconformist religion was still strictly observed, and therefore the *gwerin* held sway. While there are, of course, some overlaps in these divisions, 'upper-class or English Wales' can be seen to be an area that formed a largely rural borderland region between the administrative one drawn on the map between England and Wales and what we presume to be the bona fide Welsh regions. This anglicised identity can be traced to the Norman incursion into Wales after 1066, and the establishment of the self-governing area known as the Welsh marches, and the resultant division of land into the 'Englishry' (based in the lowlands) and the 'Welshry' (based in the uplands). This is an enormous area that can be traced on the map from Flintshire in the North East, down to Monmouthshire and then along the coastal strip of Glamorgan. It continues beyond Swansea, taking in the Gower peninsula and all of southern Pembrokeshire. This south-western section is known as 'Little England beyond Wales'.

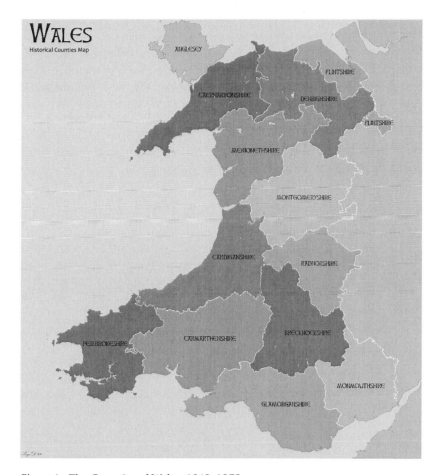

Figure 4   The Counties of Wales, 1543–1973

Source: Map courtesy of XrysD, *Creative Commons Licence – CC BY-SA 3.0.*

The tight south-eastern corner of Wales, containing Glamorganshire and Monmouthshire, and holding around two thirds of its population, was host to the United Kingdom's only upland coalfield and dominated by the culture of Zimmern's 'American Wales'. With its narrative of pit accident and social unrest set against the scenery of its real or imagined hills and waste tips, it became a perfect site for working class melodrama in both American and British cinema, from *The Citadel* (Vidor, 1938) to *Blue Scar* (Craigie, 1949). As Gareth Stanton puts it, the 'valley' became 'a trope for an idealised community living out a certain tension with the world of work' (2002: 80). Stanton here is referring to the negotiation that two films in particular – *The Proud Valley* (Tennyson, 1940) and *How Green Was My Valley* (Ford, 1941) – made between a pastoral simplicity on the one hand and the realities of a mining society on the other. For him there emerged from this refining process a sharpened and, therefore, distinctive image of nationhood that resulted in 'a familiar vision of Welsh community', where 'industry effaces the green of memory and bucolic Wales, yet reinforces this community in the rose-tinted version of the industrial past' (2002: 81). This 'tension' occurs most conspicuously, I will posit, in the Oscar-winning Hollywood film, *How Green Was My Valley*. However, 'the problem' of industrial Wales in the cinema, I suggest, predates *How Green* by at least six years. The first Welsh-language talkie, *Y Chwarelwr/The Quarryman* (Owen Edwards, 1935), and the documentary films *Today We Live* (Ralph Bond and Ruby Grierson, 1937) and *Eastern Valley* (Paul Rotha and Donald Alexander, 1937), therefore will be employed to argue the case for cinema's patronage of the *gwerin* over and above the *working class*, and to consider the legacy of the Romantics and the influence of nationalism in imagining Wales. Finally, I will reconsider the role of *The Proud Valley* and suggest that it is a unique, if flawed, attempt to introduce to the field of the cinematic feature, a sympathetic portrait of an ideologically conscious Welsh working class.

At the beginning of John Ford's *How Green Was My Valley*, the montage establishes both the past tense of the title and the vague time 'before all this' that the flashback-framed narrative is set in, suggesting a frightening present. In these opening shots (which are also the film's final images) industry is central to the film's oppositional thematic structure and, as in *Metropolis* (Lang, 1927), it is presented as a demonic and all-consuming force that leaves only zombies in its wake. Thus the streets are empty except for wistful old ladies and broken child labourers who pass by, heads down. The wind whips up a dust cloud and above it all the pyramid of the slag heap bears down upon the village. A line of men bent double feed this hungry beast by depositing more and more

Figure 5 'Here once was Wales': despoliation in the opening shots of *How Green Was My Valley* (John Ford, 1941)

debris. We can see their silhouettes standing out against the grey sky, as they march antlike up and down its slopes. This contemporary vision of South Wales during the Great Depression (the novel, *How Green Was My Valley*, by Richard Llewellyn was first published in 1939) is introduced to us via the thoughts of a middle-aged Huw Morgan. He is the youngest of the Morgan family and is about to leave the valley after the departure of his siblings to the four corners of the earth and the death of his father in a pit blast. A dissolve then casts out the present, and we are brought via Huw's voice-over narration into the still-green valley of his childhood and equilibrium is temporarily restored:

> In those days the black slag, the waste of the coal pits had only begun to cover the side of our hill. Not yet enough to mar the countryside nor blacken the beauty of our village. For the colliery had only begun to poke its skinny fingers through the green.

The feature-length flashback that follows is a nostalgic reminiscence presented to us through the eyes of the young Huw (played by a 12-year-old Roddy McDowall in his first film role). Anders Wilhelm Aberg notes, when arguing for the Stockholm archipelago as a domestic (Swedish) Arcadian space – as seen in the Swedish children's TV series *We are Seacrow Island* (1964), and in the book *Seacrow Island* that followed – the 'pastoral ideal' is 'the space of childhood'. He goes on to say that this is 'supported by a typically pastoral pattern of composition first and foremost of the structuring opposition between Arcadian space and its Other (the urban, complex, corrupt, inauthentic etcetera)' (Aberg, 2010: 130). Likewise we are presented by the flashback structure in *How Green* with the memory of the Rhondda Valley before the corruption of adulthood (which equates to the period of the second industrial revolution; the period from 1870 to the First World War). In the Rhondda (where the novel and film are identifiably set), this was a period when the deep mines of the valley were sunk to replace the less-invasive drift mines that existed during the first phase of the industrial revolution. The earlier industrial period, however, is located here outside of any historical verisimilitude (i.e., within the life span of Huw). And because of this the film has been dismissed by Welsh critics and labelled 'a mythical Shangri-La' (Stead, 1986: 172). We might therefore consider John Ford's construction of South Wales in the film as a dry run for the 'soft primitivism' of his later film, *The Quiet Man* (1952). Quoting the art critic Erwin Panofsky, Gibbons opines that *The Quiet Man* 'conceives of primitive life as a golden age of plenty, innocence and happiness – in other words, a civilised life purged of its vices' (1988: 198).

How Green Was My Valley's often 'Oirish' version of the Welsh pastoral, complete with Irish actors, Irish accents, Irish drinking songs and Irish peasant dress, is established by an 'outsider' director who 'derived from his own family memories and from Irish tradition', observing, 'The Welsh are just another lot of micks and biddies, only Protestant' (quoted in Richards, 1997: 217). However, while the accents have their origins in Ford's ancestral home, the setting does not. Filming on an 80-acre set in what is now Malibu Creek State Park in California, with the peaks of the Goat Buttes clearly visible, Ford returns Wales to Richard Wilson's Arcadia and the alpine sublime of the Gwynedd of the Romantics. This, again, is landscape as national redoubt.

This can be evidenced in the opening frames of Huw's flashback, which establishes the village as being *above* the valley floor with the land falling away on all sides to offer elevation and thus picturesque views all around. The *gwerin* presented here have not lost the connection with pre-industrial rural life and, to make the point, shepherds are seen to drive sheep through the village, while in the next shot Huw's sister Angharad (played by Maureen O'Hara) yodels to him across a despoiled hillside in an otherwise verdant panorama. Unlike the 'soft primitivism' that defines the pastoral films set in Ireland, the 'valleys pastoral' (Stanton, 2002: 80) of *How Green* incorporates work into its euphoric schema alongside home life, chapel, education for the young, and the choir. It does this by presenting industry as the generator of quaint and folksy ritual: the men all handing over their wages to the Welsh Mams who wait on the doorstep, and familial bonding and play, as in the backyard tin bath scene. Meanwhile the battle between capital and labour is presented by the preacher, Mr Gruffydd, only as 'a family disagreement'. Outside of the family unit socialism appears as an alien force that is against everything that is presented as 'Welsh.' It is brought through immigration, which in the novel brings 'foreigners' whom Llewellyn describes as: 'half breed Welsh, Irish and English....the dross of the collieries' (Llewellyn, 2009: 203). To avoid perhaps any tears in the carefully constructed 'Celtic twilight' the film presents, the Irish-American team of screenwriter writer Philip Dunne and director Ford removed the xenophobia that is a key feature of the book. Indeed, previously industrialised (and therefore despoiled) Wales, in the reference to 'men from Dowlais', is the only geographical origin we are given for the increasing numbers who come into the valley to undercut the wages of the locals (and to eventually bring idleness).

While *How Green* is in English, it seems clear that we are to assume the characters are in fact speaking Welsh. In the book the threat to the language is writ large: before Huw can go to 'the national school', his family are told: 'He must on no account be allowed to speak that jargon in or out of school' (Llewellyn, 2009: 178). In the film the threat to the language is implied cinematically through the long walk Huw makes out of the *Cymric* valley to reach a school in 'upper class or English Wales', which is filled with the English accents and manners of his fellow pupils. And also by the actions of Mr Jonas, the brutal Anglo-Welsh teacher (Jonas maybe a pun on Judas) with the clipped English accent, who masquerades as the coloniser and refers to Huw as 'our little coal mining friend'.

Unlike *How Green,* which presents a surrogate North Wales, the first Welsh language talkie, *Y Chwarelwr*, is framed by Gwynedd's jagged peaks. An amateur story-documentary based on the narrative premise of 'a day in the life' (with a lost epilogue that takes place a few days later) of a slate quarryman called Tomos and his family, the film was made by first-time director Sir Ifan ab Owen Edwards. Owen Edwards was the founder in 1922 of Urdd Gobaith Cymru (Welsh League of Youth), now known simply as Yr Urdd (The Youth). The roles of the slate workers are played by slate workers, and the other roles are played by members of the amateur drama company that Owen Edwards ran in the town. Made on location in Llechwedd Quarry and the town of Blaenau Ffestiniog in Caernarvonshire, it cost £3,000 to make, and Dave Berry comments that it was 'a primitive operation which harked back, endearingly, to the pioneer days of the "bioscope men"' (1996: 6). This, however, does not necessarily undermine the film's verisimilitude in the eyes of an audience, for as Berry notes, the film was very popular in the Welsh-speaking towns and villages where Owen Edwards toured with it in a van and, as Bruzzi convincingly argues when discussing documentary aesthetics: 'there is an inverse relationship between style and authenticity: the less polished the film, the more credible it will be found' (2000: 6). This point can be considered by comparing the film to the 'travesty' (McLoone, 2000: 39) of the re-staging of long-died-out practices for the purpose of 'authenticity' found in its contemporary, *Man of Arran*, made by the Irish-American documentary filmmaker Robert Flaherty in the same year. Like *Man of Arran*, however, the film was ideologically positioned within the philosophical sphere of a socially conservative nationalism; in this case, the values that in 1925 gave rise to *Plaid Cymru* (The Party of Wales). And just as *Man of Arran* projected an 'ascetic nationalism' (McLoone, 2000: 39) that was in line with the de Valera government's re-imagining of Irish cultural nationalism, so did *Y Chwarelwr* – albeit without the artistry of Flaherty – respond to a perceived cultural threat through the representation of a noble national archetype. The art historian Peter Lord argues for the influence of the nonconformist church when he says that *Y Chwarelwr* was a belated response to the nonconformist preacher and Welsh-language scholar, D. Tecwyn Evans who, at the National Eisteddfod in 1925, called for the cinema to be used to 'win back the 'comparatively uneducated *Gwerin*', who were 'turning their backs on the indigenous culture' (quoted in Lord, 2000: 396). The 'uneducated' *gwerin*, however, as *Y Chawarelwr* suggests, were in fact:

> a cultivated, educated, often self-educated, responsible, self-disciplined, and respectable but on the whole genially poor or perhaps small-propertied people, straddling groups perceived as classes in other less fortunate societies. (Williams, 1985: 237)

This is, however, well removed from the 'against all the odds' 'hard primitivism' (Gibbons, 1988: 201) offered by Flaherty in *Man of Arran*

and, rather, we are presented in *Y Chwarelwr* with an industrial community that has reached a rapprochement with nature, landscape and
tradition. However, it would be incorrect to describe what happened
in North Wales in the slate industry as an industrial revolution per se.
As R. Merfyn Jones notes, for example, many slate workers were also
'cottagers' who rented and farmed small plots of land (1982: 117).
Rather then, towns like Blaenau Ffestiniog were isolated pockets of
development, and there was little or no migration into the slate mining
areas, as was the case in South Wales coalfield. The relative isolation in
the North meant that the workers' society remained Welsh speaking,
Liberal and nonconformist, and the cultural practices transferred and
applied to the new situation from the rural environment. This accommodation can be read in the opening credit sequence of *Y Chwarelwr*
via a panning shot that introduces first the peaks of Snowdonia, then
the fastness of Blaenau Ffestiniog surrounded on all sides by mountains
of broken waste, an industrial sublime offering a facsimile of nature's
jagged geometry. Similarly, disavowing any acknowledgement at all of
an industrial identity, a caption (possibly added much later) reads 'the
folk life of Wales' and the images are backed by the sound of the pre-
industrial Welsh triple harp. This then is an ethnographic valorisation
of a very particular people – the *gwerin* – and, unlike in *How Green*, their
victory over the contradictions of work and place that surround them.

Here, the depression leaves the community untouched and work is
therefore central. However, it shares the day in equal measure within
the film's pattern of interdependence with home life, chapel, education
for the young, cultural pursuits and the rituals of courtship. Unlike in
the British film documentary movement's *Coal Face* (Cavalcanti, 1935),
where the unskilled Welsh colliers hue and shovel away, stripped to
the waist – the film celebrates the physicality and brute strength of
the working class – the slate workers in *Y Chwarelwr* are shown to be
highly skilled artisans. There is a central scene, for example, which
stands outside of the simple plot that revolves around the slow demise
from silicosis of the heroic figure of the father, Tomos. Featuring the
eldest son, Will, and a fellow worker this parallel narrative shows how
the quarrymen prepare the large slabs in the workshops and then cut
and dress the smaller sections into roofing slates for export. This idea
of a skilled worker was important in the construction of the *gwerin* of
the slate industry as part of a craft-based community, a central trope
in nationalist ideas of the time as to what sort of society qualified as
'Welsh'. For example, in the novel (but not the film) *How Green Was My
Valley*, Huw leaves the collieries and becomes a carpenter.

Writing in 1921, Iorwerth C. Peate spoke of the importance of 'that rural wisdom' that manifested itself in 'the village smithy or the carpenter's shop and at the shoemakers bench. Anyone who knows the real Wales well can estimate the importance of these craftsmen in the life of their communities' (quoted in Lord, 2000: 390). Another important element that in the film distinguishes the *gwerin* of the North from a working class in the South is the institution of the *caban* (cabin in English). This is the cabin often high on the hillside that the men use as a meeting place and to have their breaks in. It is here that so-called *caban* culture developed far away from the seats of power of the English quarry masters below, and this again establishes the hills as a focus for Welsh national culture. The *caban* developed its own committee, chairman and even policemen to enforce the rules. Jones describes the *caban* as being organised for 'educational, cultural and at times agitational activity' (1982: 57). Here, the focus is on the cultural role of the *caban* as the site for the semi-final of an Eisteddfod competition featuring Will singing the humorous song *Defaid William Morgan* ('William Morgan's Sheep').

While the North remained intact, the destruction of South Wales through industry and inward migration had, however, already been established as something of a cinematic trope outside of the feature film, and well before *How Green Was My Valley*, via two British documentary movement films set in the depression-hit South: *Today We Live* and *Eastern Valley*. Both these films can be seen, as Sylvia Harvey suggests when discussing the documentary on British miners, *Coal Face* (Cavalcanti, 1935), as 'an investigation of social anthropology, a view from above and outside, a middle class journey into the "darkest England" of the working class' (Harvey, 1986: 228). The documentary movement itself then had its own 'grand tour' in mind: 'as Grierson himself put it, this was a project to "travel dangerously into the jungles of Middlesbrough and the Clyde"' (quoted in Harvey, 1986: 228). Both documentaries set in the South feature Paul Rotha's signature bombastic *March of Time* style prologues as examples of where

> an introduction in which a quick résumé is given of a happier and more beautiful rural past, which gives way to the dark, noisy and ugly advent of some form of power, requiring a re-adjustment to bring man back into better harmony with his environment. (Low, 1979: 127)

In *Eastern Valley* the introductory section of the film is framed within the narrative of the life of a stream. The camera sweeps across the high pastures accompanied by the Trehafod Male Voice on the soundtrack, while the voice-over laments: 'once it was a farming valley where men and women lived the primitive but independent lives of peasant farmers'. Sure enough, two duly emerge to discuss catching trout in the river. The voiceover then interrupts to tell of the 'mighty storm' of industry that came 'with a torrent', as fire laps the screen, and chimney stack and winding gear replace the trees and sheep of Arcadia. Then a montage sequence begins, full of the dread of outsiders – 'they came from all over England and Wales' – and the deskilling of the *gwerin* that the mines brought, together with the temptations of free time; 'they accepted routine jobs in the hope that they could live more richly in their hours of leisure'. On the screen, the images flit from miners getting their wages, to their becoming seduced by 'American Wales': queues at the turnstiles, greyhounds being led to the racetrack, images of posters for rugby matches, fetes and firework displays. Then we see images of men on street corners and of unstable slag heaps engulfing filthy terraces; contagion stalks the land as 'sanitation was unknown', and 'offal from the works and dwellings lay in open drains or poured into the stream. They catch no more fish in Afon Llwyd'. What follows has the biblical scale of Sodom and Gomorrah as the destruction on screen increases, and the voiceover informs us that 'the houses are being swallowed up by the slag tips or collapsing as the land subsides into the collieries beneath them'.

In both *Today We Live* and *Eastern Valley*, the pastoral idyll is destroyed in seconds. These rapid changes, according to the voiceover of *Today We Live*, left a 'community with nothing in common except a sameness of landscape and a willingness to work'. In these opening sections the worldview of the British documentary movement's Paul Rotha comes to the fore. As Robert Kruger notes, Rotha never committed himself to the Left and was instead 'the quintessential English radical in the mould of Orwell or William Cobbett – a true nonconformist enemy of all Establishments, Left, Right or Centre and of compromise' (1999: 27).

I have made a point here to underline the 'outsider' status of these documentary filmmakers in terms of their class. In doing this I am extending the 'outsider' designation given to the mining cycle of feature films by scholars in Wales (see Barlow et al., 2005: 81). Notable in this designation is, of course, *How Green Was My Valley*, which is seen as being key in 'the Orientalized images, created by large American and English studios during the middle years of the last century, that have taken root permanently in the international imagination' (Woodward, 2006: 54). This concentration on stereotype and creative personnel, however, ignores the fact that there was a strong political consensus within Wales which chimed with the ideological thrust of these films. For example the opening establishing scenes of the documentaries under discussion, dominated by Paul Rotha's nostalgic English radicalism, dovetails with the romanticism which lay at the heart of the fledgling Welsh nationalist party, Plaid Cymru. The author of *How Green*, Richard Llewellyn, was an early member. And the physical and cultural devastation of South Wales depicted in the British documentary movement's films and also John Ford's adaptation mirror the sensibilities expressed by Saunders Lewis, Plaid Cymru's founder and its president from 1926 to 1939, as expressed in his 1939 poem, *The Deluge*:

> The tramway climbs from Merthyr to Dowlais,
> Slime of a snail on a heap of slag;
> Here once was Wales, and now
> Derelict cinemas and rain on the barren tips.[2]

The imagery the poem shares with *How Green*, with its dehumanised working class traversing the spoil heap above the village, demands that both texts be read in terms of a vanishing world and culture. Thus these simplifying images, this 'rhetorical observation', as Raymond Williams observes when discussing the poem, 'protected within the common sense of devastation and dereliction, becomes an outline of history';[3] an all-encompassing grand narrative of decline.

While *How Green* suggests only the romance of the diaspora as a way out, the South Wales that *Eastern Valley* offers in replacement to the industrial model would have fitted the nationalist vision better. For, as Gwyn Alf Williams notes, Plaid Cymru at the time 'called for a nation of "small capitalists", co-operation, the de-industrialisation of South Wales and the restoration of agriculture as the basic industry of Wales' (1985: 281). Likewise the Society of Friends, who sponsored the making of *Eastern Valley*, shunned state intervention for those who have, according to the voiceover, 'become a problem'. Instead they looked to a utopian scheme (the 'Brynmawr Experiment') of self-help born out of a paternalistic tradition from the previous century, where the men were reunited with craft skills and with the land. It was, according to one of its architects, Peter Scott, nothing less than a 'new order of society....in which production by the consumer, planned economy, quality of mate-rials and workmanship, leisure, and the right human relationships, can all have their true value' (quoted in Ffrancon, 2004: 118). Dai and his 'butties' in *Eastern Valley* work at the farms set up by the Quakers to produce fruit and vegetables for the community, which runs its own butchers and bake house. As Ffrancon observes, '*Eastern Valley* is thus an uncritical hymn of praise to the land, agriculture and the virtues of cooperative life. Both Iorwerth C. Peate and Saunders Lewis would surely have relished watching it' (2004: 122).

Increasingly however 'American Wales' was coming of age. Evidence of this can be found in 'the first flowering' of Welsh writing in English and the emergence of the Welsh industrial novel. These were usually working class, Left-wing, South Walian writers, who had more often than not spent time as colliers themselves. They wrote from and about the Welsh working class which, as Jeffrey Richards argues, was taking over from the *gwerin* as 'the Welsh style':

> It was English speaking (Welsh speakers declined from 40% of the population in 1911 to 20% in 1960) and American cultured with cinema a particularly strong influence. American English was the language of popular culture, the wider world and political struggle. This Wales was strongly communal, centred on the Working Men's Clubs and miner's institutions, the collieries and the 'Fed' (South Wales Miners Federation), on rugby and boxing, choral societies. It generated its own legends every bit as potent as Madoc and the Druids. (Richards, 1997: 216)[4]

One of the most successful of these writers was the novelist, playwright and trade union official, Jack Jones. His popular blend of historical melodrama and realism can be seen in his most successful novel, *Rhondda Runabout*, which responds to the effects of the 1926 general strike. The *Proud Valley* was written for Paul Robeson by his stage director at Unity Theatre; Herbert Marshall, together with Marshall's wife, the sculptor Alfredda Brilliant. Jones was invited to contribute to the screenplay alongside the director (Tennyson) and Louis Golding. In particular Jones added significant sections of dialogue. It is not fanciful, therefore, to consider the film's 'curious mixture of realism and stereotype, of radicalism and soap opera, of innocence and sharpness' (Stead, 1991: 117), as being in some small way down to his involvement.

Importantly, while the film was an Ealing Studios production and therefore very much within the circle of 'outsider' representations identified, for example, by Barlow et al. (2005), unlike *How Green*, it is a film sympathetic to the values of an industrial society. Ostensibly this is because it was made by a Left-leaning creative team led by a committed trade unionist in director Pen Tennyson, who initially wanted the film to be called 'One in Five' to represent the injury rate for miners. In the original script, for example, the miners take over the colliery and run it as a cooperative. However, the coming of war turned the antipathy toward the owners outward toward Germany, and the film becomes a compromise whereby the strikers persuade the owners to re-open the pit in the service of the war effort. The unfulfilled radicalism of the film led the writer and broadcaster Mathew Sweet to claim it had the potential to be 'the most uncompromisingly Marxist picture ever produced in Anglophone cinema' (2006: 172)

The film is of course a vehicle for the singing voice of Paul Robeson, and its folksy style comes to the fore when his character, David Goliath, is invited in because of his ability to sing (in the Blaendy male voice choir). However at the same time *The Proud Valley* replaces the pastoralism of *How Green* with nascent codes of social realism. As Stephen Bourne notes, some location shooting took place in the Rhondda, and, unlike *How Green*, there is no embellishment of living conditions: 'you may not see the loo in the Parrys' backyard but you know it's out there' (Bourne, 2005: 35). The location shooting establishes the valley via the trip Robeson's unemployed black stoker makes looking for work en route from Cardiff to the fictional Blaendy, after jumping an empty coal train. Here the alpine peaks and verdant valleys of the imagined North are replaced by long whalebacks, and the sight of forestry plantations on the hills tells of a coal society that was already in the process of reinvention. Within this frame the slag heap (when it appears as a site for David and his unemployed 'butties' to scavenge for pieces of coal) is not a devouring monster but, ironically, the very opposite: a measure of what was being lost by a Welsh industrial working class that depended on coal. While reproducing Ealing regional stereotypes, the working class ensemble is presented as a collective and is pitted against those outside the class. This is notably apparent with the unwelcome call of the rent man at the Parry household, and in the characterisation of the local shopkeeper and postmistress 'whose petty bourgeois sense of superiority to the community is revealed as snobbish and selfish' (Hill, 2004: 102).

The film constructs tropes familiar from *How Green*: the role of the choir and the Eisteddfod, the Welsh Mam, the centrality of education to getting out, and the well-meaning pit owners (while leaving out direct reference to the chapel in an increasingly secular South Wales). Importantly, however, we are not afforded the point of view of the native as in *How Green*, but instead are introduced to the valley via the perspective of the incomer, and therefore we judge the valley through

Figure 6 'Dam and blast it, man, aren't we all black down that pit?' The pithead
confrontation in *The Proud Valley* (Pen Tennyson, 1940)

our empathy with Robeson's David Goliath. The nationalist position
of the outsider as threat established in *How Green* is, therefore, almost
immediately dismissed. It is replaced by what can be read as proletarian
internationalism – a man who tries to stop David working in the pit on
racial grounds is unanimously overruled after his landlord and Blaendy
choirmaster Dick Parry, intervenes with: 'Damn and blast it man, aren't
we all black down that pit?' While the trades union movement is absent
from the film, ideology is not: 'When the move beyond the community
is made – in the form of the men's march to London – it is as a collective
rather than as individuals pursuing solitary goals' (Hill, 2004: 102). The
march the men take to London to ask the owners to re-open the pit after
an explosion has echoes, in its knapsacks and banners, of the media's
images of the hunger marches of the general strike and the depression.
On this march, the massed male voice reprises what appears to be the
theme tune of the film: 'They Can't Stop Singing' (part chant, part
hymn, and sung to the tune of the folksong 'All Through the Night').
Its significance is identified by Jeffrey Richards when discussing David
Goliath's multiple identities: 'David is working class and sings with his
mates "They can't stop us singing", the "them" and "us" underlying the

existence of a class society' (1997: 78). The singing may seem 'cloyingly sentimental', says Stead, but as he reminds us: 'the censors did not want unions and so choral singing became one way of suggesting solidarity' (1986: 171). Overall, as Hill notes, despite the film's political reserve, it 'remains a testament to a certain kind of longing for a new society based on the principles of decency, mutual support and honest Labour which the film locates within the industrial working class' (2004: 102).

In conclusion, in this chapter I have attempted to establish how, during the period of study, industrial Wales presented particular problems for filmmakers in the representation of a 'Celtic' nation. In North Wales, as we have seen, an indigenous amateur filmmaker successfully managed in *Y Chwarelwr* to negotiate a compromise between nature and industry in his construction of the *gwerin* for the purpose of cultural propaganda. The cultural liminality of a new identity produced by coal society in the South Wales valleys (Zimmern's 'industrial/American Wales'), standing as it did between the ethnic orthodoxies of 'Welsh Wales' and 'English Wales', proved more difficult to negotiate. Instead, British documentary filmmakers in the prologues of both *Today We Live* and *Eastern Valley*, followed later by Hollywood's *How Green Was My Valley*, established a dichotomy that ignored this new national character and instead instigated the destruction of an Arcadian South Wales as both national narrative and indicative landscape on a par with that of the famine-scoured West Coast of Ireland and the Jacobite Highlands of Scotland. These 'outsider' representations, as in Ireland, summoned up romantic tropes that either tallied with or directly reflected indigenous nationalist convictions at the time around perceived threats to the 'pure' nation from Anglo-American penetration.

This threat was most fully developed and ideologically advanced in John Ford's adaptation of the Richard Llewellyn novel, *How Green Was My Valley*, while the documentary, *Eastern Valley*, sketched out an 'approved' agrarian response. The film *The Proud Valley* reverses this, however, in that it is an 'outsider' film from the Left, working within the limitations of the day in representing the world from the point of view of that threat. In so doing it seeks to release, via its codes of realism, a working class that would be recognised by the inhabitants of 'industrial/American Wales'. It thus replaces the romantic narrative of national destruction with the glimpse of an altogether different narrative, one represented by a progressive Welsh radicalism, which is itself located in an internationalism that is telegraphed by the presence of Paul Robeson.

Notes

1. Raymond Williams 'Welsh Culture', originally a talk on BBC Radio 3, 27 September 1975, in Williams (2003: 6).
2. Saunders Lewis, *Y Dilyw 1939* (translated as 'The Deluge 1939'), originally published in 1942, quoted in Raymond Williams, 'Remaking Welsh History', *Arcade: Wales Fortnightly*, No. 4 (12 December 1980), pp. 18–19, published in Raymond Williams *Who Speaks for Wales? Nation, Culture, Identity*, Daniel Williams (ed.), University of Wales Press 2003, p. 69.
3. See above.
4. Here Richards is referring to the myth that a Welsh Prince (Madoc) was the first to reach America in the Middle Ages and to the Druidic caste of scholars/ poets and keepers of pagan religion from prehistory, who are honoured every year at the national Eisteddfodau.

References

Aberg, Anders Wilhelm (2010) Seacrow Island: Mediating Arcadian Space in the *Folkhem* Era and Beyond. In Erik Hedling, Olof Hedling and Mats Jönsson (eds) *Regional Aesthetics: Locating Swedish Media* (Stockholm: National Library of Sweden).

Balsom, D. (1985) The Three Wales Model. In John Osmond (ed.) *The National Question Again: Welsh Political Identity in the 1980's* (Llandysul: Gomer Press), 1–17.

Barlow, David, Mitchell, Philip and O'Malley, Tom (2005) *The Media in Wales: Voices of a Small Nation* (Cardiff: University of Wales Press).

Berry, Dave (1996) *Wales and the Cinema: The First Hundred Years* (Cardiff: University of Wales Press).

Bourne, Stephen (1998) *Black in the British Frame, Black People in British Film and Television 1896–1996* (London: Cassell).

Bruzzi, Stella (2000) *New Documentary: A Critical Introduction* (London: Routledge).

Ffrancon, Gwenno (2004) Documenting the Depression in South Wales: Today We Live and Eastern Valley, *Welsh History Review*, Vol. 22, No. 1, 103–125.

Gibbons, Luke (1988) Romanticism, Realism and Irish Cinema. In Kevin Rockett, Luke Gibbons and John Hill (eds) *Cinema and Ireland*, (London: Routledge), 219–221.

Harvey, Sylvia (1986) The 'Other Cinema' in Britain, Unfinished Business in Oppositional and Independent Film, 1929–1984. In Charles Barr (ed.) *All Our Yesterdays: 90 Years of British Cinema* (London, BFI Publishing), 225–251.

Hewison, Robert (1987) *The Heritage Industry* (London: Methuen Press).

Hill, John (2004) A Working Class Hero Is Something to Be? Changing Representations of Class and Masculinity in British Cinema. In P. Powrie, A. Davies and B. Babington (eds) *The Trouble with Men: Masculinities in European and Hollywood Cinema* (New York: Wallflower Press), 100–109.

Jones, Gareth Elwyn (1995) *Modern Wales: A Concise History* (Cambridge: Cambridge University Press).

Jones, R. Mervyn (1982) *The North Wales Quarrymen, 1874–1922* (Cardiff, University of Wales Press).

Kruger, Robert (1999) Paul Rotha and the Documentary Film. In R. Kruger and D. Petrie (eds) *A Paul Rotha Reader* (Exeter: University of Exeter Press), 16–44.

Llewellyn, Richard (2009 [1939]) *How Green Was My Valley* (London: Simon and Shuster).

Lord, Peter (2000) *The Visual Culture of Wales: Imaging the Nation* (Cardiff: University of Wales Press).

Low, Rachael (1979) *Documentary and Educational Films of the 1930's* (London: George Allen and Unwin).

McArthur, Colin (1982) Scotland and Cinema: The Iniquity of the Fathers. In C. McArthur (ed.) *Scotch Reels: Scotland in Cinema and Television* (London: BFI), 40–69.

McLoone, Martin (2000) *Irish Film: The Emergence of a Contemporary Cinema* (London: BFI Publishing).

Moore, D. (1979) The Discovery of the Welsh Landscape. In D. Moore (ed.) *Wales in the Eighteenth Century* (Swansea: Christopher Davies).

Richards, Jeffrey (1997) *Films and British National Identity: From Dickens to Dad's Army* (Manchester: Manchester University Press).

Stanton, Gareth (2002) 'New Welsh Cinema as Postcolonial Critique?', *British Journal of Popular Cinema*, Vol. 5, No. 5, 77–89.

Stead, Peter (1986) Wales in the Movies. In T. Curtis (ed.) *Wales: The Imagined Nation (Essays in Cultural and National Identity)* (Bridgend: Poetry Wales Press), 161–179.

Stead, Peter (1991) *Film and the Working Class: The Feature Film in British and American Society* (London: Routledge).

Sweet, Mathew (2006) *Sheperton Babylon* (London: Faber and Faber).

Williams, David (2003) Introduction: The Return of the Native. In D. Williams (ed.) *Raymond Williams, Who Speaks for Wales?* (Cardiff: University of Wales Press).

Williams, Gwyn Alf (1985) *When Was Wales* (London: Penguin).

Woodward, Kate (2006) 'Traditions and Transformations: Film in Wales during the 1990's', *North American Journal of Welsh Studies*, Vol. 6, No. 1, 216–231.

Zimmern, Alfred E. (1921) *My Impressions of Wales* (London: Mills and Boon).

3
A Poetics of the North: Visual and Literary Geographies

David Forrest and Sue Vice

In this chapter we explore different media in our approaches to the North, including a pair of linked television plays presented under the title *The Price of Coal* (Ken Loach, 1977), written by Barry Hines; these are alongside two literary texts, Philip Hensher's 2008 novel, *A Northern Clemency*, and David Peace's *GB84* of 2004. We argue that a dynamic poetics of the North emerges as both an aesthetic trend and a critical tool when viewed within such cross-medium understandings of region. The notion of a poetics of the North might appear to be a contradictory one, given critical assumptions about the region's associations with a realist form and its accompanying bleak social and political content. However, as Katherine Cockin has argued, the North 'generates oxymoron or paradox, a tension between desolation and depth, defying the literal and logical and intimating the poetic powers of the unconscious' (Cockin, 2012: 5–6). Here, we use the apparently archetypal examples of television drama and fiction, which centre on representations of the mining industry in the South Yorkshire region in order to argue against such a polarised view. We argue, instead, that our chosen texts not only blur the boundaries between visual and literary media as part of a specifically Northern aesthetic, but that they draw on a wide range of such strategies in their representation of a particular location and its history, doing so for symbolic ends. Mikhail Bakhtin's notion of the chronotope is helpful in relation to our argument about the specifically aesthetic construction of place,[1] one that is generated by what he describes as 'spatial and temporal indicators' (Bakhtin, 1981 [1937–1978]: 84). Such an effect is apparent in our chosen texts in what could be called a 'chronotope of the North'. Bakhtin argues that in chronotopic formations, 'Time, as it were, thickens, takes on flesh, becomes artistically visible; likewise, space becomes charged and responsive to the movements of time, plot and history' (Bakhtin, 1981: 84). The combination of historical time, ranging in these texts from the mid-1970s to the mid-1980s, and the space of South Yorkshire, is particularly charged both politically and aesthetically and, in Bakhtin's phrasing, allows the region to become visible 'artistically' rather than simply in documentary terms. Approaching a region in spatial terms is one way of substantiating this broad approach. Literary space can be seen as engaging with theatrical, filmic and televisual space, and in dialogue with image, thus destabilising medium-specific tropes and generic motifs of place and space.

Narratives of mining

Our first example of such a northern chronotope occurs in the pair of linked Play for Today dramas, titled *The Price of Coal*, written by Hines and directed by Loach, and shown on BBC1 in 1977 ('Meet the People', on 29 March 1977; 'Back to Reality', on 5 April 1977). The first, 'Meet the People', concerns the elaborate preparations made at the fictional Milton Colliery for an impending royal visit, while the second, 'Back to Reality', centres on the more familiar scenario of a mining disaster at the same pit. The continuities between the two plays include the same cast and setting, as well as a thematic trade-off with an ironic and political meaning: the expenditure incurred in 'Meet the People' is set against the cutbacks in safety measures that contribute to the fatal accident in 'Back to Reality'. While one of the pit managers, Geoff Carter (Duggie Brown), envisages the newspaper headlines drawing on such an irony – 'Disaster at Royal Visit Pit' – the local National Union of Mineworkers (NUM) official (Max Smith) takes a different view, and sardonically refers to the visit and the accident as 'two disasters in a row'.

The location in the North of *The Price of Coal* is clear in visual, aesthetic and political terms, as can be seen in the film's opening credits, with their juxtaposition of the two kinds of Northern space, which are fundamental to both films: a peaceful rural backdrop and the distinctive shape of pit winding-gear. The intertitle, 'Two films set in South Yorkshire', appears over this opening sequence, drawing attention to the double-faced imagery. Beneath the intertitle appears the extra subtitle, 'A film for the Silver Jubilee', which makes the film historically and politically specific, yet also symbolic as a narrative explicitly concerned with class relations and the human cost, or 'price', of heavy industry. The action takes place after the miners' strikes of 1972 and 1974, which are mentioned several times in the dialogue, and the story inevitably seems to look forward to the strike of 1984–1985, for instance in the equally frequent invocations of the NUM president, Arthur Scargill.

As the counterpart to such historical specificity, the contrasting Northern spaces of countryside and pit are central to the films' concern with broader themes of social equality and justice. Both dramas are characterised by alternating between exterior shots of a summer-time rural mining village – filming occurred during the record-breaking hot summer of 1976 – and those taken beneath ground in the pit itself. The second film, 'Back to Reality', opens on a scene in which the brothers Mark (Haydn Conway) and Tony Storey (Paul Chappell) are playing cricket, the sound of their voices set against that of clearly audible bird-song. This may seem a surprisingly idyllic introduction to a play about the 'reality' of mining-related death. However, in both plays sport (in this case cricket) assumes the role of symbolising community life and self-expression and is contrasted visually and narratively with the under-ground world of the mine and its representation through particular kinds of mise-en-scène and camera movements. Cricket's symbolic func-tion in the play is revealed when Mark's father, Sid (Bobby Knutt), gives his son a pair of tickets for a test match ten days hence, constituting a stake in the future, which is given a tragic twist when Sid goes missing in the pit accident. A journalist's demand for news in the wake of the disaster –'What is the situation?'– is met with the response from one of the miners: 'Well, the last I heard Geoffrey Boycott was a hundred and seventy-seven not out, if that's any use to you'. Such a reply acknowl-edges the miners' lives and interests outside their work, as well as giving a satirical brush-off to one of the 'bloody vultures', as Alf (Tommy Edwards) calls the journalists. The stereotypical press depiction looks only for tragedy. In similar terms, the death of Frank (Phil Askham) in the explosion is signalled by the discovery among the debris in the pit of torn and bloodstained pages from the racing formbook he had been studying earlier. The phrasing of Frank's declaration that the book is a 'mine of information' about profiting from betting, if only he had the capital to invest in it, reveals that it offers a fantasised means of escaping the mine in which he works, and constitutes a small instance of the play's deployment of crossovers between verbal and visual punning in the service of its hard look at class relations and work.

The film's representation of cricket and leisure activities is contrasted with the mise-en-scène below ground, where confused and shadowy sequences, lit only by miners' lamps and torches, are filmed with a handheld camera. Indeed, the difficulty of seeing becomes a trope that further unites the specific and symbolic elements of *The Price of Coal*. The colliery itself may seem to be represented in an entirely realist manner, yet it appears in the highly mediated form of combining two different pits, one diegetically and one semiotically (Burt, 2002: 11). The plays were filmed at the disused Thorpe Hesley mine in Rotherham, since demolished, but were based on the history of Silverwood Colliery, which the Queen visited in 1975, a year before *The Price of Coal* was made. The spectator's curiosity about what the pit itself looks like underground is part of a thread of comments in 'Meet the People', which suggests that it cannot be seen or adequately represented in any sense: Prince Charles will only experience a spruced-up version created especially for him, and even the local community can only go down to view it on formal open days. On their way to work, the miners Sid and Jimmy (Michael Hinchcliffe) come upon a noticeboard at the colliery gates, newly erected for Prince Charles' benefit, which features the National Coal Board's motto 'E Tenebris Lux', 'Out of the Darkness, Light', and their dialogue about this takes on a simultaneously realist and symbolic form. In the face of Jimmy's confused exclamation, 'Bloody hell!', Sid explains: 'Latin, that. It means, out of the shadows comes the light'. Not only is the motto enlisted in the play's structuring binary of dark pit and light countryside, but it also stands for an impassable route out of work in the mines. Sid knows the meaning of the motto from his son, Tony, who studied Latin at school; but, in answer to Jimmy's question about why Tony is still working down in the pit when he has such knowledge (the same question Frank's colleague put to him), Sid can only say that his son never gained enough qualifications. The themes of youthful aspiration and the importance of education that characterise all of Hines's work from *Kes* (Ken Loach, 1969) to *Looks and Smiles* (Ken Loach, 1981) are clearly present here.[2] They reappear in the next scene, in which Pete (Tony Graham), an apprentice, is planting trees as part of the royal preparations but complains about his gardening activities, since, as he puts it, 'I came here to be a miner'. The dialogue in this scene, in which, as in the previous one, the fate of a young man is debated, appears to resolve the opposition between countryside and mine, 'lux' and 'tenebris'. As Sid says, the trees will eventually become coal, and Pete's work in planting them is ensuring the 'economic future of the mining industry for the next two million years'. Yet such a sentiment can only resound with proleptic irony, since in less than a decade the 'economic future' of the mining industry would be effectively over. In the play's present, Sid's comic hyperbole emphasises the impossibility of reconciling work and nature, just as his ironic description of the miners' 'enlightened employers' – who give their staff, like Pete, training in different skills – implies that the NCB (National Coal Board) are definitely in the shadows.

In the first film, 'Meet the People', the conceit of the literal white-washing of the pit extends to become a challenge to viewers, in considering whether we can 'see' what the film shows us. The pit above ground is described in terms of impossible oppositions: the refurbished road leading to it is likened to that of a stately home, and it is said to resemble the Peak District rather than a pit-yard when the slag heap has been planted with grass seed. A manager reprimands some apprentices, when they are repainting an old building, to remind them that they are working for the National Coal Board and not the National Art Gallery, invoking differences in landscape and location that are, in all these examples, also differences of class. Such hints at the mine's unrepresentability continue in 'Back to Reality' in relation to the accident, in which family members have to wait above ground for news of lost miners, whose bodies then can, only with difficulty, be identified.

Releasing and establishing information about the accident becomes a way of indicating power relations, expressed in verbal versions of the visual. While Phil (Bert Oxley) insists that the families of missing miners must be informed because 'we can't keep them in the dark', the pit manager Mr Forbes (Jackie Shinn) protests innocence in the face of questions from the NUM official about the faulty motor which caused the blast: 'We're as in the dark as you'. The quick cuts between highly contrasting scenes above- and below-ground themselves enact a kind of violence that is evident explicitly in the form of the explosion, implicitly in that of class relations under capitalism.[3] Such crosscutting also characterises scenes in which the knowledge of disaster is imparted. Tony tells his mother Kath (Rita May) about Sid having gone missing, and a slow close-up on her weeping face is followed by an abrupt change of scene to the mine, where a rescue team is filmed with a handheld camera. Equally, Mark's return home from another game of cricket, which he eagerly describes to his sister, Janet, is a sun-filled scene tainted with the dramatic irony of our knowing more than he does. When Mark learns of his father's fate, his insistence on leaving the house is followed by Janet's worried plea, 'Don't go too far', a warning that we know will be disregarded when it is followed by a quick cut to the underground world of the mine, where all we can see is the indistinct movement of miners' headlamps in the darkness. The cut itself reveals that this is Mark's destination. *The Price of Coal* thus relies on a chronotopic intertwining of visual effects with verbal effects in its deployment of social and geographical specificity for a wider effect. As Alyson Buckman argues, drawing on the work of Janice Best, the chronotope 'generates not only the events of the text but also its symbolism' (Buckman, 2014: 171), in the sense that the latter's repertoire is drawn from the social world depicted. Thus, where the northern landscape seems most realistic, it is at its most symbolic.

The miners' strike

As a particularly prominent narrative within the northern cultural and political imaginary, and one which follows the pattern of using northern signifiers for symbolic ends, as identified in the previous section, the miners' strike of 1984–1985 provides a rich case study for the cross-medium spatial poetics of region. The strike's representation within British popular and literary cultures has tended towards a Civil War-like narrative that depicts a class conflict, with this discourse undoubtedly evoking in addition a sense of a regional war between North and South. The strike's use within fictional narratives such as Peter Flannery's *Our Friends in the North* (1995) is partly as a device to enable this regional dialectic for wider ideological purposes, with the Metropolitan Police pitted against striking Geordie miners (see Forrest, 2011: 227), and in a similar vein Dave Russell sees the strike as consistently narrated as 'a battle between a radical, almost colonised North and an oppressive South' (Russell, 2004: 279). In the unambiguous nature of this geographical discourse, therefore, the strike is imagined in spatial terms, embodying what Bakhtin describes as 'the intrinsic connectedness of temporal and spatial relationships' (Bakhtin, 1981 [1937–1938]: 84) in this northern formation. Philip Hensher's *The Northern Clemency* (2008) is an expansive novel that follows the lives of two middle-class families from Sheffield over a 20-year period, between the 1970s and 1990s. Naturally, the miners' strike of 1984–1985 is well represented within the novel's narrative arc, although it is by no means dominant. In this sense, the strike is used, just as it is in *Our Friends in the North*, as a historical event that affects the characters in significant ways but which nevertheless serves primarily to authenticate and render realistic the fictive elements of the historical plot. This functional approach to the strike might be seen as reducing a recent, traumatic episode of northern collective memory to mere backdrop. With this in mind, *The Northern Clemency* is unusual in that the story of the strike is retold and reimagined from a middle-class perspective, with the account of 'The Battle of Orgreave' coming from Tim, a young political radical from the affluent suburbs of Sheffield. This privileging of a middle-class voice has also been seen as contributing to an unbalanced, manipulative and fetishised narrative use of the conflict, embedding the fictional perspective within what Nick Howard criticises as 'middle class comfort zones' (Howard, 2008). Such a view might be seen to cohere with the aforementioned rigidity of the strike as a northern spatial narrative, which aligns the North within a working-class symbolic system in opposition to the middle-class South. Hensher, however, self-consciously invokes his own bourgeois identity to argue for a more complex northern aesthetic:

> Behind the whole thing is a popular stereotype about the difference between life in the north and life in the south; one warm, neighbourly, friendly, emotionally open and hugger-mugger, creating pop musicians and comedians; the other fenced off, cold, withdrawn, detached, creating novelists and string quartets.
>
> ...
>
> For me, when I think of Sheffield, I am 18, and taking a pile of Nabokovs out of the library. The Hallé is coming to play Penderecki's *St Luke Passion* at the City Hall tonight. Only in the north. (Hensher, 2013: 36)

The *Northern Clemency* reflects this middle-class perspective with the same unapologetic tone. It self-consciously renders the strike as an event to be witnessed and experienced from the perspective of its middle-class characters, and Hensher frames his bourgeois subjects as spatially distanced, passive observers, or as inauthentic interlopers on the fringes, imagining the strike as something to be 'looked at' passively with a 'dreamlike strangeness' (Anon. 2008):

> Katharine was right: it was all about the coal strike. There was a shot of the prime minister, then a shot of the miners' man, while the reporter talked over the top about the day's particular failure. The pair of them looked far too pleased with themselves; Malcolm wondered, too, and not for the first time, which of them got through more Elnett to keep their hair in place. (Hensher 2008: 409)

Here, the strike is presented as a series of images constructed and narrated within both a national and regional iconography. The strike is visualised as a news report interspersed with fictional lives and narratives, adding a temporal dimension to a cross-medium approach to regional aesthetics by evoking the events through their twenty-first-century presence as archived news image. This distance, one that is both spatial and ideo-logical, has meant that the text has been criticised by scholars of the strike and its cultural representation: as Shaw suggests, the novel's focus on the narratives of its middle-class characters renders the strikers (and the strike) a voiceless 'plot device' (Shaw, 2012: 154). While such a posi-tion is defensible, it seems rather that an approach to the text on the basis of its construction of regional space, with a broader understanding of regional narratives from across the media in mind, can enable more nuanced readings of the ideological implications of the novel's use of the strike. As Tim prepares for what will become known as 'The Battle of Orgreave', Hensher writes:

> If it hadn't been more trouble than it was worth, and likely to raise the house, he'd have fried some bacon and made a bacon butty with the HP sauce he'd made his mother buy. It was the sort of breakfast a man on a picket line deserved. But he ate the breakfast he had made for himself in the kitchen of the house with its view of a neat front garden, with its Italian tiles on the walls and its specially air-pocketed flooring, warm and yielding under bare feet in the winter. (Hensher, 2008: 467)

Here, the fetishisation of working class culture, including the invoca-tion of brown sauce, the source of class contention between Ken Barlow and his father in the first-ever episode of *Coronation Street*, is made conspicuous through the spatial construction of middle-class imagery with which it is placed in obvious ironic juxtaposition. This, in turn, initiates the means by which Hensher implicates and renders explicit the middle-class construction of working class space, place and, in this case, history, through a set of iconographic, regionally specific images. We see here, ostensibly, the same tools of representation as those which appeared chronotopically in *The Price of Coal*, used to render the spatial authority of the middle-class gaze:

> They quickly left the western suburbs, the blackened stately villas of Broomhill with their remains of railings like cut-off blackened teeth. Nobody was about; the morning was high and blue and slightly steaming, the dew smoking above the municipal garden. (Hensher, 2008: 471)
>
> ...
>
> And now the roads were widening out, leaving Sheffield behind. The carriageway. The carriageway ran like a mournful mountain pass

behind high peaks of slag, lowering and black. Down in the valleys, the palaces of the steel-makers, vast and cubic and full of fire; up here, the unworking coal-sorters, high and yet frail, their sides dustily clamped with metal stairs, like drawings executed in dust. (Hensher, 2008: 472)

Here, the spatial imagery is deliberately lofty and grandiose, evoking an earnest northern poeticism as imagined via an idealistic (and flawed) middle-class gaze, an emphasis that is developed as Tim and his friends arrive at their destination:

It was a beautiful morning – you couldn't help thinking that. The landscape was torn away in slag heaps and pylons and this fat grey slash of a motorway, but there were trees, too, and green hills as if it were the English countryside. Torn and scarred, it still swelled and dipped like Gloucestershire. Once, people might have come here to admire the scenery; the earth had been beautiful before it had proved useful. If they had their way, Tim thought with deliberation, it would only be beautiful all over again, and useless, and filled with the ragged foraging unemployed. But you couldn't help responding to the lovely morning. (Hensher, 2008: 474)

Descriptions of place and space as mythical constructions, as regional chronotopes, are here deployed with playful self-consciousness. The use of the second person pronoun at the end of the passage confirms and renders the reader complicit in the explicitly middle-class and intentionally problematic construction of, and intervention in, the strike narrative. The iconography of poetic regionalism is recycled for parody and rendered as unstable in the process.

What emerges, then, is a subversive middle-class northern aesthetic; this can also be seen as part of the novel's own paratextual construction – thus the cover of the US paperback edition features a mundane suburban home with a neat garden, connoting a private, geographically non-specific middle-class aesthetic that jars against the eponymous 'Northern' and the expectations it raises of working class iconographies of communal external space.

An awareness and subsequent use of this topography of northern poeticism is equally fundamental to David Peace's novel *GB84* (2004), but it is an altogether more radical manipulation of the northern chronotope that carries the reader's attention in Peace's novel. As in *The Northern Clemency*, cultural symbols abound in the form of cross-medium signifiers of strike history. Specifically, song titles and lyrics from the popular music of the period are combined with explicit descriptions of well-known photographs and news images, to reconstitute and territorialise the fictive elements of the narrative: this is most clearly identified in three of the novel's four sections, entitled: 'Ninety-nine red balloons' (Peace, 2004: 1); 'Two tribes' (Peace, 2004: 117); and 'There's a world outside your window and it's a world of dread and fear' (Peace, 2004: 349), all of which appear against grainy black and white documentary images. Thus the novel itself operates as a dynamic cross-medium text, re-circulating strike imagery already embedded within the national popular imagination – doing so in order to, as Katy Shaw states, 'defamiliarise' fixed conceptions of the strike's narrative as history (Shaw, 2011: 77). Peace's section titles both recreate and critique the strike's place within this historicised, documentary aesthetic, echoing Hensher's use of a televisual retrospective iconography. In both cases, a spatial and temporal distance from the event is actively established. The disorientating deployment of cultural texts is therefore a prominent aspect of the novel's use of space, with the strike's position being what Peace calls 'one single history, with one single narrative' (Peace, 2011: x) challenged through this intertextual dispersal.

This disruption of the stereotypical northern chronotope is furthered by Peace's enlisting of the graphic representation of text as a poetic tool. Each chapter is prefaced by the documentary accounts of two striking miners, Peter and Martin – their stories are visually represented (here, in obviously biblical form) and in narrative terms removed from the core elements of the novel. Their accounts are fragmented and staccato in tone and thus invert the expansive, figurative iconography of regional space that we might associate with a poetic realist North:

> Lion's mouth was open – Now or never. Bloke side of me said, Wish I'd wore me boots – Now: half-nine – Lorries coming back out. Loaded up. Police fucking drivers. Royal Corps of transport. HGV licences still fucking wet – Saluting as they left. TWO fingers – Us trapped right in the middle of push. Meat in sandwich we were. (Peace, 2004: 136)

Despite their physical displacement within the text, the poetic tone adopted by the miners' narratives inflects the overall complexion of *GB84*. Where more conventional expositions of the regional chronotope rely on a spatial and ideological distance from its subjects, enabling the figurative register to emerge, in *GB84*, the blunt sentences and fragmented prose spatially refigure the most typical of northern subjects, the industrial landscape:

> Neil Fontaine gets back in his car. He follows the lorries back down to Sheffield. He comes to the black chimneys. To the giant ovens. He parks. He walks about –
>
> He listens. He hears. He inhales. He smells. He watches. He sees –
>
> Railways. Roads. Slag heaps. Disused workings – (Peace, 2004: 78)

Expansive industrial space as the default source for the poetic northern landscape is resisted here. The poetry of this northern space is apparent due to the absence of what Philip Dodd terms 'the Lowryscape', an elegiac, painterly landscape of the urban North, 'a settled place, with its own iconography' (Dodd, 1990: 17). In its stead, there is a move towards a subjective and disrupted regional aesthetic, 'a poetry stripped of all lyricism' (Fisher, 2008) and which remains conscious of northern poetics while refiguring their spatial and temporal constitution. What occurs in both texts, then, is a self-reflexive recasting of northern, cross-medium poetic tropes resulting in a spatial distancing designed to render unfamiliar, hitherto dominant, narratives of the strike. Like Shaw in her criticisms of *The Northern Clemency*, Sue Owen takes issue with this formal disruption of (what we would argue) operate as spatial and ideological tropes of regional and class identity in *GB84*: 'the novel's postmodernism, its resistance of direct narrative strategies, or conventional character and plot, actually works against it speaking on behalf of working class people' (Owen, 2011: 180). Yet, if we read these 'postmodern' approaches in line with a wider understanding of northern poetics we might unify Peace's and Hensher's regional aesthetic strategies so that they can be read, despite their idiosyncrasies, as emerging from within and not in opposition to existing narratives of space and place in the region.

Conclusion

Following Bakhtin's formulation, in the chronotope of the North we have identified here that 'time and space markers are combined in an aesthetic whole' (Bakhtin, 1981 [1937–1938]: 84). The representation of mining, and of the pit itself, in *The Price of Coal*, *The Northern Clemency* and *GB84*, have a different political and symbolic meaning dependent on the moment in British history, as the title of David Peace's novel emphasises. Yet such industrial and regional specificity serves aesthetic and political ends that have a global significance in blurring the boundaries between verbal and visual narratives and critiquing a world in which Sid's observation to his son Mark in *The Price of Coal* is a distant aspiration: 'It's got to be the same for everybody'. Rob Shields describes 'nationalism' as 'a myth of space', and we have suggested that regionalism, and more specifically northernism, can be understood in similar terms: the 'inherent ideological cues, interpellations, and discourses which manipulate metaphors of people and land' can be made apparent through an approach that identifies the literary in relation to the filmic (Shields, 1991: 222). Just as national allegiance is 'mythic', so regionalism itself is constructed by means of realist elements used for symbolic ends. Such spatial, poetic characteristics and narratives can be better understood by acknowledging a regional aesthetic composed of a set of symbolic and cultural codes that transcend categorisation by medium and appear, instead, in a variety of temporal and generic categories.

Notes

1. Bakhtin's examples are notoriously limited to fiction, but critics have convincingly argued the case for the applicability of his theories to visual media: see for instance Stam (1989) and Flanagan (2009).
2. Hines recounts a similar story about his own decision to give up his first job, as an apprentice mining surveyor, when a fellow miner reacted with 'disgust' that a 'boy with a grammar school education should end up down the pit' (Hines, 2009: 20).
3. Some elements of 'Back to Reality' unexpectedly foreshadow those in Hines's nuclear attack drama, *Threads* (Mick Jackson, 1984), since in both films a shocking explosion is followed by the disappearance of central characters, and viewers are called upon to reach judgement on the polyphonic debate that takes place between characters on the significance of the malfunctioning pit motor, and the threat of nuclear warfare.

References

Anon (2008) Philip Hensher's Sheffield, BBC South Yorkshire, October 2008: http://www.bbc.co.uk/southyorkshire/content/articles/2008/10/29/philip_hensher_northern_clemency_feature.shtml (Accessed 27 June 2014).

Bakhtin, M. (1981 [1937–1938]), Forms of Time and Chronotope in the Novel. In M. Holquist (ed.) *The Dialogic Imagination: Four Essays* (Austin: University of Texas Press).

Buckman, A. J. (2014) "Wheel Never Stops Turning": Space and Time in *Firefly* and *Serenity*. In R. J. Wilcox, et al. (eds) *Reading Joss Whedon* (Syracuse, NY: Syracuse University Press), 169–184.

Burt, J. (2002) *Animals in Film* (London: Reaktion).

Cockin, K. (2012) Introducing the Literary North. In K. Cockin (ed.) *The Literary North* (Basingstoke: Palgrave Macmillan), 1–21.

Dodd, P. (1990) 'Lowryscapes: Recent Writings about 'The North', *Critical Quarterly*, Vol. 32, No. 2, 17–28.

Fisher, M. (2005) 'A World of Dread and Fear', *K-Punk*, September 2005: http://k-punk.abstractdynamics.org/archives/2009_03.html (Accessed 27 June 2014).

Flanagan, M. (2009) *Bakhtin and the Movies: New Ways of Understanding Hollywood Film* (Basingstoke: Palgrave Macmillan).

Forrest, D. (2011) '*Our Friends in the North* and the Instability of the Historical Drama as Archive', *The Journal of British Cinema and Television*, Vol. 8, No. 2, 218–233.

Hensher, P. (2008) *The Northern Clemency* (London: Fourth Estate).

Hensher, P. (2013) 'Beyond Bet Lynch', *The New Statesman*, 29 November to 5 December 2013, 34–36.

Hines, B. (2009) *This Artistic Life* (Hebden Bridge: Pomona).

Howard, N. (2008) '*The Northern Clemency* – Book Review', *Socialist Review*, May 2008: http://www.socialistreview.org.uk/article.php?articlenumber=10399 (Accessed 27 June 2014).

Owen, S. (2012) "They May Win But God Knows, We Have Tried": Resistance and Resilience in Representations of the 1984–1985 Miners' Strike in Poetry, Fiction, Film and TV Drama. In S. Popple and I. W. Macdonald (eds) *Digging the Seam: Popular Cultures of the 1984–1985 Miners' Strike* (Newcastle-upon-Tyne: Cambridge Scholars Publishing), 170–187.

Peace, D. (2004) *GB 84* (London: Faber and Faber).

Peace, D. (2012) 'Preface'. In Simon Popple and Ian W. Macdonald (eds) *Digging the Seam: Popular Cultures of the 1984–1985 Miners' Strike* (Newcastle-upon-Tyne: Cambridge Scholars Publishing), ix.

Russell, D. (2004) *Looking North: Northern England and the National Imagination* (Manchester: Manchester University Press).

Shaw, K. (2011) *David Peace: Texts and Contexts* (Brighton: Sussex Academic Press).

Shaw, K. (2012) *Mining the Meaning: Cultural Representations of the 1984–1985 UK Miners' Strike* (Newcastle-upon-Tyne: Cambridge Scholars Publishing).

Shields, R. (1991) *Places on the Margin: Alternative Geographies of Modernity* (London: Routledge).

Stam, R. (1989) *Subversive Pleasures: Bakhtin, Cultural Criticism, and Film* (Baltimore: John Hopkins University Press).

Part II

Urban Subcultures and Structures of Feeling

4
The Sons and Heirs of Something Particular: The Smiths' Manchester Aesthetic, 1982–1987

Peter Atkinson

This chapter highlights continuities between the aesthetic evident in the songs and related material of the popular music group, The Smiths, in the 1980s and a Left-wing aesthetic found in a range of creative work produced in Manchester in the 1930s and up until the late 1950s. The Smiths brought unique properties to popular music in the wake of the emergence of a regional punk music scene in Manchester from 1976, and represent an ideal case study for the discursive and mythic construction of what I term the 'implied' place – Manchester – that has emerged through a series of representations of the city in popular culture. I engage Raymond Williams's concept of 'structure of feeling' as a theoretical way of understanding practices, experience and feelings that may be common in a specific community, such as in Manchester, or the Greater Manchester conurbation. I demonstrate that The Smiths' music was antithetical to the cosmetic 'New Pop' of 1983 and articulated an oppositional discourse to Thatcherism in which 'Manchester' was portrayed as a dystopian consequence of political oppression. The discursive agenda and the Manchester aesthetic in The Smiths' work is examined, and I demonstrate that their approach is a legacy of the political work in the agit-prop theatre of Ewan MacColl and Joan Littlewood. I then continue to observe a similar commitment to political expression of issues facing the working class in the work of BBC North Region radio under the directorship of E. A. ('Archie') Harding and the contributions Littlewood, MacColl and the documentarist Denis Mitchell made to this commitment. I conclude by noting textual continuities of this legacy in The Smiths' work.

The Smiths' time and town

The Smiths were very much of their time, which marked the 'end of an era', Mello suggests (2010: 135). The period in which they recorded and released records 'roughly corresponded' with Conservative Prime Minister Margaret Thatcher's second term in office (1983–1987), as Brooker notes (2010: 22). Their time therefore coincided with the period in which the politics of the Thatcher government divided Britain, presiding over a formal end to the nation's industrial heritage and imposing new mythologies of privatisation, enterprise, individualism and authorised selfishness. Thatcherism was 'a particular way of managing the transition from production to consumption – Britain's old manufacturing base...to an economy of services and transactions', Brooker argues in the context of his analysis of The Smiths (2010: 31). The group articulated an oppositional position to such politics from within the field of popular music. Of their time, then, The Smiths were also very much of their town, Manchester, and were the sons and heirs of a heritage of left-wing creative production in that city and its surrounding townships, as examined below. The connections are firm between the political strife of the 1930s and that of the 1980s, when Thatcher dismantled the welfare state, and are relevant in the context of The Smiths' textual output. Raymond Williams's concept of 'structure of feeling' is useful here in consideration of the dynamic experience and representation of place. Taylor, Evans and Fraser, in their study of regional local difference between Manchester and Sheffield, heed Williams's observations about the taken-for-granted 'social practices' that must be thought of as connected practices, part of an 'ensemble' of social relations. These exert great power 'over individual belief' (Williams paraphrased, Taylor et al., 1996: 5). Williams referred to going 'beyond formally held and systematic beliefs' and considering 'meanings and values as they are actively lived and felt' and the variable 'relations between these and formal and systematic beliefs' (1977: 132). Taylor et al. suggest that this concept may be applied to the 'character' of cities, as they are, both, socially experienced and represented in folklore and media representation (1996: 6). With this in mind, I will now comment upon the constructed nature of media representations of Manchester and highlight problems in relation to the socio-geographical distribution of these representations.

The implied place: 'Manchester'

In the critical discourses attendant to the work and social and cultural effect of The Smiths, the tendency is to refer to Manchester as if it is a place with an homogenous character: Halfacree and Kitchin write of 'Manchester itself' as they observe links between geography and 'indie' music (1996: 50); Simpson writes of the 'damp, dank, melancholy' town (2004: 34); Reynolds writes of the city's 'gloom and decay' seeping 'deep into the fabric' of the sound of some of its 1970s bands (2005: 174); and Pordzik writes of Morrissey, 'more than any of the other local "bards" or pop and punk celebrities', demonstrating how to 'really transform the drab Mancunian landscape into something more fertile in art' (2007: 331). Such representations essentialise Manchester and foreground aspects of that city that have been portrayed in a series of high-profile media contexts: in films, literature, radio and television shows and in popular music. The Smiths' work, and Morrissey's lyrics in particular, re-use and capitalise on these. As Power notes, the music of The Smiths, their videos and their photographs reference the remains of industrial Manchester: arched and iron bridges, derelict 'factories, smokestacks' and the 'cobbled streets and red-brick terraced houses, which have been a part of how people see Manchester going back to the descriptions of Engels and Dickens' (Power, 2011: 103).

This is a selective representation of 'Manchester'. It is a process similar to that employed when dialect is used to represent northerners in popular media. This 'not only demarcates an imagined community but also regulates the target group of consumers', Ehland observes (2007: 22). The Smiths used and reworked clichéd images of Manchester and the North, and added extra dimension to them so that they were meaningful as 'opposition' to the 'Thatcher rhetoric' of their time (Brooker, 2010: 24). Bottà notes that popular music is able to 'autonomously reshape place-images and representations' through signifying processes of layering 'textscapes' (lyrics and song titles referring to people and places), of 'soundscapes' (the way a place shapes a band's distinctive sound and also the use of local dialect, accent or city sounds) and of 'landscapes' (the 'place connections' in a band's visual material – CD covers, posters, photographs, video, stage design and clothes) (2008: 288–289). Brooker refers to the 'layered intertextuality of Morrissey's heritage' (2010: 36). However, 'Manchester' is not a fact in these representations, it is a rhetorical construction.

In the current geographical spread termed Greater Manchester, Manchester is a relatively long, thin strip of territory bordered by eight metropolitan boroughs – Bolton, Bury, Oldham, Rochdale, Stockport, Tameside, Trafford, Wigan – and the city of Salford. The latter has traditionally been Manchester's poorer neighbour. In an early example of the self-deprecating humour featuring in representations of the area, nineteenth-century working class Radical Samuel Bamford labelled the main bridge linking the cities over the River Irwell as 'the Bridge of Tears', in an ironic comparison with Venice's Bridge of Sighs (quoted in Taylor, Evans and Fraser, 1996: 56). The (lack of) distinction between Manchester and Salford is problematic in interpretation of The Smiths' work, and that of other bands who may be commonly considered to be from 'Manchester'. Goddard and Halligan (2010: 11) talk of a 'splintering of the received histories, social and cultural' of the two cities (see also Hannon, 2010; Witts, 2010). For clarity in this chapter I suggest that the 'Manchester' referred to in discourses pertaining to and surrounding The Smiths' work, is an 'implied' place. This follows the work of Rimmon-Kenan, who noted that in the narrative communication model in novels, the 'implied author' and 'implied reader' are 'substitute agents' for the real author and reader. These agents are positioned in the process of the communication of the text as it is consumed by the real 'reader' (through whatever means: reading, watching or listening). For Rimmon-Kenan this act of substitution (of the real with the implied) is 'the source of norms embodied in the work' (1983: 86). Morrissey, and The Smiths, are implied authors as their discourse emerges through text(s): their discursive impact, their 'psychological complexity', are greater than that of the individuals who comprise the actual group (1983: 86). Thus, to use Chatman's theory of communication in fiction, these implied authors ('The Smiths') instruct us 'silently, through the design of the whole, with all the voices, by all the means' that they have 'chosen to let us learn' (Chatman, 1978: 148). In such a structure it follows that the 'Manchester' under discussion *in relation to* The Smiths' work is an implied place, constructed as their texts interact dialogically with an extensive range of discourses and media representations of that place. It is more than a mythological place (Barthes), or an imagined place (Anderson) because, in this context, it is brought into being as a subject through the work of The Smiths. For example, The Smiths made Salford Lads Club, on the real-life Coronation Street, iconic after it featured on the inside gatefold sleeve of their album *The Queen is Dead* (1986). Its Victorian façade, the fact that local film star Albert Finney attended the club as a boy, the insinuation of enforced masculine community, and the implication of gay bonding associated with the building's name in the context of its use as a Smiths image, all give the site intertextual resonance (Goddard, 2012: 373). However, the building is not *in* Manchester – it is in Salford. Still, it becomes part of the discursive construction of the implied place, 'Manchester'. Having, hopefully, made clear the distinction between the geographical fact of Manchester and the place of the same name that is produced in discourse, I signal the constructed nature of the latter wherever possible in the analysis below or refer more accurately to the wider conurbation, Greater Manchester.

Vat of agit-prop, melody and self-culture

A key time politically in Britain, the period of The Smiths' inception was also a key time in the development of popular music and the media landscape. Punk impacted significantly. Its do-it-yourself ethos emboldened some young people, encouraging them towards enterprise. As with the democratising effect of skiffle in England in 1958, bands sprang up across the land and music-making and performance in the provinces were energised. By the early 1980s, young people who had a combined interest in music and fashion, and encouraged by the way dress was used in punk to signify subcultural values (Hebdidge, 1979), were gathering in locations where these tastes could be shared: Pips club in Manchester; the Rum Runner in Birmingham, and Billy's, Blitz and Le Beat Route in London. The 1970s 'were preparing their last gasp', Rimmer muses in relation to these developments (1985: 19), observing that 'New Pop' emerged as participants in club nights – many of whom had been involved in the punk scene – found an outlet for their artistic aspirations and formed bands (1985: 5).

In the first two years of the 1980s, binary oppositions became apparent in music in Britain. While 'indie' music (sometimes known as 'alternative') had flourished in the aftermath of punk, 'glossy disco and polished soul' with 'lavish high-tech production' were dominating the pop charts (Rimmer, 1985: 18). The lure of commercial success tempted some habitués of club nights who had adopted punk's do-it-yourself ethos to form bands. Hence, Spandau Ballet, Visage, Culture Club and Duran Duran arrived, bridging the gap between two previously 'opposing traditions – punk and disco' (Rimmer 1985: 23). Consequently, 'alternative' music could better define its own values, trumpeting a guitar-based authenticity promoted in opposition to New Pop, which often made use of synthesiser technology in the wake of its incursion through German electronic bands and American and Euro disco (see Reynolds, 2005: xxii; *Synth Britannia*). Binary oppositions thus became apparent between commercial and alternative music: fabricated/real; colourful/grey; major label/indie label; inauthentic/authentic.

The binary of South/North also became apparent as the result of the success in the alternative music field of a number of bands from the North (see Reynolds, 2005). In Greater Manchester, the role of a couple of gigs by The Sex Pistols at The Lesser Free Trade Hall in summer 1976 (on 4 June and 20 July) in fomenting a new local music scene is heavily mythologised. Scenes representing the event feature in the films *24 Hour Party People* (Winterbottom, 2002, a story mainly about Tony Wilson and his Manchester enterprise, Factory Records) and *Control* (Corbijn, 2007, a biopic of Joy Division's Ian Curtis) as well as in some television documentaries and in the considerable array of publications on the subject of the post-1976 Greater Manchester music scene. By late 1976 young local journalist/musician Paul Morley was able to report for the national *New Musical Express* on the 'hot new phenomenon' of a 'small series' of 'arranged' punk rock gigs in Greater Manchester (Morley, 1976). In 1977 the local group, Buzzcocks, gained a reputation for their celebrated independent EP single, *Spiral Scratch*, which seemed to epitomise the DIY spirit of punk. As Haslam observes, with some London punk bands now being signed to major labels, 'their rhetoric of anarchy and revolution' sounded hollow, but Buzzcocks demonstrated a productivity 'working outside the normal structures', hence adhering more to the original punk ethos (Haslam, 2000: 114). Buzzcocks sang of 'boredom' and of life as 'very humdrum' (*Boredom*) and they were at the forefront of a batch of bands from the area that began to gain the attention of the national rock press and specialist radio programmes such as John Peel. The most prominent of these, arguably, were Joy Division (formerly Warsaw), The Fall, Magazine (created by former Buzzcock Howard Devoto) and A Certain Ratio.

The emergence of these bands *suggested* an homogenous 'Manchester' scene, characterised by a bleak, realist aesthetic. Black and white photographs of Joy Division by Kevin Cummins for a January 1979 *New Musical Express* cover 'were key to framing the bleak intensity of the band's image', *The Telegraph* recently wrote (Lachno, 2014). One of the black and white photographs is on a snow-covered pedestrian bridge in Hulme, South Manchester, near where Morrissey once lived. The band is positioned in the background of the photo, with the foreground being a white expanse of snowy nothingness, in what Gatenby and Gill describe as an 'Un-Rock & Roll' picture (2011: 67). The image has connotations of a bleak East European city prior to the fall of the Berlin Wall, and Joy Division's music was influenced by David Bowie's 'Berlin period', when he was influenced by a number of German electronic bands, including Kraftwerk and Neu! (see Reynolds, 2005: xxi). The suicide of Joy Division's Ian Curtis in May 1980, and the poignancy of their single *Love Will Tear Us Apart*, which achieved chart success immediately afterwards, embedded the myth of 'Manchester' as an alternative music city distanced from London's hegemony. Thus it could be said that a

'Manchester' aesthetic was produced across a set of images and discourses in a particular time and among particular circumstances. This may be associated with the 'structure of feeling' that Williams writes of. Greater Manchester's physical environment is a legacy of the onslaught of the Industrial Revolution. However, the first industrial city 'had become one of the first to enter the post-industrial era', and images of dereliction and the disenfranchisement of its people in 'the dole-age' (*Some Girls are Bigger Than Others*, The Smiths, 1986) of spiralling unemployment had resonance at the onset of the 1980s (Reynolds, 2005: 174).

The Smiths associated the geographical reality of Greater Manchester, and the discursive domain of the implied place, 'Manchester', with a radical stance. In their work the 'rhetorical recourse to the North is insistent', Brooker observes (2010: 28). As Whiteley contests, their politicised lyrics locked into 'the social and cultural divide caused by Thatcherism', shaping 'Manchester' as a site of political opposition to that agenda and its privileging of south-east England (2010: 105). Simultaneously, their adherence to, and musical referencing of, the 'authentic' rock style of the 1950s and 1960s intertextually linked them to the '1960s counter-culture' (Whiteley, 2010: 105). This emphasised the polarity between the cosmetic New Pop and what Bannister terms the 'purity' of 'indie', or 'alternative', rock music in 1983 (2006: 87). The quality of The Smiths' northern music legitimated the latter while perpetuating the political discourse of the north/south divide in England. However, partly because of the new platforms opened for rock/pop music at the time – and, partly because of their initial minor chart success – The Smiths found themselves in autumn 1983performing on television alongside New Pop acts.

By 1982 the pop video was becoming a significant medium in pop music. Coinciding with this, the opening of Channel Four Television in Britain provided a new and distinctive platform for music. The Smiths were profiled on Channel Four's *The Tube*, on 4 November 1983, 20 days before their first appearance on *Top of the Pops* – on both occasions they performed *This Charming Man* (1983). Highlighting the enclosed male world represented in the song, the latter appearance was described by David Stubbs in *Uncut* as 'an unexpectedly pivotal cultural event in the lives of a million English boys', and from this time. The Smiths' 'Manchester' aesthetic shapes itself as a national discourse (Stubbs, quoted in Goddard, 2004: 53). Morrissey eloquently observes it:

The groups from Punk's overspill continued to rabble-rouse in large armies, but The Smiths drew a line under the past with a detachment that presented a confidential perspective, and one that would never snap. The vat of agit-prop, melody and self-culture all mish-mashed into a strong autonomous weapon that seemed on the face of it academic, yet appealed to heavily scarred jostlers. (2013: 151)

Despite this, their styling, performance and iconography ensured that they attracted the attention of the style-conscious: in the *Top of the Pops* performance Morrissey sported a fashionably exaggerated, retro 1950s quiff; Marr had a fringed haircut and wore clothes redolent of the English beat groups of the 1960s. Just before playing their first gig at the Hacienda in February 1983, Morrissey wielded a bunch of gladioli like a whip – flowers being employed, initially, 'to kill off that 1982 Factory aesthetic, of concrete and steel', Marr contends (Marr, quoted in Robb, 2010: 198). With the *Top of the Pops* appearance, however, they signified an otherness to the programme's synthetic glamour and connoted a charged oppositional agenda amplified by Morrissey's yelp in between verses. To consider the discursive impact of *This Charming Man* in these contexts: the song features multi-tracked guitars and is a musical hybridity that fuses elements of Motown, country, jazz and blues (Goddard, 2004: 52). However, the exceptional nature of The Smiths' engagement with their world is signified in the lyrics of the song. These portray a scene in which a young man is stranded on a remote hillside, his bicycle tyre having suffered a puncture. It is implied that a man with considerable charm stops to help and that the two have sex on the seat of his tasteful car, as suggested by the lines, 'Why pamper life's complexity/ When the leather runs smooth on the passenger's seat?' (*This Charming Man*, The Smiths, 1983). Campbell and Coulter identify the 'Rustic homoerotic desire' that gives the song a 'subversive potential' (2010: 2). As they note, such 'subversive aspects of the band … stretched far beyond the specific establishment objects of the vocalist's ire and into a realm that was more specifically aesthetic'. Many of their songs 'invite the listener beyond the constraints of the everyday' and remind them that 'another world is possible' (2010: 6). To pamper life's complexity, briefly, the thematic territory that the song shapes is a tension between nature and culture, but one compounded by the homoerotic aspect (see Marr, quoted in Robb, regarding The Smiths' involvement in the Manchester gay scene, 2010: 199–200). A number of questions revolve around the line in the song, 'Will nature make a man of me yet?' (*This Charming Man*, The Smiths, 1983), and its relation to human pursuit: Is the protagonist seeking health through taking exercise in the country? Is it sex with another man that ensures that nature has taken its course? Is he struggling to *become* a man? Or is it that he feels that he can only become a man by escaping the city? For the hillside is desolated in contrast to that which is not so: inhabited, cultured, city society. This is where the predatory, middle-class, cultivated charmer who helps the stranded boy hails from. He has been rewarded with sufficient capital to purchase an expensive car, his upward mobility ensuring that the contrastingly immobile boy is there for his taking. Given The Smiths' 'controversial elegy' to the victims of the Moors Murderers (*Suffer Little Children*, 1984) it is reasonable to associate the desolate hillside described in *This Charming Man* with the bleak Yorkshire and Derbyshire moorlands to the East of Manchester (Goddard, 2004: 79). Morrissey discursively articulates what may be labelled a 'Manchester' structure of feeling through the Moors Murders of the 1960s, as he writes in his autobiography:

A swarm of misery grips mid-60s Manchester as Hindley and Brady raise their faces to the camera and become known to us all; nineteenth-century street life right here and now, with 1970 but a spit away. It is factual Hindley and Brady, and not our spirited Lake poets or cosy tram-travelled novelists, who supply the unspoken and who take the travelling mind further than it ever ought to have gone, sealing modern Manchester as a place of Dickensian drear. Of Hindley and Brady there would be nothing to give you heart in their complicity, as children of the poor, who had lived short and shaky lives, were led away to their tortured deaths, and the social landscape of Manchester warps forever with further reason to cry. (Morrissey, 2013: 26–27)

The victims of the Moors Murderers were snatched in Greater Manchester. The children who return as ghosts on the moors are specifically children of the poor, urban working classes of Ancoats, Longsight, Gorton, Ardwick (where Marr grew up) – all connected Victorian, inner city suburbs in east and south Manchester. These were considered slums by the 1960s, and were undergoing clearance by the City Council. One victim came from Ashton-under-Lyne, a Lancashire mill town six miles away. It is the manner in which the Moors Murders narrative maps onto the more complex discourses of class, through which such lives and their thwarted possibilities are more generally understood, that gives it its power as working class history (Pleasance, 2011: 30). As in most of the other work of The Smiths, the writing, in Pordzik's terms, 'epitomises the overlaying of individual messages with a broad variety of divergent bits of texts and meaning-bearing patterns adapted from different realms of creative thought' (2007: 327). These politicised lyrics exude 'attitude', Whiteley observes (2010: 105). This stance is informed, whether consciously, or unconsciously, by a tradition of political activism in theatre, music and radio broadcasting in Greater Manchester. I now illustrate the continuities that are evident between these and the work of The Smiths.

Taking radical theatre to the dirty old town

Academics have commented upon and analysed Morrissey's professed love of the 1961 film *A Taste of Honey* (Brooker, 2010; Goddard, 2004, 2012; Mello, 2010; Pordzik, 2007; Whitely, 2010). The film is an adaptation of a debut stage play of the same name by Shelagh Delaney, who wrote the piece as an 18-year-old Salford schoolgirl. Morrissey acknowledged Delaney as a muse; he also referred to her 'strange sexiness' and quoted from her work extensively in his lyrics (Goddard, 2012: 96–99). Like Morrissey and Marr (real surname Maher), Delaney was of Irish descent (see Campbell, 2010). The play was first staged in 1958 by Theatre Workshop, a left-wing theatre group which was then based in Stratford East, in London's East End (a run-down working class area at that time). As Lacey writes, this was unlike 'any other theatre of the period':

> The company arose out of the worker's theatre movement of the inter-war years, when its founders, Joan Littlewood and Ewan MacColl, ran a series of companies linked by a range of common concerns: a radical socialism, a commitment to performance for working class audiences, and a voracious appetite for a variety of theatrical influences and methods. (1995: 48)

The theatre companies that evolved into Theatre Workshop had their roots in Manchester (and Salford) where practitioners worked as political activists, theatre producers and performers, and as BBC radio performers and writers and, in MacColl's case, as a folk musician.

There is an initial and ostensible incongruity in a comparison between Morrissey and MacColl. The most obvious differences are the musical and generational ones. Additionally, some of MacColl's music is associated with a traditionally masculine world of (heroic) working class labour, whereas Morrissey's representations of working class life are more complex and ambiguous. The latter complicates the male position, as observed earlier, representing issues such as homosexuality, abuse and paedophilia (see Whiteley, 2010). There are similarities, however: Harper writes that MacColl, like Morrissey, 'had an opinion on everything and regularly gave the press controversy on a plate' (2006: 31). He also 'made himself visible' and 'made himself the target', as Martin Carthy has noted, as The Smiths' frontman was inclined to do (quoted in Harper, 2006: 31). Further correspondence between MacColl's work, and that of The Smiths are now outlined.

'Minstrel of the working people'

Harker recalls that two thousand people attended a concert celebrating MacColl's seventieth birthday party in London in January 1985, during the forty-seventh week of Britain's 'bitterest industrial dispute since the General Strike' (2007: 1). He notes:

> Mass unemployment; protracted industrial dispute; barricaded communities; running battles between militant workers and the forces of state; the 1980s seemed like a replay of the 1930s that had shaped him [MacColl]. He felt that recent history had vindicated his unswerving political beliefs. (2007: 3)

MacColl was born in Salford in 1915 into a working class immigrant Scottish family. Like Morrissey he engrossed himself in literature as a teenager (in Salford and central Manchester libraries) in preference to the conformity and subservience of regular employment (Harker, 2007: 36). Speaking about being unemployed upon leaving school in 1929, MacColl wrote: '[s]ince you have entered this grown-up world where nobody seems to want you or need you, you have come to regard books as your best friends, your only friends' (MacColl, 1990: 36). His reading helped him express his individuality through creative production. 'Ewan MacColl' is an alias derived from the name of the nineteenth-century Gaelic poet Eoghan MacColla: his real name is James 'Jimmie' Miller, and it was changed when he deserted during military service in World War II and hid in Urmston, Greater Manchester, for several years.

MacColl made creative use of a workers' network of institutions in Salford, including the Workers' Arts Club and Salford Workers' Film Society, where he was able to view international experimental political films by the likes of Pudovkin and Eisenstein, which influenced his future work (Harker, 2007: 16). He was also introduced to radical theatre and began to attend Communist Party meetings. He remembers how, for him, this 'transformed' the 'landscape of Salford and Manchester', which had never been the same 'since he'd read Engels' *The Condition of the Working Class in England'* (Harker, 2007: 20). Thus inspired, MacColl formed a Salford branch of the Workers' Theatre Movement in 1931 and took an interest in German and Soviet radical theatre (23). From this evolved 'The Red Megaphones', a political theatre group that performed at a series of events across Manchester and used a variety of performance styles.

In touch with theatre groups in the United States and the Soviet Union and with exiled German theatre workers, Red Megaphones toured their work to disseminate their left-wing message in working class townships, villages of the north-west and in Manchester districts (Goorney and MacColl, 1986: xxiv). In 1938 MacColl and Littlewood created the Theatre Union with the task to bring plays 'of social significance' to 'the widest possible public', particularly to those who had been 'starved' of theatre (Harker, 2007: 55). The 'theme of unemployment' ran through their play, *Last Edition: A Living Newspaper Dealing with Events from 1934 to 1940*, which 'represented a complete break with formal theatre staging' and was described as a 'living newspaper' – part 'documentary' and part 'revue' (Goorney and MacColl, 1986: xlvi).

Theatre Workshop evolved from this, operating initially from Kendal, but eventually relocating to Stratford East from where it exerted considerable influence upon English theatre and film in the late 1950s and early 1960s, as it developed stage plays such as *Oh! What a Lovely War*, *Fings Ain't Wot They Used to Be*, *Sparrers Can't Sing* and *A Taste of Honey*. Meanwhile, MacColl and Littlewood's influence in Manchester also spread to radio. Having taken to singing and to writing folk songs, MacColl would sing in the city streets, and in 1934 was spotted by a BBC radio scriptwriter, who invited him to work at BBC North Region as an actor.

E. A. Harding and the North

The BBC North Region also demonstrated a concern with social and class-related issues at the time, and continuities are evident with The Smiths' Manchester aesthetic discussed here. Scannell refers to the 'distinctive brand of regionalism' produced at the Manchester studio following the early 1930s establishment of the BBC's regional stations. This 'foregrounded ordinary working people both within the programmes and as part of the audience for whom they were made'. The 'double focus on the everyday lives and tastes of the majority' contrasted with the National Programme, broadcast from London in the 1930s (Scannell, 1986: 22). Towards the end of the 1920s the

BBC developed 'Features' programmes that combined drama and journalism, some of which incorporated Pudovkin's cinema methods of slow motion, dissolves, fades, montage and mixes – as in the work of Lance Sieveking, for example (Scannell and Cardiff, 1991: 135–136). During turbulent economic and political times, the BBC also adopted some of the methods of documentary-realist filmmakers such as John Grierson and Robert Flaherty for radio 'features' (Crisell, 1997: 36). The BBC Talks Department developed major series on social issues and 'the condition of England' from the early 1930s (Scannell, 1986: 7). These included the series *Other People's Houses, SOS* (both 1933), *Time to Spare* and the single programme *'Opping 'Oliday* (both 1934) – all of which represented social issues relating to working class life in difficult times (Scannell and Cardiff, 1991: 58, 147).

A 'purge' of Talks in 1935 followed protests from the right-wing press about the National Programme's intervention in social issues (Scannell, 1986: 14). However, programmes that documented the lives of working class people continued to be made by the BBC North Region in Manchester. E. A. ('Archie') Harding had become programme director in 1933 following his exile from the National Programme because of the nature of his left-wing work. In Manchester, Harding gathered local talent – among others, poet and writer Geoffrey Bridson – and some came from the local theatre circuit to work for the unit. In 1935, Bridson created *Harry Hopeful*, which observed the North through the lens of an imaginary character roaming the area in search of work. He produced four programmes in 1937 about the area's major industries – *Steel, Cotton, Wool,* and *Coal* – after the Manchester station acquired a mobile recording unit. Littlewood was presenter of *Coal*, she and Bridson spending a month amidst mining communities to research the scripted programme (Scannell and Cardiff, 1991: 343–344).

Olive Shapley was also innovative, recording people talking in their ordinary situations throughout the region with the mobile unit. Working with Littlewood, MacColl and Wilfred Pickles, she produced programmes on a range of human activities, including: *Pounds, Shillings and Pence: A Study in Shopping* (1938); *Homeless People* (1938); and *Canal Journey* (1939) (Scannell and Cardiff, 1991: 346). *They Speak For Themselves* (1939) was an hour long examination of mass observation that combined studio presentation and discussion with recorded actuality and music. Continuity is evident in a lineage of Manchester productions as Littlewood made Engels's *The Condition of the Working Class in England* 'the historical point of reference' for *The Classic Soil* (1939), produced by Shapley and written by Littlewood, and which made representation of working class life in Manchester a century earlier and, hence, made a comparison between the two periods. Meanwhile, MacColl also wrote for the BBC North Region; his *The Chartists' March* was broadcast on 13 May 1938, in commemoration of the centenary of that movement (Scannell and Cardiff, 1991: 353). Franklin importantly notes that the work of the BBC North Region 'more faithfully attempted to bring working class culture and voice to the microphone. Here at the edge of the BBC's empire there was less distance between producers and listeners' (2009: 32).

MacColl later worked with celebrated radio and television documentarist Denis Mitchell, who can be seen as 'an inheritor and upholder of the rich tradition of North Region feature production in the 1930s' (Franklin, 2009: 95). In Mitchell's *Night in the City* (1955), continuity is particularly evident between MacColl's experiences in Salford, his theatre work in the region, and the features work of BBC North Region. Mitchell used *Dirty Old Town*, the signature tune from MacColl's 1951 play *Landscape with Chimneys*, performed by Theatre Workshop, as the theme song, and also integrated it into the text of the programme (Harker, 2007: 94). This radio documentary was an attempt to capture the atmosphere of Manchester at night and made use of the recorded voices of people in the hidden 'layers within society almost entirely ignored or forgotten in public life' (Franklin, 2009: 103). This was typical of 'Mitchell's urban ethnography for the BBC North Region' (94). Franklin notes the 'bleakness' of the programme, and this illustrates the consistency in the structure of feeling that spans decades of media production in Manchester (109). With their mobilisation of comparably bleak images and social commentary, The Smiths emphasise this continuity. It is notable that Ewan's daughter, singer Kirsty MacColl, became a close friend of The Smiths and 'irreplaceable' to Morrissey (quoted, Goddard, 2012: 234). She sang backing vocals on *Ask* and *Golden Lights* in 1986 and worked individually with both Smiths songwriters before her tragic death in 2000.

Manchester militancy

Campbell and Coulter note 'the radical politics and aesthetics' of The Smiths, arguing:

> [T]he songs of Morrissey and Marr undermined the mores and practices at the very heart of the prevailing social order – the work ethic, the cult of the consumer, the imperatives of inherited privilege, the

instrumentalism of the culture industries and so on. The critique of bourgeois society tendered by the Smiths was always, therefore, likely to provoke the wrath of the political and cultural establishment'. (2010: 6)

This radicalism is a legacy of MacColl's and Littlewood's activities in Manchester, Salford and regions, and the texts they produced. Whether unconsciously or consciously, Morrissey retrieved and reactivated this legacy via an intermediate 1950s/1960s structure of feeling around Shelagh Delaney, Free Cinema, British New Wave and the social-realist soap, *Coronation Street*, of which he was a fan and had submitted script ideas to it as a boy (Goddard, 2012: 80).

The influence across generations is discernible in Morrissey's song, *Margaret on the Guillotine*, from his first solo LP *Viva Hate* (1988) and MacColl's song, *Dirty Old Town*, from his play, *Landscape with Chimneys*, a portrayal of northern industrial life and which predates by several years the English 'kitchen sink realism' of the late 1950s early 1960s. The lyrics of this now well-known folk song about the Salford of MacColl's youth include the lines, 'I'm going to make a good sharp axe', and 'We'll chop you down like an old dead tree' (*Dirty Old Town*, MacColl, 1949). The sentiment, which suggests a revolutionary response to appalling social conditions, is the same as in *Margaret on the Guillotine*, which was originally the title of The Smiths' LP *The Queen is Dead*, released in 1986 when Thatcher was at the height of her political power. The 'death sentence' pronounced in *Guillotine* showed that the implied author, Morrissey, similarly hankered 'after violent reprisal' (Brooker, 2010: 26–27). Like MacColl, he was interviewed by Special Branch Task Force to gauge whether or not he posed a security threat (Morrissey, 2013: 226; see also Smith, 2012; Harker). Meanwhile, an association can also be made between the heritage of MacColl's and Littlewood's radical left-wing, agit-prop theatre in Greater Manchester and The Smiths' song, *A Rush and a Push and The Land is Ours* (1987), which demonstrates a commitment to revolution with Irish nationalist connotations. The title is derived from a revolutionary call to arms written by Oscar Wilde's mother under the pseudonym of Speranza in 1848 (Goddard, 2012: 370).

Harker reports that the members of MacColl's and Littlewood's Theatre Union regarded it as a 'cause', and that '[s]hoplifting from the petit bourgeoisie was sanctioned'; anything 'to assist the theatre of the future' was considered 'fair game' (2007: 57). The Smiths' song *Shoplifters of the World Unite* (1987) exhibits very similar sentiments. That it features the word 'Unite', from the end of Marx's Communist Manifesto confirms, as Goddard observes, that the song is a call to revolutionary activity (2010: 388). A personal recollection by Morrissey is illustrative of the structure of feeling associated with a downtrodden Manchester city centre. The singer recalls that when his aunt Rita became upwardly mobile and acquired a manager's job at Chelsea Girl in Piccadilly, she could 'often be spotted chasing shoplifters through [the adjacent] Piccadilly Gardens' (Morrissey, 2013: 144). Again, in this observation Morrissey recalls local detail with a bathetic twist. As with other Smiths' songs, *Shoplifters* makes a political comment through the apparent portrayal of working class ordinariness (petty pilferers), and the statement of an otherness that must remain hidden, as illustrated in the line, 'My only weakness is...well, never mind, never mind' (*Shoplifters of the World Unite*, The Smiths, 1987). This unwillingness to disclose otherness, to decline to open-up, represents a common inhibition and denial of voice among the class-bound lower orders.

It has been seen that The Smiths' work was politically motivated and was a reaction against the political oppression that was being exerted during their time, particularly against the working class and those involved in industrial labour and the public-service sector. In a milieu in which the do-it-yourself ethos of punk rock had, among some practitioners, evolved into the founding of bands with enterprising, commercial agendas, binary opposition became evident in British rock/pop between New Pop and 'alternative' rock. A strong provincial punk scene in Manchester gave birth to a number of bands with diverse styles, linked largely by their geographical origins in Greater Manchester but also by a dystopian imagery. The Smiths evinced a wider cultural perspective, their music incorporating a range of diverse influences, their lyrics demonstrating literary qualities. Self-conscious regarding his own background, the lyricist Morrissey reconstituted images of Manchester and other aspects of British life, in the creation of songs that critiqued many aspects of contemporary eighties life. In doing so, The Smiths focused on certain aspects of Manchester life, particularly those associated with working class culture and the Manchester of the late 1950s and the 1960s. I have used Williams's concept of 'structure of feeling' as a theoretical tool with which to summarise areas of activity and feeling that are lived and felt, but which are often submerged or which elude definition. I have pointed out here the continuities between the work of The Smiths and the radical working class theatre produced by Ewan MacColl and Joan Littlewood. It has been seen that this Manchester and Salford heritage of political activism and left-wing representation was also a feature of productions the BBC North Region in the 1930s. Finally, a continuity of some themes in this body of work is demonstrated to have been incorporated into The Smiths' lyrics. The rain may regularly fall in the region of Greater Manchester – indeed this was instrumental in its industrial ascent (Taylor et al., 1996: 46) – but its heritage of radical creative production, upheld in the work of The Smiths, strongly argues against the town being 'humdrum'.

References

Albiez, S. (2006) Print the Truth, not the Legend. The Sex Pistols: Lesser Free Trade Hall, Manchester, 4 June 1976. In I. Inglis (ed.) *Performance and Popular Music: History, Place and Time* (Aldershot: Ashgate), 92–106.

Anderson, B. (2006) *Imagined Communities: Reflections on the Origin and Spread of Nationalism* (London: Verso).

Bannister, M. (2006) 'Loaded': Indie Guitar Rock, Canonism, White Masculinities, *Popular Music*, Vol. 25, No. 1, 77–95.

Barthes, R. (1972) *Mythologies*, trans. by Annette Lavers (London: Jonathan Cape).

Black, B. (1983) 'The Smiths: Keep Young and Beautiful', *Sounds*, 19 November. Available at www.rocksbackpages.com (Accessed 15 February 2015).

Bottà, G. (2008) Urban Creativity and Popular Music in Europe since the 1970s: Representation, Materiality and Branding. In M. Heßler and C. Zimmerman (eds) *Creative Urban Milieus: Historical Perspectives on Culture, Economy, and the City* (Frankfurt: Campus), 285–308.

Brooker, J. (2010) 'Has the World Changed or Have I Changed?' The Smiths and the Challenge of Thatcherism. In S. Campbell and C. Coulter (eds) *Why Pamper Life's Complexities? Essays on The Smiths* (Manchester: Manchester University Press), 22–42.

Campbell, S. (2010) 'Irish Blood, English Heart': Ambivalence, Unease and The Smiths. In S. Campbell and C. Coulter (eds) *Why Pamper Life's Complexities? Essays on The Smiths* (Manchester: Manchester University Press), 65–80.

Campbell, S. and Coulter, C. (2010) Why Pamper Life's Complexities?: An Introduction to the Book. In S. Campbell and C. Coulter (eds) *Why Pamper Life's Complexities? Essays on The* Smiths (Manchester: Manchester University Press), 1–21.

Chatman S. (1978) *Story and Discourse*, (New York: Cornell University Press).

Crisell, A. (1997) *An Introductory History of British Broadcasting*, (London: Routledge).

Cummins, K. (2012) *Manchester: Looking for the Light through the Pouring Rain* (London: Faber & Faber).

Devereux, E., Dillane, A. and Power, M. J. (2011) Introduction: But Don't Forget the Songs That Made You Cry and the Songs That Saved Your Life. In E. Devereux, A. Dillane and M. Power (eds) *Morrissey: Fandom, Representations and Identities* (Bristol: Intellect), 15–18.

Franklin, I. (2009) Folkways and Airwaves: Oral History, Community & Vernacular Radio, unpublished Bournemouth University, PhD thesis.

Gatenby, P. and Gill, C. (2011) *The Manchester Musical History Tour* (Manchester: Empire Publications).

Goddard, M. and Halligan, B. (2010) Messing up the Paintwork. In M. Goddard and B. Halligan (eds) *Mark E. Smith and The Fall: Art, Music and Politics* (Farnham: Ashgate), 1–15.

Goddard, S. (2004) *The Smiths: Songs That Saved Your Life*, 2nd edition (London: Reynolds and Hearn).

Goddard, S. (2012) *Mozipedia: The Encyclopedia of Morrissey and The Smiths*, 2nd edition (London: Ebury Press).

Goorney, H. and MacColl, E. (eds) (1986) *Agit-Prop to Theatre Workshop: Political Playscripts 1930–50* (Manchester: Manchester University Press).

Halfacree, K. H. and Kitchin, R. M. (1996) 'Madchester Rave On': Placing the Fragments of Popular Music, *Area*, Vol. 28, No. 1, 47–53.

Hannon, K. (2010) The Fall: A Manchester Band? In M. Goddard and B. Halligan (eds) *Mark E. Smith and The Fall: Art, Music and Politics* (Farnham: Ashgate), 33–39.

Harker, B. (2007) *Class Act: The Cultural and Political Life of Ewan MacColl* (London: Pluto Press).

Harker, B. (2009) Mediating the 1930s: Documentary and politics in Theatre Union's 'Last Edition' (1940). University of Salford website: http://usir.salford.ac.uk/12133/ (Accessed 24 November 2014).

Harper, C. (2006) *Dazzling Stranger: Bert Jansch and the British Folk and Blues Revival*, 2nd edition, with foreword by Johnny Marr (London: Bloomsbury).

Harris, J. (2003) *The Last Party* (London: Harper Perennial).

Haslam, D. (2000) *Manchester, England: The Story of a Pop Cult City* (London: Fourth Estate).

Hebdige, D. (1979) *Subculture: The Meaning of Style* (London: Routledge).

Lacey, S. (1995) *British Realist Theatre: The New Wave in Its Contexts, 1956–1965* (London: Routledge).

Lachno, J. (2014) Kevin Cummins Q&A: 'I saved Joy Division from being Bon Jovi', *The Telegraph* online: www.telegraph.co.uk (Accessed 14 February 2015).

MacColl, E. (1990) *Journeyman* (London: Sidgwick & Jackson).

Mello, C. (2010) 'I Don't Owe You Anything': The Smiths and Kitchen-Sink Cinema. In S. Campbell and C. Coulter (eds) *Why Pamper Life's Complexities? Essays on The Smiths* (Manchester: Manchester University Press), 135–155.

Morley, P. (1976) Review, 'The Buzzcocks, Eater: Holdsworth Hall, Manchester', *New Musical Express*, 2 October 1976.

Morrissey, S. (2013) *Autobiography* (London: Penguin).

Pleasance, H. (2011) Lost Children, the Moors & Evil Monsters: The Photographic Story of the Moors murders 1, *Image & Narrative*, Vol. 12, No. 4, 18–38.

Pordzik, R. (2007) Of Popular Spaces: Northern Heterotopias, Morrissey and the Manchester Britpop Scene. In C. Ehlan (ed.) *Thinking Northern: Textures of Identity in the North of England* (New York: Rodopi), 325–346.

Power, M. J. (2011) The 'Teenage Dad' and 'Slum Mums' Are Just 'Certain People I Know': Counter Hegemonic Representations of the Working/Underclass in the Works of Morrissey. In E. Devereux, A. Dillane and M. Power (eds) *Morrissey: Fandom, Representations and Identities* (Bristol: Intellect), 95–117.

Reynolds, S. (2005) *Rip It Up and Start Again: Postpunk 1978–1984* (London: Faber & Faber).

Rimmer, D. (1985) *Like Punk Never Happened: Culture Club and the New Pop* (London: Faber and Faber).

Rimmon-Kenan, S. (1983) *Narrative Fiction: Contemporary Poetics* (London: Routledge).

Robb, J. (2010) *The North Will Rise Again: Manchester Music City (1976–1996)* (London: Aurum).

Scannell, P. (1986) 'The Stuff of Radio': Developments in Radio Features and Documentaries Before the War. In J. Corner (ed.) *Documentary and the Mass Media* (London: Arnold), 1–26.

Scannell, P. and Cardiff, D. (1991) *A Social History of British Broadcasting: Volume One, 1922–1939 – Serving the Nation* (Oxford: Blackwell).

Simpson, D. (2004) *Saint Morrissey* (London: SAF Publishing).

Smith, J. (2012) *British Writers and MI5 Surveillance, 1930–1960* (Cambridge: Cambridge University Press).

Smith, M. E. and Middles, M. (2008) *The Fall*, 2nd edition (London: Omnibus Press).

Synth Britannia at the BBC (2009) Dir. Benjamin Whalley, BBC Productions.

Taylor, I. K. Evans and Fraser, P. (1996) *A Tale of Two Cities: Global Change, Local Feeling and Everyday Life in Northern England. A Study of Manchester and Sheffield* (Abingdon: Routledge).

Whiteley, S. (2010) A Boy in the Bush: Childhood, Sexuality and The Smiths. In S. Campbell and C. Coulter (eds) *Why Pamper Life's Complexities? Essays on The Smiths* (Manchester: Manchester University Press), 104–120.

Williams, R. (1977) *Marxism and Literature* (Oxford: Oxford University Press).

Witts, R. (2010) Building Up a Band: Music for a Second City. In M. Goddard and B. Halligan (eds) *Mark E. Smith and The Fall: Art, Music and Politics* (Farnham: Ashgate), 19–31.

5

Away and Raffle Yourself! *Still Game*, Craiglang, Glasgow and Identity

Mary Irwin

Over six decades Jack and Victor have watched their Glasgow neighbourhood of Craiglang turn from a site of optimistic regeneration into a 'toatal [total] shitehole' which they now cast their cantankerous gaze over from either side of a landing high in the Osprey Heights tower block.[1]

Figure 7   Jack and Victor, *Still Game* (BBC Scotland, 2002–2007)

Introduction – background to *Still Game*

BBC Scotland's comedy series, *Still Game* (BBC Scotland, 2002–2007) chronicled with ebullient and scathing humour the day-to-day exploits of a group of working class pensioners living in the fictitious, rundown Craiglang housing estate on the outskirts of Glasgow. Authentically written in vernacular Glaswegian, the series was linguistically rich and inventive, underpinned by a nuanced understanding of, and affection for, Glasgow and a specifically Glaswegian sense of identity. *Still Game* drew knowingly on a host of local cultural references and allusions, making strategic use of cameos from a range of well-known Glaswegians, from 2003 *Pop Idol* winner Michelle McManus and daytime television presenter Lorraine Kelly to internationally established figures, such as former world champion lightweight boxer Jim Watt and actor David Hayman.

The series featured an ensemble cast, but lifelong friends and sparring partners, seventy-something Jack Jarvis and Victor McDade (played by Scottish comedians and series writers Ford Kiernan and Greg Hemphill), were at the centre of the weekly half-hour-long storylines, and it is from their perspective that events were most frequently presented. Their relationship, whilst usually conducted in terms of comedy banter, petty squabbles and frequent mutual irritation, was at the same time firmly grounded in their shared experiences of growing up in and around post-war Glasgow and an adult life spent in Craiglang. Principal characters included scheming Winston Ingram (Paul Riley), miserly Tam Mullen (Mark Cox) and fount of all community gossip, Isa Drennan (Jane McCarry). In the mid-seventies, shopkeeper Navid Harrid (Sanjeev Kohli) had eloped from India to Glasgow with his wife Meena (Shamshad Akhtar) to escape an arranged marriage; his corner shop was a focal point for the Craiglang community, and Navid brought to the series the perspective of first-generation immigrants to the city. All these long-term friends (and/or antagonists) of Jack and Victor were, like them, hard up pensioners struggling to make the best of their circumstances, always on the hunt for any opportunities that might save them some money and make their lives a bit easier. Navid is the exception here; as the owner of his own small business, his circumstances are more comfortable than the others. Navid is, however, as much part of the community as the rest of the characters. His own livelihood depends on locals using the shop.

The characters were played by actors in their thirties and forties, which allowed for a robust comic physicality in performance, playing against stereotypes and expectations around screen representations of ageing.

That characters are played by younger actors is significant, as *Still Game* does not deal simply with straightforward nostalgia of those recalling their past, but rather a conscious reanimation and exploration of the pasts of previous generations of Glaswegians. It is the cast's and writers' own specific historical and cultural heritage as post-war working class Glaswegians that is being reanimated. Such lives are rarely depicted on national television, as Medhurst points out, of the northern-English-set television comedy *The Royle Family* (BBC, 1998–2012). These are 'not the type of people customarily assumed to require in-depth treatment in cultural representations. Other texts have no qualms about stereotyping such people, because such people have little or no power to contest such representations' (Medhurst, 2005: 147). Likewise, the particular Glasgow and its people *Still Game* depicts are not generally afforded much UK media attention.

Scotland in Moving Image Scholarship

There is substantial recent scholarship on film and television representations of Scottish and Glaswegian identity, from MacArthur's *Brigadoon, Braveheart and the Scots: Distortions of Scotland in Hollywood Cinema* (2003) and Petrie's *Contemporary Scottish Fictions – Film, Television and the Novel* (2004), to Blain and Hutchison's edited collection, *The Media in Scotland* (2008) and Hibberd's *The Funny Thing about Scottish Independents* (2010). There is some critical commentary on *Still Game*. Mowatt, in Blain and Hutchison, considers *Still Game's* popularity and success as part of his wider overview of broadcast comedy. Hibberd also reflects on aspects of the significance of the series in terms of BBC Scotland's Comedy Unit's output. The Comedy Unit is one of the most successful independent production companies in Scotland. It was established in 1995 by former employees of BBC Scotland and is based in Glasgow (Hibberd, 2010: 74). Neither Mowatt's nor Hibberd's work, however, has *Still Game's* particular representation of Glasgow as its central focus. This chapter uses Mowatt's and Hibberd's analyses as starting points, drawing on their observations to examine in detail the rich comedic depiction of the strand of Glaswegian life the series offers. *Still Game* represents a rare televisual insider perspective on the city,[2] and this rareness chimes with Mills's reflections on television comedy as a genre and the contradictory notion of an all-encompassing 'British' comedy tradition as offered by the BBC:

> In order to be a national broadcaster the BBC must deny certain kinds of comedy content, and humorous voices, as much as it promotes

others. For the regions and communities of the United Kingdom this can be seen to be problematic. (Mills, 2010: 72)

Indigenous humorous perspectives on Glasgow circulating out with Scotland are few in number, with BBC Scotland's *Rab C. Nesbitt* (discussed more fully later in the chapter) the only notable exception. *Still Game* syncretises characters, geographical locations and issues around class and identity that have experienced limited, partial and frequently problematic representations in mainstream media. Glasgow remains consistently poorly served and little understood by national broadcasters who have a limited sense of both the specificity of contemporary Glaswegian life and Glasgow's own history. The city is frequently and lazily deployed as cultural shorthand for the most violent and deprived of UK communities, its native accent often cited as a byword in belligerent incomprehensibility. A recent radio documentary on accents, *Speak Britannia* (BBC Extra, 12 July 2014), had teenagers cite the Glaswegian accent as one of the most aggressive in the UK. The comments were based less on any familiarity with the accent than the limited media exposure to the accent they had experienced.

Medhurst's *A National Joke: Popular Comedy and English Cultural Identities* provides a useful framework for examining *Still Game*'s articulation of Glaswegian cultural identity. He writes of comedy 'which explores the relationships between popular comedy, social context and shifting configurations of ideas of Englishness' (Medhurst, 2005: 10) as well as highlighting the 'neglect of comedy in academic debates over the meanings of cultural identity' (Medhurst, 2005: 15). He interrogates the nuancing of particular kinds of Englishness within the comedy genre, for example looking at the specificity of northern English identity in comedy series such as Victoria Wood's *Dinner Ladies* (BBC, 1998–2000) and Caroline Aherne's and Craig Cash's *The Royle Family* (BBC, 1998–2012). Medhurst suggests 'comedy is a short cut to community' (Medhurst, 2005: 121). This chapter approaches *Still Game* similarly, considering the way in which, within the context of a sitcom format, the series explores and documents a particular strand of Glaswegian identity, situating it within the wider contexts of other extant mobilisations of notions of Glasgow and Glaswegianness. Raymond Williams's critical term 'structures of feeling' is also significant here in articulating what it is that *Still Game* achieves in capturing, comparing and contrasting the specific cultural climates of Glasgow's present and past. At the same time, *Still Game* taps into wider discourses around nostalgia, old age and community, which give it a resonance with more universally recognisable experiences and an application and reach beyond the specifics of life in Glasgow.

Still Game and the Comedy Unit

Still Game needs first to be considered in the context of a number of other contemporaneous comedy series that have emerged from, or have been developed by, The Comedy Unit and its offshoot, Effingee Productions. Effingee productions is a television production company founded in 2000 by Greg Hemphill and Ford Kiernan and based in Glasgow, These series depict Glasgow life from the perspective of the insider writing from within the context of the city. The best known is *Rab C. Nesbitt* (BBC Scotland, 1988–2014), created by Glaswegian writer Ian Pattinson. *Nesbitt* offered a dark, nuanced reading of the bogeyman figure of the uncouth, workshy, untameable Glaswegian. The series charted the alcoholic, unemployable Nesbitt's wrangles with authority and law and order set alongside the daily grind of life on the dole. Nesbitt, as street philosopher, revelled in his unconditional and unadulterated 'two fingers up to the world' stance, displaying at the same time a fierce reflective intelligence shot through with acute, mordant humour. A little-considered irony is that the highly articulate Nesbitt is often dismissed as incomprehensible by those unfamiliar with Glasgow accents, language and pronunciation. Yet verbal virtuosity and linguistic ingenuity is a key part of the character and the vibrant working class Glaswegian oral culture from which he emerges is best represented by comedian Billy Connolly, recognised internationally as one of the world's most gifted funny men. Nesbitt's eloquence in describing his own plight and behaviour, while at the same time castigating the folly of society, is shrewd and insightful, belying Nesbitt's sardonic representation of himself as 'scum'.

The character of Rab C. Nesbitt allows Glaswegian viewers to wrestle with aspects of their own identity and their own attitude towards it. There is space for knowing, self-reflexive laughter at the complexity of Glaswegian identity, a consciousness of a perverse pride in Glasgow's ability to produce such a grotesque, yet also recognition of the accuracy of the writing and performance, which make Rab so much more than the stereotypical 'hard man' that he might be in the hands of outsiders. Where the series differs from *Still Game* is that, despite its genuine connection to Glasgow life and language, it mobilises a highly stylised version. Nesbitt is an exaggerated and, at times, almost surrealistic portrayal of a particular kind of Glaswegian folk devil in line with the figure of the wise fool who challenges and disrupts the social order.

This figure is part of the socially unruly and upended world that, *pace* Medhurst, a Bakhtinian reading finds in Rabelaisian accounts of periods of medieval carnival where the grotesque body, the opposite of the classical ideal, is in charge. Medhurst cites characters such as bawdy English comedians Frank Randle and Roy 'Chubby' Brown, who exemplify such a notion and who here have their Glaswegian corollary in Nesbitt (Medhurst, 2005).

Dear Green Place (BBC Scotland, 2007–2008), produced by Effingee Productions, is both in its writing and performance style closer to the more naturalistic style of *Still Game* than the dazzling stream of consciousness monologues and fantastical scenarios that make up Nesbitt's world. Set amidst the daily working world of local council park attendants, as in *Still Game*, the focus is on the details of everyday life in and around the city. Noticeable here is the presentation of Glasgow as a city of parks, rivers and well-preserved historical landmarks. This contrasts with a Glasgow more frequently seen as representing dark, threatening urbanity. Glasgow, in fact, is a city surprisingly full of green spaces and places.[3] *Dear Green Place* makes visual use of these little-seen aspects of the city, such as the historic Glasgow Green in the east end of the city, and the Necropolis, an impressive Victorian cemetery set amidst rolling parkland. The term 'dear green place' is itself a translation of the Gaelic word *Glaschu* from which the name Glasgow derives. Another of this group of locally set and written comedies is *Happy Hollidays* (BBC Scotland, 2009), also produced by Effingee Productions. Set in a caravan park on the Ayrshire coast, it is the kind of modest resort that would be frequented by Glaswegians for holidays in the post-war period prior to the advent of the affordable package deals to Europe, and very much part of their shared family experiences and memories. As with both *Still Game* and *Dear Green Place*, *Happy Hollidays* is concerned with the textures of everyday life, depicting with relish the cultural specificity of, in this case, the Glasgow caravan holiday.

Still Game

Still Game is the most critically and popularly successful of all of these most recent Glasgow television comedies, synthesising its eye for the local with award-winning bittersweet scripts and high quality performances. *Still Game* won six Scottish BAFTAs and was nominated for three others over its television life-time. 'Flittin' (BBC Scotland, 6 September 2002), the first episode, both introduces the main characters and establishes key themes that are at the heart of the series, as well as mapping out something of the topography of the physical and emotional landscape within which the series operates. Noticeably, all the episodes have one-word titles written in phonetic Glaswegian, bringing an added linguistic richness. 'Flittin' (which means 'moving'), in Glaswegian dialect and Scots more generally, has the added sense of a move which may not be quite legitimate, undertaken often to evade debts or financial difficulties. Jack Jarvis, tired of living next door to rude and unpleasant neighbours, wants to find a council flat in the nearby high-rise block where his friend, Victor McDade, lives. A death means a flat has become available and Jack wants to move in.

The opening shot of the episode exemplifies complex structures of feeling around the 'insider' Glasgow the series presents. It opens on an overview of the Craiglang housing estate: the perspective is from the window of one of the flats in which Victor and, by the end of the episode Jack, live. The weather is grey and overcast. The image is polysemic, resonating with negative images of working class Glaswegian life. Numerous identikit grey-coloured high-rise flats are interspersed with tenements and low-rise 'four-in-a-block' developments typical of Glasgow's local authority post-war housing stock. A four-in-a-block is a building, with two apartments on the ground floor and two on the first. These are surrounded by uncultivated grassland with, in the foreground, a dank-looking canal. Indeed, if the opening titles and the writers' names are removed this image is congruent with one that might introduce television documentary or current affairs strands focusing on any of the social problems such as drug abuse, violence, extreme poverty and deprivation with which Glasgow has long been customarily associated in the media. Such an image could figure in social research on Glasgow's historical housing problems, such as Paice's *Overspill Policy and the Glasgow Slum Clearance Project in the Twentieth Century: From One Nightmare to Another?*

The episode plays out around the desirability of moving into one of those very flats pictured, flats that for the pensioners in the series represent decent and respectable homes. This points to the contrasting perspectives of locals and outsiders looking in, which is the source of *Still Game's* take on working class Glasgow life and the structures of feeling it encapsulates. The seemingly drafty isolated spaces of Craiglang, the sprawling uncultivated patches of wasteland, neglected canal, tower blocks and the identikit council housing are not straightforward sites of urban decay. Rather, they are places where the characters meet, socialise, find out about local events and news and, as in any normal existence, have good and bad times. Rundown and unglamorous as this landscape may appear at first sight, it is at the heart of an active and self-involved community with its own complex history, which is frequently drawn upon in the characters' everyday conversations and shared reminiscences. Of *Still Game* Hibberd writes: 'its popularity lies in its urban setting, a glimpse of 'normal life' in Glasgow in which the comedy derives from everyday life' (Hibberd, 81: 2010). In addition, it is worth pointing out that, reading the image as a Glaswegian viewer would do, noticeable in the background of this opening image are the local Campsie Hills, which surround the north-west of the city. These are much loved local beauty spots that point to Glasgow's closeness to unspoiled countryside within easy travelling distance.

The socio-economic and cultural identity of Craiglang itself is part of the wider redevelopment of post-war Glasgow, and its history ties in with the experience and memories of subsequent generations of working class Glaswegians. Situating the series precisely in this location means the characters are able to speak to and reflect upon the hopes and aspirations that the development of housing schemes such as Craiglang represented to early post-war planners and Glaswegians themselves.[4] In this first episode, Jack and Victor ruminate on the ways in which the new housing scheme they moved into offers living conditions and opportunities significantly better than those within the overcrowded city, with its dilapidated tenement housing, where they and the people of Craiglang came from. Like many Glaswegians, Jack and Victor were enthused by the space and modern accommodation such overspill housing estates offered. What drives their discussion is the way in which the houses, and, to some extent, the wider Craiglang community, have deteriorated since those times. They quote from the kind of publicity material they remember being written about Craiglang when it was first built: 'Craiglang: developing for the future; Craiglang: modernity beckons; Craiglang: tomorrow's already here'. This facet of the cultural climate of post-war Glasgow, in which developments like Craiglang represented the city's belief in better lives and opportunities for working people, plays no significant part in any wider extant representations of the city. Whilst the present day Craiglang has changed from those idealistic early days, and its modernist concrete aesthetic has not worn well, neither has it deteriorated into an urban nightmare of boarded-up, uninhabited flats with drug dealers peopling the landings. It remains a place in which people live ordinary, manageable and happily uneventful lives. There are sites within the estate, such as the Clansman pub, the corner shop, the local butcher, bookmakers, laundry and the flats and houses of friends and neighbours that offer community and companionship. The landings on which the characters' flats are located are inhabited domestic spaces rather than empty places to be avoided. Isa, one of Jack's and Victor's landing neighbours, can be seen on occasions cleaning or rearranging one of the displays of plastic flowers that sit outside. Jack places a 'welcome' mat outside the front door when he moves into a new flat at the end of the episode.

Craiglang is also the site of many significant memories for Jack, Victor and the other characters. Frequently recalled throughout the series are scenes of an earlier Craiglang, when the main characters themselves were younger, bringing up families and looking toward the future with optimism. Craiglang has its own distinctive personal and social historical structures of feeling for this group. In the scenes where we see Jack finally leaving the home in which he had lived with his now deceased wife, this sense of the life he has had in Craiglang becomes poignantly apparent.

More broadly, running through *Still Game* is the structure of feeling of a particular type of working class Glaswegian lived experience, one that goes unremarked in outside representations of Glasgow life. It is in this respect that younger actors playing older people is significant not merely for the laughs to be had watching older people behaving badly. The cast and writers, in recalling the Glasgow of their parents' and grandparents' lives are reinserting their own little-documented cultural inheritance into current media discourses. Ford Kiernan was interviewed in 2008 on Radio Scotland's *Stark Talk*, a series of in-depth 30-minute interviews with influential contemporary figures, the focus being on prominent and successful Scots. He talked about the cultural significance of a happy working class upbringing in the city, his memories of this, of family and friends, and the sense of connectedness that he felt to it all. He made clear that, although a move to London might be beneficial career-wise, he could not live anywhere but Glasgow. It seems reasonable to suggest that, for its material, *Still Game* draws upon 52-year-old Kiernan's perspective of Glasgow life from his own fondly remembered experiences of growing up in the 1960s and 1970s and beyond, whilst building on the memories of family, which stretch back to the 1930s, 1940s and 1950s. Co-writer 45-year-old Hemphill, as explored a little later in the chapter, makes similar use of the stuff of his own life.

The social, historical and cultural contexts of post-war Glasgow is most frequently considered in relation to the decline of heavy industry and the city's subsequent struggles to readjust to a post-industrial climate. Yet, as *Still Game* demonstrates, time and again characters' memories of living and working in and around the city do not consist of relentless grinding poverty and unhappiness, but of jobs, holidays, family celebrations and normal ups and downs, like any other ordinary British citizens of the period. In *Still Game*, the textures and cultures of a contemporary Glaswegian world are connected to the reanimated socio-historical lived experience of the post-war Glasgow of which the fictitious Craiglang pensioners are part. While *Still Game* is a comedy with no claims for social realism or explicit sociological or historical commentary, its well-crafted and observed recreation of its characters' lives and environment brings back many significant memories of working class Glaswegian lives which are not figured in any widely circulated national accounts of Glasgow. This recreation is done on a micro level through the mobilisation of the wide net of close personal and social relationships binding Craiglang residents together, and which emphasise the deep, tightly knit roots of this working class community. These relationships are best exemplified by the gossip Isa's convoluted monologues, which invariably encircle a new piece of Craiglang news with where she heard it, who told her and a potted synopsis of memorable anecdotes related to them. While the bystanders are often irritated by these lengthy outpourings, everyone always knows the characters she mentions.

Just as the internal connections that underpin local Craiglang life are woven across the series, so too are the familiar links for Glaswegians to their city's past and present. One such example is frequent mentions of Yarrow Shipbuilders, located on the Clyde and a major employer in the city. One of the main characters, Winston, makes a number of proud references throughout the series to having worked for Yarrows as a 'Clyde fitter' for 35 years. In Episode 6 of Series 2, 'Scran' (broadcast on 2 May 2003), the plot revolves around Winston's bad blood with another former Yarrows employee, Vince Gallacher, played by David Hayman. This comment is, of course, understood by all the characters and a local audience, and also acts to colour outside understanding of the shipyards, which are usually represented from the perspective of strikes and closures rather than the source of local employment, pride and belonging, which they represented for many years.

'Shooglies', a reference to the trams, which were a major part of Glasgow's transport system (broadcast on 9 May 2003), brings together another set of iconic Glasgow institutions, memories and images. Jack and Victor take a trip into the city centre to celebrate their 60-year friendship. What the trip memorialises in particular is the Glasgow that was the backdrop to this relationship, pointing to it as a place of fond and happy memories. Jack and Victor, and by extension the writers Hemphill and Kiernan, are rehabilitating an earlier Glasgow, bringing back to life the times and experiences of older Glaswegians, parents and grandparents.

This set of memories is complex. The pair walk around the city centre – George Square to be precise – noting missing landmarks. Jack points to where there used to be a tobacconist, a fur coat shop, a haberdasher's and Birrell's confectionery shop. All of these are businesses connected to an earlier era and also recreate a little of the landscape of Glasgow of the 1950s and 1960s, when Jack and Victor would have been in their twenties and thirties and most likely to have been frequenting the city centre. At the same time, the episode is not only nostalgic for the past, because we also see Glasgow city centre is currently a bright and prosperous place in its own right. There is a comedy montage of Jack and Victor in the John Lewis department store, surrounded by an array of consumer goods, and later we see them in a state-of-the-art restaurant, converted from a Victorian bank. This is itself a symbol of a postmodern Glasgow refashioning a post-industrial future from the industrial past. A young waiter takes pity on them when they say that they cannot afford the prices, although his promise to wipe their bill does not work out and they have to pay for what they eat. That said, they both agree that it was worth it for the experience, memories and chance to be in the city full of memories, both of what it was and what it is now.

The trip also has the two visit the city's transport museum, a much-loved local resource with a collection of historic vehicles and recreations of the contexts in which the vehicles operated. The museum has been situated in various key locations around the city in its 50-year history and is now housed in the new Riverside Museum (2011), designed by award-winning architect Zaha Hadid. Jack and Victor are particularly attracted by a recreated Glasgow shopping street that serves as the location for a tram. Jack speaks of the memories of Glasgow life that this brings back – and of their own lives, especially – saying it was 'some flashback the old caur' [tram car] and that 'they should have never done away with thae [those] things, smashing things'.

In 'Hoaliday' (holiday) (broadcast on 7 May 2003), Jack and Victor have been invited by Jack's daughter, Fiona, to Canada where she and her family have relocated. Once again the episode shifts between different Glaswegian memories and experiences, in this case the experience of emigration to Canada as represented by Jack's own family. The episode crystallises the relationship between Jack and his daughter, his late wife, Craiglang, Scotland and Canada. He and Victor are very much impressed by the affluent lifestyle Fiona and her family now lead. Underpinning much of this episode is Fiona's desire for her father to come to Canada and live what she sees as a better life than the one that he has in Craiglang. Their discussion mobilises a picture of the Craiglang that she remembers and the Craiglang for which Jack and Victor and the rest of the cast are often nostalgic. Jack says 'It's not the place you remember. Your ma used to take you up to Mrs McCain's shop on Napier Road and put you on the counter'. He continues 'I'd take you to the park'. He is quick to point out that the shop has gone and the park now neglected. At the same time, he also recalls that he and his wife were themselves on the point of emigrating to Canada, as were 'thousands of young people but wur [our] bottle went'. At the same time Jack makes it clear to his daughter that his life is in Craiglang, and that for him the ties of friendship and the rootedness of his life there are more significant than moving to Canada for all the attractions it can boast. Greg Hemphill was part of this exodus in real life, his family moving to Montreal when he was six. Hemphill returned to Scotland as a teenager to study at the University of Glasgow. In the depiction presented of Scots settlers' lives in Canada, Hemphill draws upon his experiences of life there.

'Party' (broadcast on 31 December 2006), the Series 6 finale special, does more than have characters merely reminisce about the Craiglang and Glasgow of the past; a large part of the action is actually set in 1975. The main ensemble cast, trapped in a lift, reminisce about the last time the lift got stuck – Hogmanay, 1975. In Scotland, and Glasgow in particular, the celebration of New Year's Eve has special significance. New Year's Day, rather than Christmas, was the main seasonal holiday, and Christmas Day was not a public holiday in Scotland until 1958. Traditionally, the last day of the year was spent ensuring that the whole house was spotlessly clean for the coming year, and after midnight neighbours would go to each other's houses to celebrate. To return to the episode, we flashback to 1975, and Victor's and his wife Betty's Hogmanay housewarming party; Victor's newly decorated flat is kitted out in the height of seventies chic with dramatically patterned voguish wallpaper, lava lamps, a hostess trolley and, Victor's pride and joy, that seventies *must-have*, an avocado bathroom suite. Jack says, 'you've landed on your feet here, boy, this is like Hugh Hefner'. The main characters and the party guests are confident, lively, fashionably dressed 30 somethings, and both they and Craiglang represent a modern, go-ahead Glasgow looking to the future. This segment demonstrates a quite different seventies Glasgow from the more familiar images of a dark, depressed and hopeless city. Flash forward to the present, and Jack points out: 'we had it all in front of us back then, not a care in the world'. The episode ends with counting down to 'the Bells' (the first stroke of the chimes of the New Year) and the sound of ships' foghorns on the river Clyde, another Glasgow Hogmanay tradition.

This mid-seventies scene is connected with yet older Glasgows by the continuation of these long-seated traditions. In turn, it is connected with contemporary Glasgow, as the cast break the fourth wall to wish the viewers a happy New Year, a celebration still very much part of Glaswegian and Scottish tradition, and the source of many family memories. The location of the party in the seventies allows the cast, in effect, to become their parents' generation, playing out and honouring the traditions that they are likely to have experienced as children and bringing this period back to vivid life.

Conclusion

Of course, *Still Game* is predominantly a light-hearted comedy series, one which derives much of its popular appeal from the antics of younger actors playing mischievous, unruly Glasgow pensioners, saying and doing things that would not be expected from the over-seventies. As this chapter demonstrates, the series works well beyond such generic expectations. Drawing its subject matter from the rich and complex cultural source of twentieth-century Glasgow, a source little explored by national media beyond the well-worn and oft-repeated tropes of poverty and violence this chapter has identified, *Still Game* offers a space in which Glasgow and Glaswegians have the chance to make the jokes about themselves and their culture rather than stand as the subject of others' laughter. Concurrently, *Still Game* amidst the laughter acknowledges and values the little-celebrated or understood world of working-class Glasgow and its citizens.

Notably, the series, which was last broadcast in 2007, was recently revived by its creators in September 2014 as a stage play at Glasgow's Hydro Arena. The *Daily Record* newspaper reported that it sold out all 21 performances, attracting audiences totalling 210,000.[5] The year 2014 was of especial significance for Glasgow and Scotland, as August saw Glasgow successfully host the 20th Commonwealth Games, relishing the opportunity to be in charge of how the city presented itself on a world stage, whilst in September the Independence Referendum gave Scots the opportunity to decide whether they wished to remain part of the United Kingdom. All these events, each in its own way, spoke to vibrant contemporary Scottish national discourses around self-representations that moved beyond those offered by Britain and all-inclusive British identities. The response to the independence referendum, as evidenced by the 84.5% voter turnout, demonstrated Scots' eagerness to take control of deciding what a future Scotland might look like. Despite the majority 'no' vote, post-referendum, the specificity of Scotland and of Scottishness are now an undeniable part of the wider UK national debate. Clearly, this recognition is of vital interest to Scots. More than ever, in post-referendum times a Scottish media text such as *Still Game*, with its wryly authentic, comic presentation of urban working class life encapsulates Scots' desire to speak for themselves and in their own voices.

Notes

1. BBC Comedy, *Still Game*, http://www.bbc.co.uk/comedy/stillgame/, accessed 30 June 2014.
2. At the time of writing (2014) Glasgow was in the world media spotlight due to holding the Commonwealth Games in the city. This situated Glasgow as the subject of a global media event, and world media spaces were made available for the city's own representation of itself as 'the Games' city This was an atypical situation for Glasgow, and it will be difficult to ascertain for some considerable time what kind of lasting measurable impact that this has had on Glasgow's national and international image.
3. 'With 91 parks – Glasgow has more per head of population than any other European city'; from *The Council's Magazine for the People of Glasgow*, http://www.glasgow.gov.uk/CHttpHandler.ashx?id=9064, accessed 3 November 2014.
4. The history of the redevelopment of post-war Glasgow, and how the city should be reshaped for the better in the period of reconstruction, is complex. The driving force was the immediate shortage of housing and the wider aim to provide clean modern homes for people in contrast to the decaying housing stock of the inner city. One strategy was the development in the 1950s of council overspill schemes on the far edges of the city, such as Drumchapel to the north and Castlemilk to the south. Residents who moved there from the inner city were delighted with the green open spaces and newly built spacious houses with desirable amenities like inside toilets and running hot water. Jack's and Victor's Craiglang is clearly identifiable with such a scheme. Over the years, a number of economic, social and cultural factors meant that such schemes did not deliver what they initially promised. *Still Game* explores the tensions between such expectations and disappointments. See 'Unveiling a futuristic vision of a Glasgow that might have been', *Sunday Herald*, 11 August 2013, http://www.heraldscotland.com/news/home-news/unveiling-futuristic-vision-of-a-glasgow-that-might-have-been.21839645, accessed 3 November 2014; and *Dreaming the Impossible Unbuilt Britain*, Season 1, Episode 3: 'A Revolution in the City' (BBC, 11 August 2013).
5. John Dingwall, '*Still Game* pulls in £6 million from 21 sell out shows at the hydro, paving the way for a new TV series', *Daily Record*, 11 October 2014, http://www.dailyrecord.co.uk/entertainment/celebrity/still-game-pulls-6-million-21-4417745, accessed 12 February 2015.

References

Blain, N. and D. Hutchison (eds) (2008) *The Media in Scotland* (Edinburgh: Edinburgh University Press).

Hibberd, L. (2010) 'The Funny Thing about Scottish Independents', *Media International Australia*, Vol. 134, 74–83.

MacArthur, C. (2003) *Brigadoon, Braveheart and the Scots: Distortions of Scotland in Hollywood Cinema* (London: I. B. Tauris).

Medhurst, A. (2005) *A National Joke: Popular Comedy and English Cultural Identities* (London: Routledge).

Mills, B. (2010) 'On Television Comedy as an Invented Tradition', *Media International Australia*, Vol. 134, 64–73.

Mowatt, I. (2008) Broadcast Comedy. In N. Blain and D. Hutchison (eds) *The Media in Scotland* (Edinburgh: Edinburgh University Press).

Paice, L. (2013) 'Overspill Policy and the Glasgow Slum Clearance Project: From One Nightmare to Another?', *Reinvention: A Journal of Undergraduate Research*, Vol. 1, No. 1, 1–19.

6
Topological London

Kris Erickson

In 1931, Henry Charles Beck's map of the London Underground revolutionised urban transport by offering passengers the ability to visualise their journey as a series of interconnected transfer points rather than a tangle of separately operated railway lines, which it was in actual fact. Beck aimed with his representation to simplify the task of charting one's route through unfamiliar terrain, and he did this by straightening out paths along horizontal, vertical, or diagonal lines, adding tick marks to denote stations and diamonds to symbolise interchanges (see Figure 8). By systematising the graphic design and jettisoning dependence on cartographic accuracy, Beck invented a new language for urban mobility that was rapidly copied by other cities around the world.

At the same time that London has risen in prominence as a global financial centre, the Tube map has itself become a commodity in the networked information economy, where symbolic exchange, more than the movement of actual, tangible goods characterises economic production in late capitalism. The London Underground has become a ubiquitous and iconic symbol of interconnected twenty-first-century life, along with other trappings of frictionless globalisation: airport coffee shops, familiar consumer brands and 24-hour news.

The status of economic, social and political life in the age of interconnected global capitalism has been a topic of intense academic study since the 1970s, with a vast body of work exploring the articulations, disconnections and transformations wrought by the transition from Fordist production in the early twentieth century to post-Fordism and the rise of the information economy by the end of the century (Jessop, 1988; Harvey, 1989; Lash and Lury, 2007). Theorists turned to the concept of the network to make sense of connections between actors and places that seemed to operate according to a capricious logic, rewarding some nodes (New York–London–Tokyo) while punishing others (the hinterland, the Global South), depending on one's position in the spatial or social order (Castells, 1996; Latour, 2005). Urban centres became locked in competition as they sought to secure investment from global capital, which circled the Earth like a plague of locusts (Mitchell, 2003: 165). Cities and regions responded with 'cultural planning', efforts to emulate the success story of places like California's Silicon Valley by attracting young, hip and digitally literate creative people (Florida, 2005; Kovacs, 2011). The traces of this approach are visible in the curious non-places such as those surrounding London's 'Silicon Roundabout' cluster. By the early 2000s, the network had become social as well as global, making us entrepreneurs and curators of ourselves, enjoining us to 'add' new connections and reward our friends with 'likes'. Our lives increasingly reflect the topological interconnections of Beck's vision for modern city life.

Although we now routinely reside and act within them, global information networks remain largely inaccessible to local political governance and critique. In light of controversy surrounding surveillance activities by the National Security Agency (NSA) and tax-sheltering techniques used by American Internet firms, the problem is acutely experienced by European citizens. Scholarship on political activism has remained focused on the urban (and its network linkages) as a significant and contestable site of struggle, evidenced recently by the Occupy movement and other social-media augmented protests in opposition to economic austerity (Castañeda, 2012; Dowling et al., 2012).

Mobile networked technologies are implicated in this contemporary urban politics. Protests in London in the summer of 2011 were widely reported to have been coordinated over social media networks such as the Blackberry Messenger (BBM) service (Fuchs, 2012). Much of the scholarship on urban politics has focused on the role of networked technologies in facilitating and coordinating offline social movements, to understand changing and co-constitutive relationships between personal, everyday technologies and society. A smaller but growing body of work draws attention to the way mobile technologies are themselves contestable, and besides routing political action through their networked architectures, are themselves potential sites of political movement, struggle and understanding. This chapter contributes to discussions on the politics of technologically mediated urban mobility by examining possibilities offered to users of mobile applications (apps) in London.

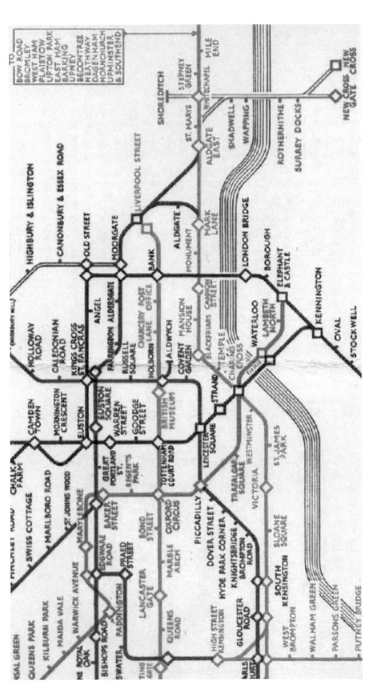

Figure 8 Detail of 1933 printed edition of *Beck's London Underground* map

Source: Copyright Transport for London.

In this chapter, I argue for an interpretation of technologically mediated contemporary London, not as a space of networks, or a virtualised
space, but as a topology. Drawing upon recent theory by Lash (2012)
and Lury (2013), which develops a historical post-Cantorian interpretation of topology as a space of social imaginary, I argue that certain
mobile technologies enable movement beyond the virtual, with its own
challenges for political subjectivity, towards a new and highly abstract
space where possibilities for political engagement with the urban are
re-ordered according to a topological, relational logic. This way of
thinking and being in the world is compared with earlier critiques of the
alienating effects of symbolic capitalism by members of the Situationist
International (SI). Situationist strategies of the *dérive*, *détournement* and
rencontre were developed to confront the Euclidean geometric closures of
monumental urbanism, which were seen to inhibit possibilities for real
connection between human beings and their built environment. The
predictable geometric ordering of urban space was seen as anathema to
disorderly, authentic encounters between people, and promoting such
encounters became a key aspect of the situationist project. Today, the
problem is rendered more complex for urban dwellers who hold in their
hands devices that can re-arrange and cut across space according to soft-
ware-coded logics, in some cases rendering the city as a topology. But
what are the opportunities for political and social connection in topological space? Proceeding from the situationist dissatisfaction with older
geometric urban cartographies, I propose a methodology for assessing
the capacity of new mobile interactive applications to promote encounters between Londoners and their city.

Distinguishing virtual and topological abstractions

In the discussion of mobile and spatial information technologies that
will follow, it is necessary to distinguish between different technological
visions of the city, of which the topological is only one configuration
(albeit increasingly important).

When personal computers entered mainstream consumer culture,
they were accompanied by a discourse of virtuality, expressed in hacker
fantasies of zooming through 'cyberspace' as a disconnected avatar.
This conception of empowered individual netizen was offered against
prevailing cybernetic visions of centrally commanded intelligent systems.
Perhaps the most famous of these was British cyberneticist Stafford
Beer's effort to build an omnipotent computerised command room for
the Chilean government in the early 1970s (Axelrod and Borenstein,
2009). However, the rise of virtuality as popular entertainment eclipsed

its use as a technique for governing complex social relations, distorting public opinion about what it meant to live in virtual space as a political subject. Commonplace invocations of the virtual relegated it to a kind of escapism, through which one might leave the 'real' and achieve satisfying but ultimately illusory fulfilment in the unreal world of the computer. Of course the advent of 'increasingly personalized computing' achievable through mobile and wearable technologies renders escapist critiques less salient and less possible (Wilson, 2014; also see Deuze, 2011).

Rob Shields (2003, 2006) suggests that we understand the virtual, not as an opposition to the 'real' but rather as its immaterial although highly effective twin. For Shields, following Deleuze and Proust, the virtual is 'real without being actual, ideal but not abstract' (2006: 284). Although not materially actualised, the virtual exists in direct relation to the materially real. After all, Shields reminds us, a virtual office is as much a real office in its purpose and effects. So, too, might a virtual representation of a city have effects for its residents: as a model, a *maquette*, a projection of traffic flows and future growth upon which planners decide. London was extensively virtualised in advance of the 2012 Olympic Games, both to plan architectural development and to prepare security forces and emergency responders (see Figure 9).

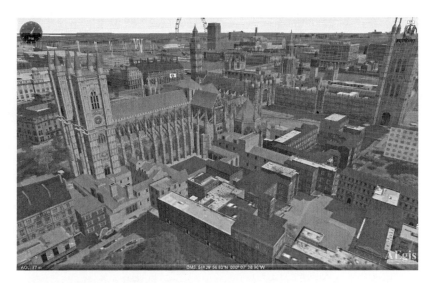

Figure 9   A virtual projection of London used to prepare security forces in advance of the 2012 Olympics

Source: Image credit: Aegis Corporation.

Virtual representations are possible to render via mobile technology, but not all mobile-enabled visualisations are virtual. In contrast with the 3D projection of London above, Beck's Underground map is not a virtual representation of the city, but a topological one. With enough determination, one might reconstruct a material replacement for London by working from the plans contained in Aegis Corporation's 3D software. The same is not true of Beck's representation, which in fact does not represent London at all, but a series of possibilities contained within its network of underground tunnels.

For Lash (2012) these topological spaces warrant further attention and differentiation from virtual spaces in order to advance what he considers a 'mathematical turn' in social theory leading from Badiou's project of translating Georg Cantor's mathematics of set theory into philosophy (2012: 263; see Badiou, 2009). Cantor's contribution to mathematics, further refined in axiomatic set theory and expanded in topological mathematics, offers to Badiou an ontology which is consistent with multiplicity while also being internally consistent and formalisable (Bowden 2012). Set theory enables comparison of seemingly incomparable groups (such as infinite series of numbers) by describing correspondence (bijection) between elements of multiple sets. Sets can be described topologically according to corresponding properties and transformed in such a way that elements retain their topological relationship (homeomorphism). Topological spaces are abstract constructs built out of equivalences between the properties of points, which can be arranged in relational space. Lash refers to the philosophical status of topological space as a 'self-organising socio-technical imaginary', in order to distinguish it from Euclidean abstractions, including those we might consider 'virtual':

> In topology the virtual does not generate the actual.... A circle and a square are topological equivalents. They are not topographically equivalent, yet they belong to the same topological set. This is the set of their shared properties, such as being planar and having an inside and an outside separated by a boundary.... The movement, the process at stake is not the generation of an actual by a virtual, but the deformation of, as it were, two actuals into one another via their topological properties. (Lash, 2012: 265)

Lash's project is partially to think through the implications of the cultural object as topological figure. Cultural objects, which are the exchange commodities of the global culture industry, are topological in the sense that they deform into one another via equivalences in their properties. For Lash, the underlying framework for the topological equivalence of brand images is intellectual property and, in particular, the trademark. The relationship between two brands as protectable IP is the 'shared property of the morphing contemporary cultural object.' (2012: 277).

Of course, corporate brands and trademarks are only one set of symbols used and exchanged in the information economy. The mobile technologies and devices that underline daily lived experience are, on one hand, reducible to their brand markings. But these technologies also permit topological deformations in other ways: mobile devices function as converged platforms, capable of accessing software applications which, due to the shared language of programming and information protocols such as GPS, are able to communicate with other applications. The reimagining of the city and, indeed, of all social space into the so-called Internet of things is facilitated by the confluence of these two sociotechnical conditions of convergence and equivalence.

Three main features of topological space differentiate it from other kinds of material and virtual space, with implications for the politics of urban mobility:

(1) Topological spaces are not real or virtual, but imaginary.
(2) Topological mappings re-order space according to functional equivalencies.
(3) Topological objects deform into one another according to these equivalencies.

First, topological spaces are imaginary as opposed to virtual spaces, which are idealisations or extensions of the real. In that sense they are, according to Lash, a kind of 'social-imaginary'. The political meaning of the imaginary status of topological space is difficult to discern and is still emerging from this new literature. One thing which is not clear is how much correspondence matters between a topology and real space. In the London Underground map, the City branch of the Northern line is shown to lie east of Mornington Crescent station, when in actuality it passes to the west. That fact does not seem to alarm Londoners who rely on the topological information contained in the map in their daily commute. On one hand, topologies can only exist by consensus obtained from users of the topological figure in social practice. On the other hand, the imaginary status of the topological map seems to offer potential for new politically productive imaginings and configurations.

Second, rather than describe Euclidean geometric forms and distances, topologies describe relational information between elements residing in sets with equivalence. In Lash's deployment of topology as analytic to understand political subjectivity in the information economy, making things equivalent renders them easier to transact. This is the basis of the processes of economic and cultural globalisation (digitalisation, standardisation, protocols, logistics). Continuing with the London Underground example, in the topological configuration, Finsbury Park and Shepherd's Bush become equivalent to one another because they lie in Zone 2. This functional equivalence elides other non-equivalences in the socio-cultural reality of lived experience in these places. Topological ordering promotes a kind of totalism, which extends the software-sorting of places predicted by 'big data' algorithmic governance (Dodge et al., 2009). The latter makes reference to data inductively generated from 'real' transactions and behaviours, while the former is a deformation of space to correspond to a social imaginary.

Third, topological space enables the deformation of objects into one another according to their shared properties (Lash, 2012: 264). This vertigo-inducing feature makes topological organisation generative for informational capitalism. From the perspective of Transport for London, all passengers in the network are interchangeable. Topologically, I deform into you because we are both ticketholders of a two-zone fare. Never mind that I am travelling to Islington while you are going to Kensington. This de-formational movement, enabled by topological ordering, may engender new kinds of political subjectivity or it may reproduce certain kinds of subjects (e.g., consumers of Transport for London's services).

Topological systems are, like the London Tube map, designed to cut through the messy friction of the real. They both permit and exalt systematic and relational thinking. Topologies are imaginary spaces, but imagined by whom? In order to achieve consensus as social-imaginaries, topological understandings must be collectively sustained by social actors. But topological orderings also reflect the imaginations of people working in a particular software design paradigm, one which appears to be animated by a distaste for friction and disorder. There is, in a topological model, nothing that cannot be relationally 'fixed' within the boundaries of the figure. The topological design paradigm for mobile information services emerges both from the functional limitations of computer code and from a cultural progression of the Californian Ideology and the more diffuse startup ideology which has superseded it (Barbrook and Cameron, 1996).

Despite the efficiencies that mobile technologies seem to apport to everyday life, they have become the focal point for popular critiques, some of which have achieved the level of moral panics. These appraisals have variously characterised mobile technology as frivolous, addictive, antisocial, fetishistic and co-incident with a disaffected and dangerous urban youth culture. Critiques have tended to deploy either the medicalised discourse of addiction or a criminological rhetoric of anonymous anti-social behaviour. Perhaps, however, mainstream anxiety about mobile technology is driven less by fear of virtual escapism, and rather by its tendency to present anti-Euclidean political opportunities.

Mobile applications have the potential to disrupt not only the geometric capacity of authorities to monitor space, but they also disrupt markets and social relations. For example, the anonymous dating application *Grindr* leaps across spatial and social boundaries to create information linkages and opportunities for erotic couplings that are independent from material infrastructure of social interaction. The popular transportation app *UBER* does the same for taxis and is also independent of the regulatory, policy and material infrastructure that organises the taxi-driving profession. Using Lash's language, the geolocational capability of the mobile phone transforms the problem of finding a taxi and the problem of finding a mate into functionally equivalent topological problems. Mobile application developers, speaking the language of networked information services, are geared up to solve these problems using the same approach: anonymised geolocative matchmaking.

The kinds of problems and opportunities opened up by mobile technology are reflected in earlier dissatisfaction with urban space and social relations articulated in another era by the situationist movement, which sought to reconnect the lives of everyday people with a built environment seen to increasingly reflect the interests of commercial exchange rather than individual human agency. The following section outlines some of the tactical and methodological responses developed by the situationists in response to issues that resonate with present-day anxieties about mobile technology: its capacity to produce disconnection and abstraction from the built urban environment.

The Situationist International encounters London

In September 1960, the fourth conference of the Situationist International was held in London at the British Sailors Society hall in Limehouse. Situationism, which grew out of the avant-garde movement of lettrism in the late 1950s, circulated through a countercultural network connecting

Paris, Berlin, London, Brussels, Geneva and a cluster of other European cities. The movement united an interest with the traces of contemporary capitalism on the urban landscape and the development of tactics for resisting the geometric and temporal patterns of life imposed by the spectacular capitalistic society. These tactics grow largely from the practice of psychogeography, a method of exploring space, which invited participants to relinquish prior expectations and commitments and drift (*dérive*) through space according to chance, along the way sensing the psychological atmosphere of each portion of the landscape. The purpose of this technique, along with other techniques of engagement promoted by the situationists, was to destabilise the expectations, rhythms and ordering of capitalist urban existence.

A unit of philosophical importance for the situationists was the encounter. Encounters were seen to encapsulate authentic connections between individuals as well as their surroundings, in opposition to the routinised interactions that characterised most of life in the modern city. Psychogeography and more aggressive tactics of *détournement* and the construction of situations, were above all pursued as a means to promote the emergence of new encounters, thus actively subverting other kinds of spatiotemporal order.

On the first day of the London conference on 24 September 1960, SI member and urbanist Attila Kotányi proposed a radical means of statistically measuring, until that moment, the efficacy of situationist efforts. If the unit of analysis was the encounter, then societies could be compared on the basis of their capacity to promote encounters, which could be objectively calculated:

> We know that, for a variety of reasons, these encounters do not produce themselves. The lack of encounters can be expressed by a concrete number, which could characterise the historical state of the world... Our activities, flowing from this analysis, must *practically* critique the reasons for why there are no encounters (independently of all 'progress' in the means of communication, for example)... This is the minimum required for the construction of situations. (Debord et al., 1960: 19)

Of particular importance in Kotányi's critique was the acknowledgement that the technologies of communication whose constant improvement characterised modern life were not sufficient, on their own, to generate new encounters of the politically productive sort he envisaged. The members then spent the rest of the day discussing the implications of such an instrumentalist approach for the status of situationism as an international social movement. If Kotányi's proposal was not uniformly endorsed by the other nine attending members of the SI (such propositions rarely were), it nevertheless cast light on the problem of empirical and objective measurement of the common activities of SI adherents, even if there was lack of consensus about rationalisation of the movement as a collective political endeavour. Kotányi himself continued to be interested in the political as well as the spatiotemporal configurations of the city, turning his attention to what he saw as the geometric imposition of urban planning, remarking in 1961 as the 'Director of Unitary Urbanism' that, 'We are living under a permanent curfew. Not just the cops – the geometry' (Kotányi and Vaneigem, 1961).

Given the challenge of characterising the political opportunities presented by topological space as presented to us via mobile technology, is it possible to extend Kotányi's search for an empirics of urban encounter? The next section outlines one possible methodology to account for and enumerate the possibilities present in different mobile spatial technologies. Taking London as the field site, as the situationists did some half-century ago, one might in this case generate a typology of ways of being in the urban environment, as well as gain a sense of the intensity and direction of movement of technologically mediated everyday life.

A method to characterise mobile encounters

Digital networks offer up a banquet of data, not only in the service of advertisers who seek to locate, track and connect with consumers, but also for sociologists seeking to understand the patterns of life as represented in traces left by users as they interact in space. In order for mobile platforms to perform tasks, they must be furnished with applications (apps), some of which, like geolocative mapping software, come preloaded on a user's device as a default. Other apps must be chosen by the user and downloaded to their device before being used. Platforms containing a selection of commercially available apps are to a certain extent open to public view and can be approached empirically.

Content analysis of some 252 mobile applications residing on the Google Play download service and containing the word 'London' in their description offers a window into the mobile practices of people living in – and moving through – the city. In order to render a wide range of software applications countable and comparable, such a content analysis technique must first decide the dimensions of individual apps to be used for comparison and, secondly, define the operationalised variables, which will be recorded in order to generate 'data' from the observations.

Much of the information available about apps on the mobile market-place is numeric or categorical and readily comparable: variables such as product type, number of downloads, price, and user rating are easily obtained. However, while useful for measuring the consumption rate and consumer opinion of these products, such information does not enable meaningful comparison of the features, much less the opportuni-ties for political subjectivity, embedded in the range of different applica-tion types.

We might then construct additional qualitative variables in order to capture aspects of software relating to its functionality. For example, 'intensity of connectivity' might be measured through comparison of the 'permissions' that an application asks of its device owner. Some applications need access to the Internet only occasionally, for example to update core components of the software. Other applications are more invasive, requesting access to the user's address book, social media profiles, and geographic coordinates, so as to continuously track the owner through space. Additionally, access to geolocational data can be more granularly sorted according to its intensity: none, approximate location (network based) or GPS coordinates.

Of particular interest here is the ability to compare applications according to their spatial configuration (in order to sort those that offer virtual representations of London from those that use topological abstraction). We might investigate this proposition by constructing a variable to record the representational perspective(s) contained in the app. For example, software interfaces may be comprised of text only, still images, moving animations, first-person perspective, overflight, carto-graphic views or topological relationships.

Consequently, it is possible to generate two separate axes for compar-ison of the body of mobile apps focused on London. One axis reflects the perspective range offered by a given application, derived from human coding of the contents of the application according to the visual categories described above. This axis is concerned with what the appli-cation enables a user to 'see'. The second axis represents the functional capabilities offered by the application to its user, derived from the proxy variable of technical permissions (which assumes a two-way exchange of personal data for added functionality). This enables us to compare what applications enable the user to 'do'.

y-axis: visualisation permitted by the application

Can one see things that are there

Can one see things that are there, from a perspective not normally allowed (virtual)

Can one see things that are not there, relationships made visible in a new way (topological).

x-axis: functionality permitted by the application

Can one do things

Can one do things in a way not normally allowed (virtual)

Can one do things informed by relationships made visible in a new way (topological)

Discussion

A schema for assessing the content of apps is represented in Figure 10. The two-by-two grid contains four quadrants, and in each case a mobile application from London is offered as an example to illustrate the possibilities available to mobile users. The schema proceeds from the bottom-left, characterised by the lowest intensity of spatial abstraction and the lowest intensity of information exchange, to the top-right, characterised by intense abstraction in the spatial and informational dimensions. Top-right apps most closely resemble topological spaces, although capturing the precise moment of abstraction from real to virtual to topological can only be approximate.

Reading across the different experiences offered by apps on the Google Play marketplace, we experience London in different spatiotemporal configurations. In Box 1: *Rainy London Live Wallpaper* offers users the ability to change the background image on their mobile device to an animated photograph of London streets. Water droplets accumulate on the screen to simulate the titular rainy atmosphere. The visual perspective of the app is first-person view at street level. One could virtually imagine oneself standing in the scene, weather and all. Minimal data is given or taken by the app, with only a few permissions required to use the software.

Box 2: *Traffic Panic London* is an interactive 3D mobile game in which users control traffic lights at key intersections to facilitate the flow of traffic or initiate explosive crashes. The app presents a 'realistic' visualisation of London in three-quarters overhead view. Slightly more data

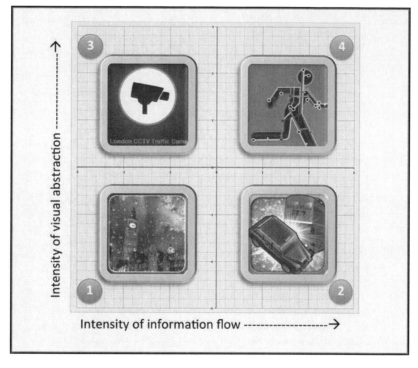

Figure 10   Typology of mobile software applications tagged with 'London'
Source: Illustration by the present author.

flows between the application and the user, with the latter required to give inputs and the former requesting a surprising amount of permissions to access. Box 3: *London CCTV Traffic Cams* localises a popular form of application, granting the user access to real-time traffic cameras throughout the city. The view may be alternated between video cameras looking down on the motorway and a cartographic representation of streets with higher or lower levels of congestion. The application requests minimal permissions from the user other than their geographic location. Box 4: *London Transport Planner* is a full-featured integrated travel app, uniting publicly available data from underground, rail, bus and cycle linkages. Users are invited to plan their trips using a series of drop-down menus that produce diagrammatic route maps and itineraries. The app demands a large number of permissions from the user, including GPS location and access to the user's stored data and contacts.

It is clear that our relationship to the built environment of the city is becoming increasingly mediated, and that mobile software applications are implicated in facilitating and intensifying new socio-spatial relationships. We might call this, as Kotányi did, 'progress in the means of communication'. However, using the situationists' criteria, it is uncertain whether applications surveyed in this brief taxonomic exercise objectively improve the capacity for authentic encounters with the urban. Virtual escapes allow us to experience the city independent of its physicality, through a wallpaper souvenir or a representational video game. Geolocative services offer efficient ways of cutting through its materiality by enabling train connections or routing us around traffic during a commute out of the city. These mobile software applications, although descriptively tagged to be for and about 'London', actually grant us access to an abstract or idealised city whose topologies might – in the case of serialised applications 're-skinned' for other global cities – be preserved under continuous deformation.

In his own experiment inspired by psychogeographic techniques, O'Doherty inscribed the words 'Order' and Disorder' on an A-Z map of Greater Manchester and then set out to walk the contours of each mathematically drawn shape through real space. By applying such an arbitrary 'order' onto the city, O'Doherty hoped to achieve what he termed 'the interruption of topology' (O'Doherty, 2013). What his experiment actually detected were the interactions of multiple, overlapping and incompatible topologies – one, his own arbitrary inscription and 'folding' of the Euclidean map; another, the topology of the daily Möbius-like progression of capitalist exchange and movement; third, an imaginary topology of Masonic symbolism centred on the Royal Exchange Theatre. Considering the political significance of his experiment, he proffers modestly that 'the resulting narrative was not without its insight into hidden forms of inhabitation and modes of organisation that is also generative of new political imaginaries in the city' (2013: 226). However, to organise such an encounter required tremendous effort and highlights the extent to which we cannot rely solely on smooth mobile technologies to 'interrupt' urban topologies, absent of significant intention.

This chapter has sought to chart a journey from early topological representations of London's Underground rail network, through situationist critiques of the same rationalised urban vision, later intensified via convergence and the global culture industry. We arrive at a present moment when mobile devices offer access not only to virtualised experiences, but also to topological imaginaries. The situationists were interested in accessing the authentic, by promoting encounters between urban dwellers and the city around them. The applications that drive mobile technology offer a range of different ways of encountering London. Some are virtual-representational, painstakingly re-presenting the street level to the viewer. Others are data-intensive abstractions, offering users the ability to encounter the city in ways not permitted by Euclidean geometry (e.g., to plan one's route based on CCTV traffic data). The city that exported a vision of topological urban mobility is now itself transformed, via the shared morphology of software design, into a topological projection of itself, a metaphorical hyperspace.

References

Axelrod, J. and Borenstein, G. (2009) Free As In Beer: Cybernetic Science Fictions. Paper delivered at the 2009 Pacific Ancient and Modern Languages Association Conference.

Badiou, A. (2009) *Logics of Worlds: Being and event II* (London: Bloomsbury Publishing).

Barbrook, R. and Cameron, A. (1996) 'The Californian Ideology', *Science as Culture*, Vol. 6, No. 1, 44–72.

Bowden, S. (2012) The Set-Theoretical Nature of Badiou's ontology and Lautman's Dialectic of Problematic Ideas. In S. Bowden and S. Duffy (eds) *Badiou and Philosophy* (Edinburgh: Edinburgh University Press), 39–58.

Castañeda, E. (2012) The Indignados of Spain: A Precedent to Occupy Wall Street, *Social Movement Studies*, Vol. 11, No. 3–4, 309–319.

Castells, M. (1996) *Rise of the Network Society* (Cambridge, MA: Blackwell).

Debord, G. et al. (eds) (1960) The Fourth Conference of the SI in London, *Internationale Situationniste*, No. 4.

Deuze, M. (2011) 'Media Life', *Media, Culture and Society*, Vol. 33, No. 1, 137–148.

Dodge, M., Kitchin, R. and Zook, M. (2009) 'How Does Software Make Space? Exploring Some Geographical Dimensions of Pervasive Computing and Software Studies', *Environment and Planning A*, Vol. 41, No. 6, 1283–1293.

Dowling, E., Feigenbaum, A., Pell, S. and Stanley, K. (2012) 'Occupy London', *South Atlantic Quarterly*, Vol. 111, No. 3, 608–615.

Duffy, S. B. (2012) *Badiou's Platonism: The Mathematical Ideas of Post-Cantorian Set-Theory* (Edinburgh: Edinburgh University Press).

Florida, R. L. (2005) *Cities and the Creative Class* (New York: Psychology Press).

Fuchs, C. (2012) 'Social Media, Riots, and Revolutions', *Capital and Class*, Vol. 36, No. 3, 383–391.

Harvey, D. (1989) *The Condition of Postmodernity: An Enquiry into the Origins of Cultural Change* (Oxford: Blackwell).

Jenkins, H. (2006) *Convergence Culture: Where Old and New Media Collide* (New York: NYU Press).

Jessop, B. (1988) 'Regulation Theory, Post Fordism and the State: More than a Reply to Werner Bonefield', *Capital and Class*, Vol. 12, No. 1, 147–168.

Kotányi, A. and Vaneigem, R. (1961) 'Basic Program of the Bureau of Unitary Urbanism', *Internationale Situationniste*, No. 6.

Kovacs, J. F. (2011) 'Cultural Planning in Ontario, Canada: Arts Policy or More?', *International Journal of Cultural Policy*, Vol. 17, No. 3, 321–340.

Lash, S. (2012) 'Deforming the Figure: Topology and the Social Imaginary', *Theory, Culture & Society*, Vol. 29, No. 4–5, 261–287.

Lash, S. and Lury, C. (2007) *Global Culture Industry: The Mediation of Things* (Chichester: Wiley).

Latour, B. (2005) *Reassembling the Social: An Introduction to Actor-Network-Theory* (Oxford: Oxford University Press).

Lury, C. (2013) 'Topological Sense-Making Walking the Mobius Strip from Cultural Topology to Topological Culture', *Space and Culture*, Vol. 16, No. 2, 128–132.

Mitchell, D. (2003) *The Right to the City: Social Justice and the Fight for Public Space* (New York: Guilford Press).

O'Doherty, D. P. (2013) 'Off-Road and Spaced-Out in the City: Organization and the Interruption of Topology', *Space and Culture*, Vol. 16, No. 2, 211–228.

Shields, R. (2003) *The Virtual* (London: Routledge).

Shields, R. (2006) 'Virtualities', *Theory, Culture & Society*, Vol. 23 No. 2–3, 284–286.

Wilson, M. (2014) 'Continuous Connectivity, Handheld Computers and Mobile Spatial Knowledge', *Environment and Planning D: Society and Space*, Vol. 32, No. 3, 535–555.

Part III
Broadcasting and Belonging

7
A Region in Microcosm: Brandon Acton-Bond's Post-War BBC Radio Features

Ieuan Franklin

Introduction: post-war regional radio

In scholarly work there is a significant discrepancy in the historical coverage of both BBC Regional broadcasting and BBC radio features. The experimental and socially conscious radio documentaries pioneered during the 1930s and 1940s by producers such as D. G. Bridson and Olive Shapley in the BBC North Region have been documented by both scholars and the producers themselves (Bridson, 1971; Scannell and Cardiff, 1991; Shapley, 1996), but there is little evidence of equivalent studies of post-war Regional programming.

To some extent, this can be attributed to the appeal of the 'golden age' of radio broadcasting for both scholarly and popular sources. There is greater coverage of the decades during which BBC radio was the main provider of broadcast entertainment and information, before the BBC's television service fulfilled its potential (demonstrated by the huge audience figures for the coverage of the Queen's Coronation in 1953) and before commercial television was initiated (ITV began in 1955). Both services seriously eroded radio's large audience base: there was a peak of 12 million exclusively radio licences in 1950. This was the beginning of a cycle whereby radio's status in the media ecology would be demoted, as it was regarded as 'too invisible, too transitory, too functional, too faceless, too passé to have a measurable impact on public life – yet, simultaneously, too "mass" in appeal to be treated, alongside film or theatre, as art' (Hendy, 2007: 141).

While the quotidian work of the individual BBC Regions was suspended during the war, this was by no means an end to programmes from, in and about the English regions, or indeed Scotland, Wales and Northern Ireland. The advent of war in 1939 – fought as a 'People's War' – obliged the BBC to represent the plural character of Britain to a greater extent than it had done hitherto. Thomas Hajkowski has complained of the scholarly consensus in which the idea of centralisation in BBC policy has assumed orthodoxy at the expense of the independence of regionally based broadcasters (2010: 110). Of course it is important to appreciate the political and historical dominance of what Sir Thomas Beecham deplored as 'the undesirable weight of power and influence residing in the Corporation's London headquarters' (quoted in Baker, 1950: 98). However, as Hajkowski points out, the post-war BBC Regions actually enjoyed more autonomy than they did before the war. The 'dead hand' of Portland Place still rested on the controls, but with a new lightness of touch (Baker, 1950: 100).

One consequence of the BBC's exalted status as a provider of news and reportage during wartime was that the subsequent response to bulletins referencing or featuring local people and places in the BBC Regions during the post-war era was overwhelming. Patrick Beech, who had spent his formative years in broadcasting as Assistant Head of West Regional Programmes, believed that this led to a new bond between broadcaster and listener, a bond that had not existed since the original and short-lived local 'metropolitan' network of the 1920s (1968: 5).

With the competition that television represented, radio eventually came to concentrate on and excel in those things that it did best. Through the diffusion of actuality (i.e., unscripted testimony or ambient sound), radio was able to report on diverse areas of human affairs in news and documentary programming quickly and with immediacy. For example, in the immediate post-war period (the particular focus of this chapter) in the BBC West Region a regular feature of the 15-minute long daily 'News from the West Country' programme was interviews recorded during the day in mobile recording cars, on the same kinds of portable disc-cutting equipment that had been used by war correspondents. As Denys Val Baker noted,

> listeners can hear... the bustle and excitement of Bampton Pony Fair, the conversation of a Wiltshire shepherd, the roar of a new engine on test in a Bristol aircraft factory, the street scene at Helston Furry Dance – sounds which give a real feeling of being present. (1950: 104)

The idea of 'sounds which give a real feeling of being present' are at the heart of this chapter, which will argue that such sounds were not just 'the stuff of radio' (to quote the title of BBC radio producer Lance Sieveking's memoirs), but also had the potential to shape and strengthen a regionalist consciousness by encouraging the recognition and awareness of inherited and shared elements of culture.

Someone who understood this potential use of broadcasting from very early on was the writer Filson Young, who wrote a weekly column for the *Radio Times*, and was 'programme consultant' to the BBC from September 1926 until his death in 1938 (Briggs, 1995: 68). Young believed that the bureaucratic and centralised nature of the BBC stifled creativity and input from the regions. He had some experience in radio production himself, as he had produced several plays written by Bernard Walke, the celebrated and controversial Anglo-Catholic Parish vicar (between 1913 and 1936) of St Hilary in Penwith, West Cornwall. This included the broadcast in 1927 – from within the church in St Hilary – of Walke's nativity-themed community play, *Bethlehem*, an idea devised by Young, which is said to be the first ever BBC Outside Broadcast or O.B. (and the first play to be produced outside of a BBC studio). This play was hugely popular, and a second was broadcast, entitled *The Western Land*, which featured an entirely non-professional cast, with a local farmer, flower grower, miner and fisherman playing themselves. The latter was produced by Archie Harding, later to become head of the North Region in Manchester. Harding would foster talent such as D. G. Bridson, Olive Shapley, Joan Littlewood and Ewan MacColl, who made great use of what might be termed 'real people' (rather than actors) in their work. The success of both these productions led Filson Young to petition the BBC to expand the quantity and quality of Regional BBC stations. It is worth quoting this memorandum at length, due to its foresight and passion:

> So many broadcasts have no bounds and no roots; they just emerge from the ether in the same shape as they are conveyed through it. The reason for the Cornish successes ... has been that they have been in a tradition – one the Catholic tradition, the other the Cornish tradition. England is full of such traditions – scores of different kinds of traditions or frameworks into which equally successful broadcasts might be built ... My plan, which would really be a substitute for the Regional organisation, and would have to be worked [out] in close conjunction with productions and an extended O.B. Department, would necessitate a completely new kind of survey of England (such as one would make in a search for geological strata) in which one could expect to discover, say, people like Bernard Walke who are more

or less sensitised to their environment and capable of expressing in some way the life in which they find themselves.[1]

Filson Young was too far ahead of his time; Reith and Eckersley (to whom this memorandum was sent) had decided, instead, to adopt a doctrine of centralisation (see Briggs, 1995: 292–293). Yet, later generations of BBC producers and executives were to come to hold ideals similar to Young's, and to conduct exploratory surveys of their own. One sympathetic executive was Gerald Beadle, controller of the West Region, who regarded the 'reflection of British society in sound…from the extensive use of mobile recording apparatus, particularly in the regions', as being a purpose of the BBC, unanticipated by the Corporation but worthy of, inclusion in its charter (1951:152).

The 'actuality feature'

There is not the scope here to sketch a history of the importance of actuality to the British radio feature, let alone the history of radio features. But for now we can observe that the genre of the radio feature was actually initiated in the BBC Regions in the 1930s. As D. G. Bridson explained in an interview with Philip Donnellan for the latter's Omnibus documentary, *Pure Radio* (BBC, 1977):

> I think one of the reasons why it got started, the Features Department, in the Regions before it did in London, was that in the Regions we were comparatively free from what I would call administrative interference.[2]

During the 1940s and early 1950s the classic model of the radio feature, a 'written piece' – depending on the nuances of the written word as interpreted by narrators, reporters or actors – was beginning to be supplanted by forms of extempore speech recorded on acetate discs, the culmination of the wish to hear ordinary people speak in their own words. This movement from the 'invented' to the 'actual' corrected some of the more pretentious literary aspirations of the radio feature. More broadly it also enhanced the claim of the radio feature to be the one genre unique to radio, and the claim of the aural medium of radio to be closer to the oral tradition than was the intervening literary tradition.

The arrival of the tape recorder in the mid to late 1950s made the collection of actuality much easier; disc-cutting machines were bulky, and the discs could contain a very limited amount of material. Editing a programme using the acetate discs was also laborious and needed considerable skills in precision and timing. In a column for *The Listener*, published 10 January 1957, Michael Swan noted that, although it had not been long since BBC radio had begun to exploit the possibilities of the portable tape recorder, instances of the use of actuality could be charted across the schedule:

> 'I am a tape-recorder' might be the cry of scores of BBC men as they make their sallies into private homes, West Indian rum-parlours, Yarmouth trawlers. (Swan 1957)

Nevertheless, as this chapter seeks to demonstrate, Brandon Acton-Bond had begun conducting similar 'fly on the wall' work using disc-cutting recorders in the late 1940s. More broadly, a 'demotic turn' in broadcasting could be detected in other types of programming, such as talks, and magazine or discussion programmes. The increasing relative power of the working class in Britain during the post-war period had determined that certain concessions had to be made to non-standard dialects in national broadcasting (Fairclough, 1989: 73). In 1944, Kenneth Adam (then the BBC's director of publicity) could boast that the audience for '[Wilfred] Pickles, for [Cecil or C.H.] Middleton, for [Robert] Blake, for [Ralph] Wightman' were numbered in faithful millions, 'gathered as much for the way they speak as for what they say', and that these men had not an 'Oxford vowel' between them (Adam, 1944: 33). In the late 1940s Pickles's demotic quiz/chat series, *Have a Go!*, reached an unprecedented audience for any British radio or TV programme – allegedly 54% of the population (Tunstall, 1983). BBC radio's need to provide entertainment for the mass audience – and later to retain a share of the working class audience attracted to television 'required a style of literary and dramatic diction and of performance which was closer to the idiom of ordinary speech'(Rodger, 1982: 39), and Pickles' programme fitted the bill perfectly.

During wartime, the BBC had drawn upon its pre-war experience in Regional broadcasting, producing a variety of programmes in which 'ordinary folk' – both civilians and army personnel – were brought to the microphone. D. G. Bridson's *Billy Welcome* (the precursor of *Have a Go!*) and *We Speak for Ourselves*, and Francis Dillon's *Country Magazine*, heralded a new impetus to bring the actual workers and farmers contributing to the war effort onto the airwaves in order to be celebrated as everyday heroes (see Black, 1972: 128–135). Of course, at this time the working class had become a major centre of attention for the BBC's morale and propaganda activities on the home front.

Rural radio: the West Region

As Sonya O. Rose has observed, the fact that British citizens heard rural affairs being discussed by agricultural workers on the airwaves in the wartime series *Country Magazine* helped to raise the prestige of the national agricultural community; indeed the series had been founded to address the concerns of agriculturalists that they were less valued members of the national community than urban dwellers and industrial workers (2003: 215). However, whereas portraying (national) unity through (regional) diversity was made essential by the war effort, it became more problematic as an aim, both pragmatically and ideologically, during peacetime. For the BBC West Region staff that had created *Country Magazine*, it was a difficult task to represent the unity of their own geographically expansive and occupationally diverse West Country. A number of programmes and series broadcast during the post-war period can be viewed as experimental attempts to widen and broaden coverage and surveillance of the region.

Before outlining these programmes, it is worth considering very briefly what the 'West Country' actually is. Invariably including the counties of Somerset, Dorset, Devon and Cornwall – and in a wider definition extending to the City and County of Bristol and to Gloucestershire and Wiltshire – the West Country is an informal and loosely defined term for the area of south-western England. It is misleading to state that the West Country 'escaped' the Industrial Revolution, but even today it is still a largely rural area. The cultural and historical identity of the region has been shaped over the centuries by imaginative and mythopoetic geographies as much as by objective and static characteristics – hence the continuing resonance of Thomas Hardy's nineteenth-century Wessex, often used synonymously with the 'West Country'.

In the immediate post-war period, the West Region became a major production centre under its new director, Gerald Beadle, and its head of programmes, Frank Gillard, the former war correspondent who would later play a key role in initiating the BBC's Local Radio network (see Linfoot, 2011). The regional structure of the BBC at this time was determined by technical considerations relating to transmitter range rather than to any social considerations (Cooke, 2007: 86). The West Regional broadcasts served a huge area stretching from Land's End all the way to Brighton. Nevertheless a historical understanding of the distinctiveness of the region was vital to the staff. In a special booklet issued in 1949, the Region's political discussion programmes were said to amount to 'something quite revolutionary in our public life':

It is not entirely fanciful to say that not since Wessex ceased to be a kingdom – which is going back more than somewhat – has the West had the means of forming any unified opinion about its own affairs. In this field regional broadcasting fills the gap between the national press and the local press, and should bring greater vitality to both. (Quoted in Baker, 1950: 103)

County Mixture, a series of seven programmes of considerable length and complexity (created by producer Desmond Hawkins, who was involved in scripting *Country Magazine* and would later become Controller of the West Region), sought to extend coverage of the region through a representation of each of the seven western counties in sound 'portraits'. It met with some acclaim from the rural audience, yet the experiment could not be sustained, because the idea was to capture the essence of a community in each programme, and the staff concluded that a county was too large a unit to be considered a true community (Beadle, 1951: 154). One of the most ambitious attempts undertaken by the West Region to reflect rural life was the series *Village on the Air*. Each week for two years a recording car was brought to a different village, and ordinary people were invited to tell their own story.

Brandon Acton-Bond's early radio work

West Region features producer Brandon Acton-Bond, who had been an actor and was a pilot during World War II, began working as features producer in Plymouth in 1947; he was interested in building on the attempts to reflect everyday life within the West Country. Acton-Bond was also a pioneer of oral history, as evidenced by the series he produced, *Fifty Years Ago in the West of England*, which was broadcast in 1950. This programme has been singled out for praise by oral historian Paul Thompson (1971) for its vivid recollections of Cornish tin mining and the clay-workers' strike of 1913.

In the late 1940s and early 1950s Acton-Bond made several features that, through documenting the daily life of a small community over a period of time, recorded what we might term, not oral history, but the 'oral present'. These features can be described as micro-local sound portraits, which presented a kind of microcosm of the region. Acton-Bond achieved this by employing two ostensibly contradictory tactics: he gained the trust of programme participants and collaborated with them over an extended period of time, and he utilised unobtrusive and discreet forms of surveillance in the recording of actuality. Acton-Bond

was a consummate 'sound hunter' (see Bijsterveld, 2004, for an explanation of this term), who, in his skilful selection of microphone placement
to catch natural sounds, employed experimental techniques (Anon.,
2006). His innovative recording methods were inspired by the natural
history broadcasts at which the West Region excelled. They often
involved recording people as the sound recordist Dr Ludwig Koch (who
conducted a great deal of work in the BBC West Region) recorded wild
birds – leaving the microphone 'in position' long enough that the birds
(or people) ceased to notice it, and then activating the microphone and
beginning the recording process (Beadle, 1951).

For example, the feature, *The School On The Moor* (first broadcast in the
West Region on 15 December 1948) was about a school in Bolventor, on
Bodmin Moor, opposite Jamaica Inn. This tiny school was attended by
only 30 children (ages 4–15) who came from cottages and farmsteads
scattered all over the moor; the headmaster, Reg Bennett, and his wife
were the only teachers.[3] Acton-Bond and his colleagues placed a number
of microphones in the two classrooms, leaving them there for a week,
after which time the children grew accustomed to them as 'part of
the furniture'. Then, without their knowledge, the microphones were
activated, and a great deal of 'eavesdropping' actuality was recorded
on acetate discs during the winter months to provide the basis for the
feature (Beadle, 1951). The range of actuality featured in the finished
programme includes arithmetic lessons; a school assembly; recitations;
nursery rhymes; piano and choral practice; playground games; and
sounds such as that of the children drinking milk from glass bottles with
straws. Bennett came to the Plymouth studio to comment on the discs,
identify the children and talk about their individual characteristics, and
so on, which formed the basis of his narration.

The programme was partly organised around a comparison of school
life today with the school life in the late nineteenth century, with Reg
Bennett quoting from the school's earliest logbook, which dated back to
1878. The programme is based entirely on first-hand experiences, and
yet a kind of thesis discreetly emerges about how little has changed over
the 70-year period in terms of material conditions and soundscapes, but
how much has changed in terms of social attitudes towards the discipline of children. Discipline is clearly less strict in the contemporary
period: Bennett is most concerned that school finishes early enough that
the children can walk home before dark, as the school and its environs
(it was at the very centre of Bodmin Moor) still does not have electric
lighting (Acton-Bond, 1948). Although the programme was only broadcast in the West Home Service 'with no ballyhoo', Frank Gillard noted in

a memo on the occasion of a repeat of the programme in 1949 that 'one or two of the national critics gave it a very big write-up'.[4]

In 1949 Acton-Bond began planning a new series of feature programmes, called *Pictures of a Road*, which began the following year. It was another attempt to represent the topography of the West Region in sound, this time involving travelogues written on the spot and then recorded and edited for transmission. It was described by Frank Gillard:

> For each programme he is choosing a stretch of road, and sending three well-contrasted observers along it independently. He will record their account of the journey and then make up his programme – thirty minutes – from their recordings, with a fourth voice to link the descriptions together. The first road is Lyme Regis-Portsmouth, and the travellers will be Ralph Wightman, Trudy Bliss and Johnny Morris.[5]

This series was popular, and several of the programmes were broadcast nationally on the Home Service. Acton-Bond expanded on the idea in the coming years by creating other programmes as a variation on the theme, such as *Pictures of a River*, *Pictures from the Air*, and *Pictures of a Railway Journey*, all of which were broadcast nationally on the BBC Home Service. In both his actuality features and the radio dramas he produced, Acton-Bond returned again and again to the topography, character and quotidian reality of village life, as his notes for a programme about a fictional village (*Sunday in West Aller*, 1953) attest:

> In our minds it has an exact geographical location. It lies inland in a part of Devon called the South Hams, a peninsula of many hills and small valleys and steep, narrow lanes...Nothing much happens on Sunday, they say, and in that it's not unlike the other villages around. Yet if one looks closely perhaps some pattern to the day emerges. The church, the milking times, the Sunday dinner, the pub, daylight and darkness all play their part in establishing the day's outlines...Almost every village has a character of its own, a character by which it is recognised in the country around. One is called a gossipy village, another is friendly, another suspicious, another is dull and dirty or charming and olde worlde, another very puritanical, another free and easy.[6]

The resulting programme was an interesting experiment as a 'real-time' radio drama broadcast in five-or ten-minute segments interspersed throughout one day's output. But, perhaps the most ambitious and experimental feature made by Acton-Bond was *Year's Round at Bolventor* (broadcast on the BBC Home Service on 27 December 1951), during the making of which he repeatedly brought recording gear to this village on the edge of Bodmin Moor in Cornwall (which had also been the focus of *School on the Moor*). This was a longitudinal portrait of the village that allowed the producer to become thoroughly familiar with the community – one which was typical of many remote villages at the time, in being, as Frank Gillard put it, 'obliged to depend on their own resources for social entertainment'.[7]

As a means of presenting an authentic sound picture of Bolventor over the course of a typical year, almost every small social event in the life of the village was recorded for inclusion in the edited feature (e.g., a christening). In *Year's Round*, Acton-Bond recorded, in addition to the events themselves, the actual preparations for most of the social events featured, as well as comments from participants and observers (such as that of Tommy Hooper and Reg Bennett as they watch a horse race at Bolventor Sports Day). In this way the listener gets a sense of work and leisure 'processes' unfolding within everyday life, with frequent examples of what Erving Goffman termed 'backstage behaviour' or 'back region' communication.

The programme is notable for this consistent attention to 'performances' that are an integral part of the fabric of social life and (presumably) not enacted especially for the production, and it seamlessly stitches together a variety of social rituals. For example: there are snatches of talk at the late night whist drive in the school (one departing participant remarks, 'I shall have my breakfast when I get home!'); a choir practice in which a swallow flies into the low porch of the chapel and has to be retrieved; the scratchy tannoy and the rumble of horses' hooves in the Bolventor Sports Day on August Bank Holiday; the auction of donated gifts at the Harvest Festival; speeches at the Women's Institute birthday party; and songs, recitals and a play at the school at Christmas.

The programme often sounds like a real-life version of *The Archers*, the long-running British radio soap opera set in a fictional farming community. With this in mind, it is significant that Acton-Bond is best known for producing the radio series *At the Luscombes*, which was about the life of a family living in a West Country village. Written by Denis Constanduros and first broadcast in the West Region in 1948, the serial was a clear forerunner of *The Archers*, which was to launch in 1951. Although it was very popular in the West Region, it was not until 21

December 1953 that the Regional station could persuade management in London to broadcast the programme on the national Home Service, and this short-lived national 'run' of the serial concluded on 1 March 1954.

Ethnography and eavesdropping

As an 'actuality feature', *Year's Round* is unusual for being so narrowly circumscribed in terms of geography – it is truly parochial, in the original sense of being 'of the parish' – and for being almost exclusively concerned with leisure rather than work. It can be observed that BBC management were always concerned about programmes that had examples of 'thick dialect', and in his skilful fieldwork (characterised by strenuous efforts to combine authenticity with intelligibility) and his rather 'safe' choice of subjects, Acton-Bond clearly had the full confidence of BBC management. *Year's Round* is one of those rare examples of a programme in which the producer set out to comprehensively record a sonic reflection of the living present, and which now functions in the modern context as 'sound heritage'. At this point it is useful to refer to field recordists Robin and Jillian Ridington and their (2006) distinction between oral history and acoustic history. Whereas oral history is an account of the past using spoken words, acoustic history is an account of changing soundscapes:

> Acoustic history is the history of events as they are heard, rather than objects as they are seen, while oral history is a narrative account of events by participants. (Ridington and Ridington, 2006: 51)

Acton-Bond's unusual production methods clearly evidence a desire to capture everyday settings, social interactions and 'naturally occurring' situations. His aim was similar to that of ethnographers, who hope to minimise their influence on the life-world that they set out to record, in order to facilitate open and unguarded expressive behaviour. One of the advantages of documenting social life in 'natural' and public settings is that there are a great many social actors whose presence and significance are countervailing to that of the ethnographer or sound recordist (see Hammersley and Atkinson, 1983: 110, 191). In this way their presence has little or no effect on the pace or content of events, and as they record extensively they are able to document many conversations and ordinary interactions with a minimum of interference (Ridington and Ridington, 2006: 79).

The 'eavesdropper model' of radio broadcasting employed by Acton-Bond has not been adequately recognised, discussed or theorised, except perhaps in discussions of radio art and sound installations. In his discussion of 'broadcast talk', Scannell asserted that the effect of listening to radio is precisely *not* that of overhearing talk not intended to be overheard, and that all radio talk is public discourse (Scannell, 1991: 1–11). While this is the normative model of studio-based discourse in radio, I would like to argue that the use of actuality in radio features and of experiments in perspective in radio drama pioneered and popularised an alternative 'eavesdropping model' of discourse. BBC radio producers have always given a great deal of consideration not just to what kind of environments might be recorded as vivid actuality material for radio broadcasting, but also the way in which the resulting actuality would itself be affected by the manner in which it was recorded, and how to counteract the inhibiting effect of the introduction of recording technology to the social environment.

Acton-Bond's experiments can, in fact, be linked to early experiments in storytelling through the atmospheric or informative use of sound. Of great relevance here is the German tradition of the 'hörspiel' – a form of radio drama in which a soundscape is constructed through extensive use of sound effects, actuality and ambient sound. As early as 1927, Otto Alfred Palitzsch had critiqued radio's tendency to act merely as a conduit for the other arts (e.g., by transmitting Ibsen and Shakespeare plays), calling for a new kind of 'pure radio play that is not somehow carried by a choir or geared to voices and music but is integrated into an acoustical atmosphere at which the hooting of the automobile and the bray of a donkey are able to find their place, just like the whistle of the wind and the chiming of devotional bells in a village church. In the place of coloured sets come tonal ones' (quoted in Albright, 2003: 96).

In Britain there had likewise been a rich tradition of attention to soundscapes in radio drama, although the same tendency in radio features (the 'sound portrait') is not so well documented. *Quayside Nights: Plymouth*, produced by Francis Worsley and broadcast by the BBC West Region on 10 August 1935, is a pre-eminent example of a sound portrait. This programme featured specially recorded actuality of tradesmen and workers on Plymouth's quayside – the sound of men at the Barbican fish market selling lots is interspersed with the sounds of cranes and winches loading pig iron. Later that same year, a radio feature called *Dinner is Served* (produced by Laurence Gilliam, devised by Gerald Coxon and broadcast on the national Home Service on 17 October) depicted through sound the organisation of the national food supply. The production and distribution of vegetables, fish and meat from source to consumer was tracked, and the programme featured, for example, the testimony of a Lowestoft herring drifter skipper and girl gutters and packers. Such programmes not only added a new dimension to radio broadcasting through their use of actuality, but they also represented 'thumbnail sketches' of work processes underlying everyday life that most people took for granted. A column in an edition of *Daily Worker* the following year (7 February 1936) chastised the BBC for the fact that this type of broadcasting was the exception rather than the rule, and asserted that the Corporation was mired too deep in its 'battleship organisation' to mingle with real people:

> The microphone could be the ear and the voice of millions, a sharing of experience by means of which people become alive to themselves. Today it is only a platform for old men to lecture at us. Just imagine listening to miners from their galleries underground, a walk round East London, a trade union meeting, soldiers talking to fishermen. (Audit, 1936: 7).

As with the later introduction of 'sync sound' lightweight cameras in documentary filmmaking, the refinement of mobile recording techniques (such as the introduction of the tape recorder) enabled radio producers to record individuals and interactions in informal settings in a way that had not previously been possible without recourse to studio dramatisation, with its intrinsic fictionalisation. This development in radio features was – again, as with documentary film – often contiguous with the avoidance of the expository or editorial commentary that had dominated the form until this time, and which had tended to conflate the voice of the narrator with that of the programme itself and, in turn, with the voices *in* the programme.

In Acton-Bond's features about Bolventor life, he negated this problem by contracting a member of that local community to perform the role of narrator and scriptwriter, so that this voice performs a constituent role within the programme, as it did within the community. Hendy has written about this technique as utilised in a latter-day programme called *Spar Boys* (transmitted on BBC Radio 4 on 11 July 2001), which is *'narrated by someone with experience of his own'* (Hendy, 2004: 179–180, emphasis in the original). Whereas presenters/narrators have increasingly been positioned as 'ordinary' co-members of the listeners' lifeworld, these radio documentaries feature presenters/narrators who are also members of the life-world represented within the programme. Thus

Acton-Bond's work can be regarded as a groundbreaking experiment in co-production and in presenting the soundscapes of an acoustic environment coterminous with that of the rural West Region listener.

The BBC's calendrical role

Finally, Acton-Bond's programmes can be said to have represented a local or regional analogue to the kind of national broadcasting perpetuated by the BBC during the 1920s and 1930s, as it sought to inculcate a sense of nationhood, belonging and community through the sustained use of outside broadcasts and an ingrained emphasis on national ritual and royal events (Mackenzie, 1986). During this period the BBC produced thousands of outside broadcasts, including such diverse fare as religious services, opera, plays and music hall entertainment, dance music, public speeches, ceremonies and sporting events. As Scannell and Cardiff observe:

> Nothing so well illustrates the noiseless manner in which the BBC became perhaps *the* central agent of the national culture as its calendrical role; the cyclical reproduction, year in year out, of an orderly procession of festivities, rituals and celebrations – major and minor, civil and sacred – that marked the unfolding of the broadcast year. (1991: 171–172)

As many of the outside broadcasts originated from London or other large cities, the Regions came to excel, almost by default, in programmes that reflected back to their audiences the culture of everyday life in the areas they served (see Scannell, 1993). They did this most successfully through the development of Regional outside broadcasts and features. Acton-Bond's experimental programmes represented a micro-local approach to the reflection of everyday life within a region, which blended these two programme genres together.

It is arguable that the life of the typical English village, as documented by Acton-Bond, could never hope to provide what might be regarded as a truly 'broadcastable' event of the kind documented by BBC Outside Broadcast staff – if it could, it would not be a typical English village (Beadle, 1951). Perhaps this was partly the point: Acton-Bond was reminding listeners that each town, village or even parish had its *own* unique calendar of ceremonies and rituals, in contradistinction to the national calendar. Acton-Bond's 'local outside broadcasts' demonstrate the way in which many aspects of popular culture exuded a sense of stability and traditionalism in the immediate post-war years – people engaged in and valued leisure activities and social rituals in much the same manner as they had before the war (Philips and Tomlinson, 1992: 9). As Denys Val Baker observed in 1950, the development of the BBC Regions occurred 'just at the right time, when people wanted to resume their normal lives – wanted to emphasise, if anything, the meaning of their familiar, local life, with all its everyday idiosyncrasies and traditions' (101). In this manner, Acton-Bond succeeded in portraying both the distinctiveness of West Country life and its imperviousness to change.

Notes

1. BBC internal memorandum, sent from Filson Young to V. H. Goldsmith (Assistant Controller), R. H. Eckersley and J. C. W. Reith, 5 November 1930. Quoted in Silvester Mazzarella, *Filson Young: The First Media Man (1876–1938)*, http://richarddnorth.com/archived-sites/filsonyoung/biography/part-7-making-airwaves-1924–30/41-pioneering-at-the-bbc/, accessed 5 January 2015.
2. Extract from Philip Donnellan's interview with D.G. Bridson, uncatalogued production file, MS1938, Birmingham Archives and Heritage, Library of Birmingham.
3. Memo from Frank Gillard (Head of West Regional Programmes) to Godfrey Adams, 2 December 1948. BBC Written Archives, Caversham, R19/1432/2 (Entertainment/Features File II/West Regional Memos/1947–1949).
4. Memo from Frank Gillard (Head of West Regional Programmes) to Head of North Region Programmes, 4 March 1949. BBC Written Archives, Caversham, WE1/75 West Region Features 'The School on the Moor' 1949–1951.
5. Memo from Frank Gillard to Controller of the Home Service, 23 December 1949. BBC Written Archives, Caversham, R19/1432/2 (West Regional Memos 1947–1949).
6. Brandon Acton-Bond, 'Article for Radio Times' script. BBC Written Archives, Caversham, WE1/85 Feature Programme: 'Sunday in West Aller', 1953.
7. Memo from Frank Gillard to Controller of the Home Service, 23 December 1949. BBC Written Archives, Caversham, R19/1432/3 (West Regional Memos 1950–1954).

References

Adam, K. (1944) Regions in Wartime. In *The BBC Yearbook* (London: BBC), 33–36.

Albright, D. (2003) *Beckett and Aesthetics* (Cambridge: Cambridge University Press).

Anon. (2006) 'Obituary: Michael Croucher', *The Times*, London, 10 June.

Audit, G. (1936) 'Moving the Mike', *The Daily Worker*, London, 7 February.

Baker, Denys Val. (1950) *Britain Discovers Herself* (London: Christopher Johnson).

Beadle, G. (1951) 'Rural England Reflected', *The BBC Quarterly*, Vol. 6, No. 3, 152–156.

Beech, P. (1968) *BBC Lunchtime Lectures, 6th Series* (London: BBC).

Bijsterveld, K. (2004) '"What Do I Do With My Tape Recorder…?": Sound Hunting and the Sounds of Everyday Dutch Life in the 1950s and 1960s', *Historical Journal of Film, Radio and Television*, Vol. 24, No. 4, 614–634.

Black, P. (1972) *The Biggest Aspidistra in the World* (London: BBC).

Bridson, D. G. (1971) *Prospero & Ariel: The Rise and Fall of Radio: A Personal Recollection* (London: Victor Gollancz).

Briggs, A. (1995) *The History of Broadcasting in the United Kingdom: Volume II: The Golden Age of Wireless* (Oxford: Oxford University Press).

Cooke, Lez (2007) BBC English Regions Drama: Second City Firsts. In Helen Wheatley (ed.) *Re-viewing Television History: Critical Issues in Television Historiography* (London: I. B. Tauris), 82–96.

Fairclough, N. (1989) *Language and Power* (London and New York: Longman).

Hajkowski, T. (2010) *The BBC and National Identity in Britain, 1922–53* (Manchester: Manchester University Press).

Hammersley, M. and Atkinson, P. (1983) *Ethnology: Principles in Practice* (London: Routledge).

Hendy, D. (2004) 'Reality Radio': The Documentary. In A. Crisell (ed.) *More than a Music Box: Radio Cultures and Communities in a Multi-Media World* (New York: Berghahn Books), 167–188.

Hendy, D. (2007) *Life on Air: A History of Radio Four* (Oxford: Oxford University Press).

Linfoot, M. (2011) 'A History of BBC Local Radio in England: c 1960–1980', University of Westminster, unpublished PhD thesis.

Mackenzie, J. M. (1986) 'In Touch with the Infinite': The BBC and the Empire 1923–1953. In J. M. Mackenzie (ed.) *Imperialism and Popular Culture* (Manchester: Manchester University Press), 165–191.

Philips, D. and Tomlinson, A. (1992) Homeward Bound: Leisure, Popular Culture and Consumer Capitalism. In D. Strinat and S. Wagg (eds.) *Come on Down? Popular Media Culture in Post-War Britain* (London and New York: Routledge), 9–45.

Ridington, J. and Ridington, R. (2006) *Why Baby Why*: A Guide to Howard Broomfield's Documentation of the Dane-zaa Soundscape. In Jillian and Robin Ridington (eds) *When You Sing It, Just Like New: First Nations Poetics, Voices and Representations* (Nebraska: University of Nebraska), 78–94.

Rodger, I. (1982) *Radio Drama* (London: Macmillan).

Scannell, P. (1991) Introduction. In P. Scannell (ed.) *Broadcast Talk* (London: Sage).

Scannell, P. (1993) The Origins of BBC Regional Policy. In M. McLoone (ed.) *The Regions, The Nation and the BBC* (London: BFI), 27–37.

Scannell, P. and Cardiff, D. (1991) *A Social History of British Broadcasting: Volume One, 1922–1939* (Oxford: Blackwell).

Shapley, O. (1996) *Broadcasting a Life* (London, Scarlet Press).

Swan, M. (1957) 'The Spoken Word: On Tape', *Listener*, 10 January, 79.

Thompson, P. (1971) 'BBC Archives'. *Oral History Journal*, No. 1, Summer, 23–26.

Tunstall, J. (1983) *The Media in Britain* (London, Constable).

8
Gi' It Some 'Ommer: ITV Regional Programming and the Performance of the Black Country

Julie E. Robinson

For those unfamiliar with the geography of Central England, the 'Black Country' is an industrial area of the West Midlands lying immediately to the west of Birmingham. It is often claimed that its colloquial name derives from the emissions of the heavy industry that once dominated the region's skyline, as well as its economy, although it may also refer to the South Staffordshire coalfield on which the area predominantly stands (Quigley, 2010: 47). According to John Fletcher (1968), local historian and founder member of the Black Country Society, it was the boundaries of the coalfield that provided the area with its geographical limits – with faults to the north, east and west confining development to a very specific locality. In the first issue of the society's journal, *The Blackcountryman*, Fletcher defines the region very precisely as comprising the towns of 'Wednesbury, Darlaston, Willenhall, Bilston, Coseley, Tipton, Dudley, Brierley Hill and the adjacent villages', plus West Bromwich, Smethwick and Oldbury (1968: 11) but, as Quigley and Shaw (2010) suggest, there is no real consensus on exactly where the Black Country begins and ends and, for convenience sake, most modern commentators equate it to the area covered by the metropolitan boroughs of Walsall, Dudley and Sandwell and the City of Wolverhampton, even though, historically, the conurbations of Walsall and Wolverhampton, like the nearby regional centre of Birmingham, have always been excluded from the definition. As this might suggest, the geography of the Black Country is highly contentious and plays an important part in shaping the perception of local and/or regional identity amongst its residents. However, for the purpose of this study, defining its precise territorial boundaries is less important than the way in which a particular *version* of the Black Country was projected in regional television programmes made and transmitted on ITV in the Midlands between the 1960s and the 1980s.

This chapter will suggest that the representation of the Black Country in ITV regional programming in this period was not entirely the vision of news editors and programme makers, but rather reflected the wider discourses taking place in the construction of Black Country history at the same time. It will argue that, at a time when many of the area's traditional industries were in decline and its ancient pastimes were under attack, there was a surge in interest, not only in recording and preserving those traditions, but also in recreating and reconstructing them, and that the ITV regional companies operating in this period did not so much invent the performative mode of representing the Black Country discussed here, but rather tapped into a pre-existing movement. Whilst it is possible to view the representation of the Black Country in regional programmes dating from this period outside of the institutional context, a brief history of ITV in the region may be useful in highlighting the more general issues surrounding the representation of local and regional identities on Midlands' screens.

ITV in the Midlands 1968–1989

The material that forms the basis of this discussion is held in the ITV regional news and programme collections now in the care of the Media Archive for Central England. The collection comprises material created by ATV and Central Independent Television for transmission in the Midlands between 1956 and 1989 and, although the deposit includes material dating back to the very earliest days of ITV in the region, for a number of reasons the decision has been taken to concentrate on the period after 1968. In terms of the underlying thesis of the chapter, it represents the start of a particularly active period for the Black Country Society, which had grown out of another local organisation with a more practical interest in preserving the area's industrial history: the Dudley Canal Tunnel Preservation Society (Smallshire, 2009). It seems, however, that Fletcher always had larger ambitions than securing the future of the canal and, within a year of its formation, the new society he had helped established 'to promote interest in the past present and future of this great and interesting region' had a membership of over 150 and had established a regular quarterly publication, *The Blackcountryman* (Brimble, 1968; Smallshire, 2009). In terms of the history of ITV, 1968 saw the implementation of the Independent Television Authority's newly revised regional structure, which meant that for the first time the Midlands had a single contractor operating for seven days a week and based, at least nominally, in the region (Independent Television Authority, 1968: 24; Sendall, 1983: 333–334).

Prior to 1968, the situation was somewhat more complicated. When the Television Act 1954 first made provision for a second television service in Britain, technical restrictions meant that there were only enough available broadcasting frequencies to provide nationwide coverage across one network, in spite of a requirement for ITV to be internally competitive, as well as providing an alternative to the BBC (Sendall, 1982: 65). In addition, the act also insisted 'the programmes broadcast from any station or stations contain a suitable proportion of matter calculated to appeal specially to the tastes and outlook of the persons served' (Television Act 1954, 2 and 3 Eliz. 2, Ch. 55) and, according to Bernard Sendall, it was the ITA's first Director-General, Robert Fraser, who came up with the solution of appointing *regional* television companies to provide a service in their own area as well as competing to supply programmes to the national network (Sendall, 1982: 64–66).

Although later described by Peter Black as 'the best single idea anyone ever had about television in Britain' (1972: 73), the complex pattern of contracts finally adopted by the ITA was not necessarily the best solution for the Midlands. In order to avoid one company becoming dominant, the broadcasting week in the three most densely populated areas – London, the Midlands and the North – were split into weekdays and weekends and divided, more or less equally, between four contracts (Sendall, 1982: 65, 68). Unlike the smaller companies, which served their regions for seven days a week, or even the other two 'majors', Associated Rediffusion and Granada, which operated the weekday contracts for London and the North, respectively, the two companies appointed to serve the Midlands were forced to split their time and resources between two regions (Sendall, 1982: 65). By the time the Midlands service launched in February 1956, ATV was already well-established as the weekend broadcaster for London and had its main operational centre in the capital, whilst ABC, as the weekend contractor for both the Midlands and the North, had decided to open its main studios at Didsbury near Manchester. A joint studio facility was developed at Aston in Birmingham with its own administrative and technical staff, but as ABC's Managing Director, Howard Thomas, would later comment, they 'never considered themselves belonging to either ATV or ABC' and neither company became 'fully localised' in the region (1977: 161).

In the circumstances, it is hardly surprising that both ATV and ABC struggled to establish a track record in producing high quality regional programming for the Midlands, compounded no doubt by the fact that, as two of what became known as the 'Big Four' ITV companies, they were also charged with producing the bulk of the programming for the network (Sendall, 1982: 68). For all the ITA's protests that 'every one of [the] fifteen companies is a regional company, the four largest companies no less than the remaining eleven' (1962: 7), in the late 1950s and early 1960s the official discourses coming out of ATV, in particular, were focused upon the company's success as the weekend broadcaster for London and its contribution to the network, with its role in the Midlands often appearing as an afterthought (Associated TeleVision Ltd, 1958: 5). Nonetheless, during this period ATV did manage to maintain a fairly robust, and occasionally innovative regional production schedule, introducing the first regional news bulletin, *Midlands News* (1956–1969), and the first lunchtime programme, *Lunchbox* (1956–1964). Following the renewal of the first ITV contracts in 1964 and the subsequent introduction of the soap opera, *Crossroads* (1964–1988), to the Midlands (and later network) schedule, regional programming was, however, mainly confined to the company's new early-evening news magazine, *ATV Today*, which also took over the remit of earlier special-interest programmes such as *Midland Farming* (1958–1964) and *Come in to the Garden* (1960–1962). The ITA was unimpressed with what it saw as ATV's lack of commitment to its regional audience, and the company found itself with a more difficult challenge than it had expected when it came to securing the new seven-day contract for the Midlands, which was due to come into effect in July 1968 (Sendall, 1983: 342). At least now the company was fully committed to developing a base in the Midlands – a brand new studio and office complex, the ATV Centre was opened in the centre of Birmingham in October 1969 – although throughout the 1970s the ITA's successor, the Independent Broadcasting Authority (IBA), continued to push the company for more regional content in its Midlands schedule, which the Authority felt was still lacking in quantity and quality and too focused on Birmingham (Independent Broadcasting Authority, 1975: 144). In the late 1970s and early 1980s, as the IBA reviewed its regional structure once again and put forward a proposal for a new dual region with separate programming for the East and West Midlands, ATV significantly increased its regional output, although not enough to satisfy the Authority, which only awarded the company the new contract on the condition that it undergo complete restructuring and adopt a name that better reflected the region it served

(Briggs and Spicer, 1986: 95; Potter, 1990: 341–342). The new franchise holder, Central Independent Television, finally divested itself of the Elstree studio, which had been ATV's main production base since the late 1950s, and, having added a second major studio and administrative facility in Nottingham to complement its existing complex in Birmingham, finally became fully established as a Midlands broadcaster, with an enthusiasm for regional programming seldom seen in its earlier incarnation (Bonner and Aston, 1998). In spite of this change in the franchise holder, however, there is both a continuity of representation of the Black Country across the ATV/Central divide and evidence of long-term relationships with some of the main contributors – relationships that date back to the very start of the ATV seven-day franchise.

Locating the performance of the Black Country

The Black Country is widely acknowledged to have a unique character, with its own traditions, humour, local dishes and dialect, and the area's idiosyncratic traditions and practices were undoubtedly a large part of its appeal to regional programme makers. What may have made it more fascinating, however, was the apparent disparity between this playful, performative side of Black Country life and the hard realities of work in the area's mills, factories and foundries. The Black Country's indigenous industries – chain and nail making and coal mining – were notoriously harsh (Quigley and Shaw, 2010), and the dominance of mining and heavy engineering in the area may have also contributed to its strong sense of community and identity. As Castells and Walton have argued:

> Regional identities are the discursive products of the collective invention and recreation of traditions, but they are also grounded in the ways in which people make their livings and live their lives. (Castells and Walton, 1998: 76–77)

As Quigley and Shaw point out, even as late as the 1970s, one in three workers in the Black Country were engaged in '"metal bashing" in one form or another' (2010: 31) and, although by the mid-1980s much of the area's traditional manufacturing base had been lost, this shared experience was still a very recent memory. Moreover, Black Country men, in particular, had a reputation for playing hard as well as working hard (Hillier and Mosley, 1976: 70), and it is perhaps because of the difficult conditions, rather than in spite of them, that performance and ritual became so important within Black Country society.

ITV regional programmes in this period tapped into the strong oral and folk traditions of the area, and the following discussion will consider the representation of the Black Country across a range of programmes and genres, considering how performance was foregrounded by regional programme makers who visited the area between the 1960s and the 1980s. In terms of defining performance, it will adopt Richard Schechner's 'wide spectrum approach', which covers a

> 'continuum' of actions ranging from ritual, play, sports, popular entertainments, the performing arts (theatre, dance, music), and everyday life performances to the enactment of social, professional, gender, race, and class roles, to healing (from shamanism to surgery) and to the various representations and constructions of actions in the media and the Internet. (2002: xi)

In particular, it will concentrate upon the areas in which the interests of the programme makers and their contributors seem to overlap most closely: the performance of history; the use of poetry as a form of social commentary; and the representation of the region's vernacular culture, specifically Black Country humour and a long-standing tradition of industrial folk songs.

Performing histories

The first sustained study of the Black Country in this period was *The Cradle of Industry* (1969), a documentary film shown on Easter Monday, 7 April 1969, in the 35-minute slot more usually occupied by local news magazine *ATV Today* (1964–1981). The impetus for the film appears to have come from regular reporter Gwyn Richards who, according to the *TV Times*, spent 12 months researching and writing the programme (Anon., 1969b). Although it is not entirely clear how Dr John Fletcher of the newly formed Black Country Society came to be involved, or how closely the Society worked with the production team on the programme's content, *The Cradle of Industry* established a number of conventions in terms of how the Black Country, and particularly Black Country history, came to be represented on screen in the subsequent 20-year period. Richards's omniscient narration provides the audience with a somewhat poetic history of the region, with Fletcher appearing in vision to fill in the practical details, such as the importance of the coalfield, both to the local economy and in terms of defining the Black Country's borders, or the area's ability to constantly adapt its industries to meet demand (*The Cradle of Industry*, 1969). However, Fletcher's role in the programme goes beyond that of simply an 'expert witness'. By locating him firmly within the industrial landscape, a connection is established between audience and place that might otherwise be missing, and Fletcher's strong regional accent and rejection of formal academic language enhances the sense that he is very much 'of' the Black Country. Although one of the key themes of the programme is change – and particularly the displacement of the Black Country's traditional industries – there is also a strong sense of continuity with the past. The only industrial work shown in any detail takes place in a traditional chain forge (rather than, e.g., the modern steelworks at Round Oak) and this connection is further reinforced by the use of old still photographs, many of which appear to predate World War I.

Several of the other themes explored by the programme would also go on to become familiar to regional audiences. The 'separateness' of the small towns that make up the area – separate not only from the surrounding districts, but also from each other – was revisited in Sue Jay's award-winning documentary, *On the Road to Nowhere* (1974), which celebrates the strong community spirit demonstrated by the residents of Lower Gornal, a village so isolated that there is literally a single road leading in and out. The traditional, but long-outlawed, sports of dogfighting and cockfighting are discussed at some length by local dog breeder Joe Mallen and broadcaster Phil Drabble, respectively (Media Archive for Central England, 2011), with more than a suggestion, by Mallen at least, that they may not have died out completely, even in the 1960s. Perhaps because of its illegality, and its sense of belonging to a 'lost' culture, dogfighting seems to have held a particular interest for regional programme makers. Mallen had previously been featured in an earlier documentary, *Joe the Chainsmith*, made by Phillip Donnellan in 1958 for the BBC (Franklin, 2014), and the topic was not only revisited by the Central's *Gi' It Some 'Ommer* (1984) in the mid-1980s, but director Mike Connor even reused some of the 1969 footage in the second programme of the series. The Black Country's unique, and often cruel, sense of humour is also alluded to in *The Cradle of Industry*, not only during a sequence in which a toothless man recounts the bizarre tale of how he once put a monkey in the oven at a local pub, but also by Fletcher's closing address to camera, a humorous poem about the first Black Countryman to go to heaven. The programme ends with a singalong and 'grey paes' (peas) supper at the George and Dragon public house at Bradley, a less formal version of the social event that concludes

On the Road to Nowhere (1974), although on that occasion the 'paes' are served with faggots rather than bacon.

The Black Country Society's approbation for the programme was enthusiastically expressed in a letter of congratulation to *ATV Today* producer Donald Shingler (Anon., 1969c), and it is not difficult to see why. Richards's televisual journey through several thousand years of Black Country history shares the fundamental idea with *The Blackcountryman*'s editorial team that history did not have to be stuffy or academic, but was rather something to be lived and experienced. A look at the content of the Society's journal in this same period not only indicates the breadth and depth of the Society's interests in those early days, but also demonstrates a similar performative mode within Black Country historiography. In addition to 'serious' academic articles, such as Stanley Chapman's review of the literature on Black Country industry or Peter Barnsley's account of 'Two Old Cradley Mills', and items on linguistics and toponymy (Barnsley, 1969; Chapman, 1969; Green, 1970; Starkey, 1970), early volumes also include personal testimony, interviews and memoirs (Anon., 1969b; Parsons, 1968; Russell, 1969), folk songs (Raven, 1969) and contributions from local poets such as Kate Fletcher and Jim William Jones (Fletcher, 1970; Jones, 1969). Many of these contributors can also be seen in ITV regional programmes on the Black Country, along with John Fletcher, who continued to appear on *ATV Today* on a semi-regular basis throughout the late 1960s and early 1970s and also presented the industrial archaeology programme, *A Present from the Past* (1975). Fletcher's approach to history is best described as 'hands on', and the programmes often involved demonstrations of industrial techniques, either by experts or by Fletcher, himself. He was even happy to be involved in more tongue-in-cheek reconstructions, most notably advising John Swallow on how to successfully emulate Joe Darby, the 'spring-jumping' World Champion from Netherton, near Dudley, for *ATV Today* (16 October 1972). Predictably, Swallow was unable to jump across the Dudley Canal in spite of Fletcher's encouragement.

Poetry as a form of social commentary

Although absent from the 1969 documentary, poetry was an important part of output of *The Blackcountryman* and also played a key role in a number of other news stories and documentaries made by ATV and Central between the 1960s and the 1980s. It is interesting to note that poetry is rarely presented as a self-contained performance, but is instead used to provide some kind of commentary, either on topical events or on the area's declining industrial and social traditions. In this period Tipton-born vernacular poet, Harry Harrison (who is also interviewed at the start of *The Cradle of Industry* and can be seen in the George and Dragon at the end of the programme), appears in a number of items for *ATV Today*, commenting in verse upon a number of topical news stories, including the closure of Cradley Heath market (16 November 1967) and the 1968 Cup Final (17 May 1968), which West Bromwich Albion won 1–0, as well as more traditional aspects of Black Country life. For example, in a news item on 'Groaty Pudding' (a local type of meat stew), shown on 13 January 1976, Harrison recites a short poem in praise of 'Grorty Dick' (an even older name for the delicacy) before discussing the prospects for that evening's 'World Championships' with reporter Peter Green (*ATV Today*, 1976a). Not all of Harrison's contributions responded directly to a particular event, however, and in John Swallow's 1978 report about Emily Hadley from Tipton, who was still doing her washing by hand with an old-fashioned dolly maid and tub, his accompanying poem combines a more gentle humour with a nostalgic longing for a way of life that was fast dying out (*ATV Today*, 4 December 1978).

Neither was poetry always used humorously. For example, the short film item on chainmaking by hand, shown on *ATV Today* on 8 June 1972, rejects the usual explanatory voiceover in favour of a verse by Jim William Jones (another local poet and regular contributor to *The Blackcountryman*). This novel soundtrack juxtaposes Black Country dialect words such as 'ommer (hammer), yed (head) and togs (clothes) alongside more conventionally poetic language to celebrate the strength and skill of the area's craftsmen (*ATV Today*, 1972a). The most sustained use of poetry as commentary, however, appears in the 1984 documentary series, *Gi' It Some 'Ommer*, a spin off from Central's business programme, *Venture* (1982–1989). In common with many Central regional programmes around this time, *Venture* adopted a magazine format with studio interviews and discussions supplemented by filmed inserts, but it also made occasional specials on film, and the last programme before the 1983 Christmas break took the form of a documentary about Alf and Jimmy Holland, a father and son from Dudley who had made their living as rag-and-bone men, or 'tatters' (12 December 1983). In recent years, Jimmy had branched out into his own business, a skip hire firm, and the film focused on the relationship between the two men and Jimmy's continuing efforts to better himself. It also exploited the image of its subjects as Black Country 'characters' with a post-credits sequence showing them arriving at the Venture studio and disman-tling the empty set. The film was directed by Mike Finlason, who also directed three programmes in the follow-up series, even reusing some of the same footage of Alf and Jimmy in programme four, *Survivors* (*Gi' It Some 'Ommer*, 1984d).

Gi' It Some 'Ommer (the Black Country transliteration of 'give it some hammer', meaning to hit something really hard) draws on many of the same oral and folk traditions as the 1969 documentary to tell the story of the region at a time when its traditional industries, mining and engineering, were in terminal decline, but nothing had yet been put in their place. Although episodes three, four and five were made by Finlason in a fairly traditional documentary style (1984c, 1984d, 1984e), the first two programmes were directed by Mike Connor, who used his characteristic montage of archive film, stills, voiceovers, interviews and reconstructions interwoven with excerpts from a musical play, *The Nailmakers*, and scenes of modern industrial activity (1984a, 1984b). What these two somewhat disparate halves of the series have in common, however, is the use of poetry to provide a running commentary on the declining fortunes of this once-prosperous, although highly volatile and dangerous, industrial economy.

The poems are written by Harry Taylor, the founding editor of 'nostalgia publication' the *Black Country Bugle* (*Black Country Bugle*, 2015) and read in dialect by local actor Ralph Lawton. As with the earlier news films, they offer both a nostalgic look back into the Black Country's colourful history and an insight into the modern day struggles of its post-industrial population. In the series opener (*Gi' It Some 'Ommer*, 1984a) a poem about the Tipton Slasher, a notorious bare-knuckle boxer, can be heard over a reconstruction one of the Slasher's brutal fights; Pat Roach, wrestler and star of the Central drama production, *Auf Wiedersehen, Pet*, assumes the role of the local legend. The fight itself, which takes place on top of a hill, is shot in at least three different planes – close up, medium shot and extreme long shot – and these are superimposed over each other as the combatants repeatedly punch each other to the ground. The poem which accompanies the sequence not only chronicles the Slasher's triumphant rise to the status of a national celebrity and his subsequent fall, but also re-affirms his connection to the Black Country; Tipton, it explains 'was allis wum' (always home). In programme five, 'Kids' (*Gi' It Some 'Ommer*, 1984e), a group of local school children visit the Black Country Living Museum and a local country park, where they contemplate the region's industrial past as well as its uncertain future, while the verse provides a commentary on the wider implications of mass unemployment and social exclusion, as well as the more direct effects on the children themselves. The museum, which opened in 1978

(Benson, 2001), is yet another example of the performative turn in the presentation of Black Country history and in the programme provides the children with the opportunity to better understand their community's history by engaging with it on a visceral level rather than a cerebral level (*Gi' It Some 'Ommer*, 1984e). In spite of its very clear lineage back to *The Cradle of Industry*, however, the series on the whole was greeted with somewhat less enthusiasm by the Black Country Society, which reported 'mixed' comments and concluded that it was 'probably not the best series to be produced on our region' (Brimble, 1984: 3).

Vernacular culture: Black Country humour and folk songs

The ubiquity and importance of humour in Black Country life and culture has already been alluded to in the earlier discussion of poetry, with both cultural forms drawing upon the audience's knowledge of their local environment and community for inspiration. Poet Harry Harrison was also a stand-up comedian and appears in this guise in *On the Road to Nowhere* (1974), alongside a number of other traditional local acts, including a spoon player. In March 1976, *ATV Today* ran an extended item on local comedienne Dolly Allen, a pensioner in her sixties, whose deadpan delivery and observational style of humour Harrison greatly admired (1976b). Most of Dolly's jokes are directed at her layabout husband, who she usually gets the better of, but her willingness to poke fun at herself as well as at others is typical of the region.

According to Jon Raven, Black Country humour is frequently concerned with rivalries between the local towns, which have always remained fiercely independent of each other, or centred on individuals, often real people, but also the celebrated Black Country characters Aynuck and Ayli, whose antics provide a commentary on 'the domestic, social and work life' of the area, and who also act as its political conscience (Raven, 1986: 135, 139). In 'Survivors', programme four of *Gi' It Some 'Ommer*, one joke told by local stand-up comedian Tommy Mundon combines all of these elements into a story about Ayli buying a goldfish from the local rag-and-bone man and going round to local property developer Roy Richardson's house to borrow a file so he can remove a lump from its head (1984d). As the story about the monkey in *The Cradle of Industry* suggests, however, it is a style of humour that can also be incredibly cruel (1969).

As well as a very particular brand of self-deprecating humour, the Black Country also has its own specific tradition of folk music. Fletcher suggests the area's 'distinctive culture' manifests itself not only through the geographical specificity of the songs, but also in their roughness and vulgarity, a trait not unsurprising in a region where the work was hard and physical, and death was ever-present (Fletcher, 1977). As in other areas, there was a long tradition of rural and agricultural songs but, following the development of the Black Country as an industrial region, these were eclipsed by a new, urbanised form, which captured the harsh realities of a working life spent in mines, foundries and chain-shops (Raven, 1969: 32). Jon Raven in particular did much to collate and rehabilitate the industrial songs of the Black Country, publishing several books on the subject in the 1960s and 1970s (Palmer and Raven, 1976; Raven, 1977, 1978; Raven and Raven, 1965), but he was also a prolific songwriter and musician, and his own work was clearly influenced by the regional traditions he was working to preserve. Raven's association with ATV in the Midlands, like Fletcher's, dates back to at least March 1968, when his band, The Draymen, provided the sound-track to a short news item about the eviction of travelling families. The film cuts together library footage of travellers being removed from a series of unidentified sites (in yet another example of the recycling of earlier footage) skilfully fitting the images to Raven's plaintive tale of a community on the margins of society (*ATV Today*, 1968).

Raven also makes an appearance in *Gi' It Some 'Ommer* as one of the cast of *The Nailmakers*, the play he co-wrote with Malcolm Totten, extracts from which appear throughout the first two programmes of the series (1984a; 1984b). Although written in the early 1970s, this 'documentary musical' (Birmingham Rep, 2013) adopts the syntax and conventions of the region's traditional industrial folk songs which, according to Raven (1969), 'tended to be more local in character and more true to life in so far as they were often about living characters and spoke frequently of local conditions'. This is illustrated by the opening song, which introduces the nailmakers of the play's title. Nail making, like chain making, was a staple Black Country industry, and the association with 'real' people is reinforced by the use of black-and-white archive footage intercut with shots of the actors. The performance itself takes place in a location that would have been instantly recognisable to many Black Country residents – the recently closed Round Oak steelworks, founded by the Earl of Dudley in the 1850s (Raybould, 1984: 68) and newly purchased by Roy Richardson and his brother, Don, for redevelopment as the Merry Hill Shopping Centre. Raven is not the only artist working in the folk tradition who appears in the programmes, however. In programme four of the series, which looks at the Black Country's 'survivors' (people who are making a living in the area in spite of its industrial decline), local businessman and singer-songwriter, Bev Pegg, performs his own song, also called 'Survivors', which is equally rooted in lived experience and tells of the peculiar resilience of the local people.

Conclusion

As this discussion suggests, a significant number of programmes made by ATV and Central between 1968 and 1989 adopted a performative mode of representing the Black Country that borrowed heavily from the region's strong oral and folk traditions. With its highly idiosyncratic customs, dialect and even industries, it is not difficult to see why the Black Country might have had a visual and aural appeal that extended far beyond its own boundaries and proved attractive to audiences, not only elsewhere in the Midlands region but also worldwide, as suggested by the success of *On The Road to Nowhere* (1974) at the San Francisco Film Festival (Anon., 1974). However, there is also evidence to suggest that the television companies' well-established relationship with a particular group of Black Country artists and performers – including Jon Raven, Harry Harrison, Tommy Mundon and Dolly Allen – may have influenced programme makers' decisions about how they represented the region. In addition, the performative mode in which the Black Country was represented on Midlands' screens can be seen as reflecting a similar movement in the historiography of the area, which gave equal weight to 'serious' academic study and vernacular culture, and promoted an active, rather than a passive, consumption of both past and present. Taking the lead from these existing discourses, programmes such as *The Cradle of Industry*, *A Present from the Past* and *Gi' It Some 'Ommer*, not only document the rise and fall of Black Country industry, but also embrace the rich cultural heritage that sprang from it; performance in this case is not simply a televisual device, but is as much a part of the landscape and fabric of the region as its factories, foundries and rolling mills.

References

Anon. (1969a) 'How the Union Came', *The Blackcountryman*, Vol. 2, No. 1, 17–19.
Anon. (1969b) 'The Black Country', *TV Times*, Vol. 55, No. 29, 31.
Anon. (1969c) 'Correspondence', *The Blackcountryman*, Vol. 2, No. 3, 68:71.
Anon. (1974) ITV Awards at San Francisco, *Television Today*, 17 October 1974, 20.

Associated TeleVision Ltd (1958) *Annual Report and Accounts 1958* (London: ATV).
ATV Today (1967) ATV, 16 November 1967, 18:15.
ATV Today (1968) ATV, 17 May 1968, 18:15.
ATV Today (1972a) ATV, 8 June 1972, 18:00.
ATV Today (1972b) ATV, 16 October 1972, 18:00.
ATV Today (1976a) ATV, 13 January 1976, 18:00.
ATV Today (1976b) ATV, 1 March 1976, 18:00.
ATV Today (1978) ATV, 4 December 1978, 18:00.
ATV Today, The Cradle of Industry (1969) ATV, 7 April 1969, 18:00.
Barnsley, P. (1969) Two Old Cradley Mills. *The Blackcountryman*, Vol. 2 No. 1, 39–46.
Benson, J. (2001) Public History Review Essay: The Black Country Living Museum. *Labour History Review*, Vol. 66 No. 2, 243–251.
Birmingham Rep (2013) *'The Nailmakers' by Malcolm Totten and Jon Raven 1973. Photograph, 1 of 2.* [online] Available from: http://www.birmingham-rep.co.uk/rep100/114 (Accessed 3 December 2014).
Black Country Bugle (2015) *Contact the Black Country Bugle.* [online] Available from: http://www.blackcountrybugle.co.uk/contact.html (Accessed 15 January 2015).
Black, P. (1972) *The Mirror in the Corner: People's Television* (London: Hutchinson).
Bonner, P. and Aston, L. (1998) *Independent Television in Britain: Volume 5, ITV and IBA, 1981–92: The Old Relationship Changes.* (Basingstoke: Macmillan).
Briggs, A. and Spicer, J. (1986) *The Franchise Affair* (London: Century).
Brimble, J. (1968) 'Society News: The First Year', *The Blackcountryman*, Vol. 1, No. 1, 6–10.
Brimble, J. (1984) 'Society News', *The Blackcountryman*, Vol. 17, No. 4, 2–3.
Castells, L. and Walton, J. (1998) Contrasting Identities: North-west England and the Basque Country, 1840–1936. In E. Royle (ed.) *Issues of Regional Identity: In Honour of John Marshall* (Manchester: Manchester University Press), 44–81.
Chapman, S. (1969) 'Black Country Industrial History', *The Blackcountryman*, Vol. 2, No. 2, 36–45.
Fletcher, J. (1977) Introduction. In J. Raven (ed.) *The Urban and Industrial Songs of the Black Country and Birmingham* (Wolverhampton: Broadside), xvii–xxi.
Fletcher, K. (1970) 'Expanairshun', *The Blackcountryman*, Vol. 3, No. 1, 51.
Franklin, I. (2014) Documenting the Social and Historical Margins in the Films of Philip Donnellan. *LISA e-journal* [online], 12 (1). Available from: http://lisa.revues.org/5606 (Accessed 19 February 2015).
Gi' It Some 'Ommer, Programme 1 (1984a) Central, 2 July 1984, 22:35.
Gi' It Some 'Ommer, Programme 2 (1984b) Central, 9 July 1984, 22:35.
Gi' It Some 'Ommer, Programme 3, Bosses (1984c) Central, 16 July 1984, 22:35.
Gi' It Some 'Ommer, Programme 4, Survivors (1984d) Central, 23 July 1984, 22:35.
Gi' It Some 'Ommer, Programme 5, Kids (1984e) Central, 30 July 1984, 18:30.
Green, H. E. (1970) 'What's Ina Name', *The Blackcountryman*, Vol. 3, No. 1, 46–47.
Hillier, C. and Mosley, J. (1976) *The Western Midlands: A Journey to the Heart of England* (London: Gollancz).
Independent Broadcasting Authority (1975) *Annual Report and Accounts, 1974–75* (London: IBA).

Independent Television Authority (1962) *Annual Report and Accounts, 1961–62* (London: HMSO).

Independent Television Authority (1968) *Annual Report and Accounts, 1967–68* (London: HMSO).

Joe the Chainsmith (1958) BBC, 7 November 1958, 21:30.

Jones, J. W. (1969) 'Little Song of the Engine', *The Blackcountryman*, Vol. 2, No. 3, 20.

Media Archive for Central England (2011) *[ATV Today: 07.04.1969: The Black Country]*. [online] Available from: http://www.macearchive.org/Archive/Title/atv-today-07041969-the-black-country/MediaEntry/1074.html (Accessed 29 August 2014).

On The Road to Nowhere (1974) ATV, 24 April 1974, 22:30.

Palmer, R. and Raven, J. (1976) *The Rigs of the Fair: Popular Sports and Pastimes in the Nineteenth Century through Songs, Ballads, and Contemporary Accounts* (Cambridge: Cambridge University Press).

Parsons, H. (1968) 'Chriss with Two Esses', *The Blackcountryman*, Vol. 1, No. 3, 29–33.

Potter, J. (1990) *Independent Television in Britain: Volume 4, Companies and Programmes, 1968–80* (Basingstoke: Macmillan).

Quigley, P. and Shaw, M. (2010) 'Characterization in an Urban Setting: The Experience of the Black Country', *The Historic Environment: Policy and Practice*, Vol. 1, No. 1, 27–51.

Raven, J. (1969) 'Discovering Black Country Folk Songs', *The Blackcountryman*, Vol. 2, No. 1, 32–35.

Raven, J. (1977) *The Urban and Industrial Songs of the Black Country and Birmingham* (Wolverhampton: Broadside).

Raven, J. (1978) *Victoria's Inferno: Songs of the Old Mills, Mines, Manufactories, Canals and Railways* (Wolverhampton: Broadside).

Raven, J. (1986) *Black Country and Staffordshire: Stories, Customs, Superstitions, Tales, Legends and Folklore* (Wolverhampton: Broadside).

Raven, M. and Raven, J. (eds) (1965) *Folklore and Songs of the Black Country: Folk Out of Focus Being a Brief Resume of the Little Known Folk Lore of the Black Country and Staffordshire* (Wolverhampton: Wolverhampton Folk Song Club).

Raybould, T. (1984) 'Aristocratic Landowners and the Industrial Revolution: The Black Country Experience c. 1760–1840', *Midland History*, Vol. 9, No. 1, 59–86.

Robinson, J. E. (2014) 'From Wales to the Wash': A History of ITV Regional Programming in the Midlands 1956–1989, University of Leicester, Ph.D. thesis.

Russell, B. (1969) 'Billy Russell Remembers', *The Blackcountryman*, Vol. 2, No. 1, 25–26.

Schechner, R. (2002) Foreword: Fundamentals of Performance Studies. In N. Stucky and C. Wimmer (eds) *Teaching Performance Studies* (Carbondale: Southern Illinois University Press), ix–xii.

Sendall, B. (1982) *Independent Television in Britain: Volume 1, Origin and Foundation 1946–62* (London: Macmillan).

Sendall, B. (1983) *Independent Television in Britain: Volume 2, Expansion and Change 1958–68* (London: Macmillan).

Smallshire, V. (2009) Chairman's (Historical) Notes. *The Legger*, No. 215, 4–11.

Starkey, E. M. (1970) 'Black Country Dialect', *The Blackcountryman*, Vol. 3, No. 1, 14:17.

Television Act 1954 (2&3 Eliz. 2, Ch. 55) (London: HMSO).

Thomas, H. (1977) *With an Independent Air: Encounters During a Lifetime of Broadcasting* (London: Weidenfeld & Nicolson)

Venture, Programme 57 (1983) Central, 12 December 1983, 22:35.

9
A Post-War History of Radio for the Asian Community in Leicester

Gloria Khamkar

Introduction: post-war Asian migration

During the post-war period, at a time of industrial labour shortage, Asian immigrants from different parts of the world – but particularly from India and Pakistan – arrived in England to seek employment. The British media were slow in specifically and fully addressing and catering to this Asian immigrant community. The BBC eventually did produce local radio programmes, either in the Asian languages or in English, which met this need; the present chapter chronicles the introduction of this programming output, with specific reference to the important contribution of BBC Radio Leicester. In order to understand this development, it is useful to understand a little about Asian migration to England, of which there is a long tradition; there had been a flow of students, lawyers, cricketers, housemaids, entertainers, governesses, peddlers and seamen stretching back to the seventeenth century and earlier. However, the extent of this migration was very small. The scenario changed drastically after World War II. During this period, England was experiencing a shortage of unskilled labour, and thus turned to the Asian countries to find people, particularly for England's industrial cities (Arnold, 2012; Ballard, 2003; Parekh, 1997; Peach, 2006). British employers, such as the National Health Service (NHS), London Transport and British Rail began to explore these sources for recruits (Ballard, 2003). As a result, many Indians – unskilled, semi-skilled and professional – migrated to England.

A significant factor behind this migration was the British Nationality Act of 1948,[1] which conferred British citizenship to all who lived in the British Empire and Commonwealth. Moreover, as a result of political pressures during this period, Indians already settled in East Africa were forced to move, because they were seen as a bar to African advancement. In the case of Uganda in 1973, President Idi Amin gave the whole Asian community 90 days to leave the country, in which time 30,000 Asians relocated to Britain (Arnold, 2012). Thus the flow of the Indian population was greatly increased by the migration of East African Asians during the 1970s.

Patterns of immigration and settlement

So, who were these immigrants? The vast majority were drawn from a few specific areas in the subcontinent. In community-specific terms, the vast-majority Asian migrant population can be placed in these broad categories: Gujarati Hindus from the Western Indian state of Gujarat; Punjabi Sikhs and Hindus from the Northern Indian region of Punjab; and Punjabi Muslims mainly from Pakistan (Ballard, 2003; Spencer, 2002). Each of these migrant groups had its own specific motivations to emigrate from Asia and Africa to Britain. To take one example, the Indian state of Gujarat was a major manufacturing hub of cotton textiles. A large proportion of cotton textiles were exported by Gujarati merchants to Europe (Chaudhuri, 1990). The peddler communities, which provided the foundation for mass migration after the end of World War II, were largely composed of Punjabi Sikhs and Muslims. There was a pre-existing affiliation because the British Indian regiments posted to France during World War I were largely recruited in the Punjab. Thus, these communities gained almost a monopoly over immigration opportunities within the British labour market (Ballard 2003).

The Commonwealth Immigrants Act 1962,[2] however, re-shaped the migration movement by tightening the regulations, permitting only those with government-issued employment vouchers, limited in number, to settle in the United Kingdom. This act made entry more difficult (Arnold, 2012). Because of this act, South Asian male immigrants were faced with the decision of whether to bring their families to join them or to return to their homeland. At the same time, the Indians forced out of East Africa in the 1970s came as family units (Peach, 2006).

The destinations in Britain for these Asian immigrants during this period were largely confined to the large metropolitan cities. Thus, the Asian groups were not only segregated from the white population, but also from each other. For example, the Indian Hindu and Sikh community was concentrated in London, Leicester, Birmingham and Wolverhampton; and the Pakistani community was concentrated in London, Birmingham, Manchester, Bradford, Leeds and Luton. These immigrants were often non-English speaking, typically lived in houses in multiple occupation, and were employed in groups rather than as individuals, working in the metal-bashing industries of the West Midlands, the woollen textile mills of West Yorkshire and the cotton mills of Lancashire (Peach, 2006).

These communities shared many common things. Many individuals were of rural origin, either peasantfarmers or craftsmen by trade, and very few had any significant educational or professional qualifications. Yet, despite the shared socio-economic background, as the years passed members of each group followed differing routes of adaptation and upward mobility.

Leicester's Asian community

Leicester had a pattern of Asian immigration similar to the other parts of England. During the post-war period, Indians were attracted to Leicester because of the labour shortage. In this case, the majority of Asians who moved to Leicester came from East African countries, particularly from Kenya, following the expulsions from Uganda. As these Asians had already emigrated from India to East Africa, they are often referred to as 'twice migrants' (Bhachu, 1985). Many were educated and possessed entrepreneurial skills; for example, many Gujarati-speaking, well-educated entrepreneurs settled in Leicester along the Belgrave Road and adapted easily to the local economy by establishing a successful Asian business sector (Buda, 1986; Vertovec, 1994). This Gujarati community led the way upwards and outwards, and most members of the older generation used business enterprise as their stepping stones to success, usually starting with the corner shop, before moving on to establish much larger enterprises in either wholesaling, services or manufacturing (Ballard, 2003).

Immigration and the British media

So what was the impact of this immigration on the existing British media landscape? In multi-ethnic societies media plays a key role in educating both the minority and the majority population; it could also manipulate and, indeed, generate conflict between ethnic minorities and the indigenous population, and in this way either encourage the integration of ethnic minorities into society or force them to isolate themselves (Anwar, 1978). There are different aspects of the relationship between ethnic minorities and the mass media. The first concerns the way ethnic minorities are projected by the institutions of the mass media, and the second concerns the extent to which these minorities are given the opportunity of using the mass media to obtain information about social institutions in the host country in order to assist their members to adjust to the new environment (Anwar, 1978: 10). However, there is also the vital issue of the extent of the actual participation of ethnic minority members in broadcasting. When ethnic minority communities become active producers, they themselves are in control, more or less, in portraying the real – and not stereotyped – image of ethnic minority communities. These communities, by becoming actively engaged in media organisations, help in obtaining and disseminating information about the host country to their community members.

According to Cottle (1998), as a Public Service Broadcaster the BBC had a particular duty to represent and serve Britain's ethnic minorities, particularly during the post-war period. This is not just because it had a responsibility to meet the needs of all the licence payers, but because the BBC is one of the key institutions through which people form a picture of the kind of society Britain is: whether it is inclusive or exclusive; whether it recognises and celebrates the value of cultural and ethnic diversity or falls back on old stereotypes and prejudice; whether it strives to increase mutual understanding and equality of opportunity or is content to allow hostility and disadvantage to persist (Cottle 1998). And certainly, the BBC has been publicly committed to serve its ethnic minority audiences, both through targeted programmes and services and through fair representation in mainstream radio and television output (Cottle, 1998: 295).

The introduction of Asian programming into the BBC's output

As the Asian immigrants became settled in England, their social needs also grew. To understand this need, in July 1965 the BBC organised a conference to discuss with Asian community representatives whether special programmes designed to assist them with the problems of integration into their adoptive country would be welcomed. This initiative was readily accepted as responding to a particular need to overcome the problems of language and cultural and environmental differences,[3] as the Asian representatives thought that the special programmes could help to break down feelings of alienation – particularly among Asian women – which resulted from differences of religion, culture and language (Anwar, 1978).

As a result of these views, the BBC at first responded to this need by establishing its Immigrants Programme Unit in October 1965 to produce television programmes for the newly arrived immigrants; this unit was later renamed the Asian Programmes Unit. The BBC began regular weekly networked radio and television programmes aimed specifically at the Asian community through this unit.[4] These programmes were mainly designed to help integrate newly arrived Asian immigrants into their new environment through practical advice (Malik, 2002). The theme of these programmes was clear in their titles, such as *Make Yourself at Home* and *Nai Zindagi, Naya Jeevan* ('New Life' in Hindi and Urdu) (Anwar, 1978). In November 1965 the Immigrants Advisory Committee was set up. This committee, and, according to the committee, the Asian community as a whole, welcomed these initiatives by the BBC and recognised their place within the BBC's sense of public service.[5] This represented a catalyst for the development of broadcasting for ethnic minorities.

BBC local radio

During this period, the BBC began to appreciate the potential for 'specialisation, decentralisation and democratisation' (Lewis and Booth, 1989: 89) with a local radio service. BBC Radio Managing Director Frank Gillard, widely regarded as the founder of BBC Local Radio, identified this very early on in his career. Michael Barton was the first manager of BBC Radio Sheffield (1967–1975) and later became the controller at BBC Local Radio (1975–1988). According to Barton (2015): 'Gillard's brainchild was to give the communities of England their own localised services'. Thus the original idea was to bring the BBC closer to the audience, which the Pilkington Committee had supported in its 1962 report (Stoller, 2010: 211). Gillard's plan for BBC local radio represented more than just a defensive move against the growing commercial lobby. Many of the elements of the definition of community radio were present in his concept of local radio (Stoller, 2010: 155). As Briggs (1995) explained, each station would undertake a continuous and detailed coverage of local news and, through a multitude of local voices, narrate in a running story all aspects of local life. This meant the inclusion of a range of voices, as Barton (2015) recalls:

> As fledgling managers, we were encouraged to reflect local life – in all its forms – as closely as possible and that we should involve members of the public in the whole broadcasting process; we were about to 'democratise' the microphone.

Frank Gillard's challenge was to ensure that his local radio stations were there to be used by the community. Immigration to Britain and patterns of settlement were now starting to make an impact in terms of the conception of the local community that local BBC stations should serve. At this time, the BBC started considering local radio as a better platform for Asian broadcasting. As a result, one of the first tasks for Barton, as a manager of Radio Sheffield, was to set up the Radio Advisory Council, the chair of which was appointed by the postmaster general. This council agreed that minorities should be represented on radio, and since Sheffield had a considerable Asian population, one of its members was appointed on the board, which helped the committee in getting a better spread of ideas and opinions from the ethnic community, which represented around 8% of the population at that time (Barton, 2015).

The idea was that the BBC's professional broadcasters would provide a framework and training, but the 'flesh on the bone' had to be provided by the community: the community was there to come forward and to actually make their own programmes. As those radio stations developed, areas with a significant Asian population who wished to make programmes found themselves on the air (Bentley, 2013). Some of the examples of these Asian radio programmes are *Milan*, *The Six O'Clock Show* and *Good Morning Leicester* on BBC Radio Leicester; *Nawrang* on BBC Radio Nottingham; and *New Londoners* and *London Sounds Eastern* on BBC Radio London.

BBC Radio Leicester – *The Six O'Clock Show*

The BBC introduced Asian radio programming output through its local radio station in Leicester in the 1970s. Owen Bentley worked as station manager of BBC Radio Leicester from 1975 to 1982. With the introduction of the BBC's Immigrants Programme Unit's programmes for the Asian migrant community informing and advising them in their daily life in Britain, according to Bentley, 'the Asian community was very willing to seek these programmes out, as there were no VCRs; though there were a few cinemas around, there was nothing like the choice of Asian media that anybody living today can access' (Bentley, 2013). Therefore, BBC Radio Leicester, with its large Gujarati-speaking audience, started taking steps to satisfy the demands of its Asian listeners, who represented about 10% of the population (Barton, 2015). As Bentley (2013) recalls, during the mid-1970s these local stations were given the responsibility of responding to the Asian need for programming:

I came to Leicester (as the Station Manager of the BBC Radio Leicester) from working two years in Africa and I listened to Radio Leicester. I said to myself, this station does not reflect the community I'm seeing outside there. I saw there was just one programme that we were doing, *Milan*, and thought, no, we've got to be bold here, we should try and get this audience on board.

Milan was a weekly half-hour programme broadcast every Wednesday at 7.02 p.m. for Asian immigrants, in the Hindustani language, a mix of Hindi and Urdu, the national languages of India and Pakistan, respectively. It was presented by Manju Mahindro, and included an English lesson, record requests, and a local news summary prepared by the newsroom and then translated into Hindustani. Also, there used to be a 'what's on' bulletin specifically aimed at the target audience, for example, notice of Indian films showing locally.[6]

In October 1976, soon after joining BBC Radio Leicester as station manager, Bentley started producing a programme called *The Six O'Clock Show*. Local Asian citizens presented this radio programme; one of the presenters was Vijay Sharma, who later became head of BBC Asian Network (Bentley, 2013). Another popular presenter was Don Kotak, who went on to become the owner and founder of Leicester's Asian radio station, *Sabras Radio*. Kotak (2014) recalls the *Milan* programme:

During 1974 *Milan* was just a short programme having the news in Indian and Pakistani languages of Hindi and Urdu, and thus a lot of people started writing about, that we need more time when the Ugandan Asians came round. From what I remember, it was a very short programme. I think it was mainly news. I can't remember listening to any music on *Milan*. Later in October 1976 *The Six O'Clock Show* started.

The Six O'Clock Show was initially broadcast three nights of the week in English, one night in Hindi-Urdu, and one night in Gujarati. Later, it was expanded to all weekdays from Monday to Friday, 6 p.m. until midnight and, subsequently, also on Saturdays from 8 p.m. until 10 p.m. (Graham, 1991; Bentley, 2013). Kotak (2014) explains how his involvement in *The Six O'Clock Show* started:

I was at university in Leicester in the '70s. I was doing some media work for the Students' Union at that time, and I got involved with Radio Leicester, who at that time had thought about creating some programming output for the large number of Asian refugees who were settling in Leicester following the Amin exodus – Owen Bentley was very instrumental in all that. It was during that period that I myself along with another presenter started a radio programme – we called it *The Six O'Clock Show*.

It was perceived at that time that it would be good to provide something for as many ethnic communities as there were in Leicester. The *Six O'Clock Show* was being broadcast two hours a week at that time to the ethnic communities, and not just for the Asian community; there was also a Caribbean spot with reggae music and Caribbean news. However, very soon the Asian population became most responsive to this programme, and therefore the programme just automatically became an Asian-directed programme. Thus the Asian programming output developed from two just hours a week to a great deal more hours, which meant that eventually quite an extensive team was built up for ethnic broadcasting. That was in fact the start of what is today known as the BBC Asian Network, according to Kotak (2014).

Kotak worked at the station for several years and became very popular. Kotak was not the only one whose radio career began at BBC Radio Leicester in the 1970s. Vijay Sharma, now former head of the BBC Asian Network, was also one of the presenters on *The Six O'Clock Show* in Leicester. When Sharma came to Leicester in 1976, she felt that, in the context of Ugandan Asians having come to the city only a few years before, there was still a need for basic information about housing, benefits, employment and about health matters (Sharma, 2014). *The Six O'Clock Show*, which came to meet some of these needs, developed into a radio magazine programme, which included Asian news – local, domestic as well as from the Indian sub-continent – discussions, music and requests (Shaw, 1987; Bentley, 2013; Sharma, 2014; Kotak, 2014). The earlier BBC's national radio and the television programmes for Asians were really about education and information only, but music was also extremely important to the Asian community, particularly Bollywood music. BBC Radio Leicester made all possible efforts to get the most recent recordings of Bollywood music; people bought them in India or had them sent out. Thus entertainment was a key feature of programming as well as information, and that was part of the success (Bentley, 2013). Kotak suggests that evening entertainment, such as music, played an important part in immigrants' daily lives:

Because the Asian migrant community obviously had just settled in this country, economic survival was the priority for this community, everybody was working during the day, and in the evenings we were providing some entertainment for them. (Kotak, 2014)

The success of *The Six O'Clock Show* is well documented. In 1986, the Special Projects section of the BBC's Broadcasting Research Department was commissioned to undertake a survey to establish the radio listening patterns amongst the Asian community in Leicester. It included the listenership survey of *The Six O'Clock Show*. This survey indicated that 65% of the Asian population in Leicester claimed to listen to radio nearly every day, and one reason was the BBC Radio Leicester's Asian programme, which had a listenership of about 82% (Shaw, 1987: 113). In 1991, the Special Projects section of the BBC's Broadcasting Research Department conducted a similar survey, which reported that the BBC Radio Leicester's Asian programme appealed across the Asian community and thus was a great success (Graham, 1991: 73).

Conclusion

The Six O'Clock Show was the main Asian programme produced by the BBC Radio Leicester during the 1970s. As the local radio stations developed, areas with a significant Asian population that wished to produce programmes were able to pursue this aim, and generally found themselves on the air (Bentley 2013). However, with the beginning of the Asian programming on local radio stations, some local radio production staffers began to report tensions they were experiencing as they worked with their local communities – tensions in terms of allocation of time slots to various communities within the locality. There were also issues about provisions for multiple minority languages. For these reasons, a number of local radio stations had set up immigrants' advisory panel, which proved extremely useful in providing both publicity and feedback in relation to Asian programmes.[7] This was an indication that centrally the BBC was attempting to coordinate its provision to make sure it accurately reflected local needs and demands and not just the prejudices of the station managers (Linfoot, 2011: 288), and thus there was a shift towards more integration across the output within the BBC.

In its 1978 report on ethnic minority broadcasting, the Commission for Racial Equality (CRE) praised BBC Local Radio for its strategy on minority programmes, but it made recommendations that special attention should be paid to improving and expanding existing programmes for the Asian listener community (Anwar, 1978). At the same time, there was a feeling amongst the Asian community that the amount of programming produced for them was not sufficient, and also that there was a need for different timeslots to reach a wider audience. There was also a demand for more entertainment and for more programmes delivered in regional languages, beyond Hindustani languages (Kotak, 2014; Sharma, 2014). Therefore, the existence of a public-service platform for Asian programming generated such interest and expectation that it did, subsequently, convert into a demand for independent Asian radio services. And, as a result, the Asian community groups started their own radio services to expand provision and tap into the market.

In conclusion, it can be asserted that BBC Radio Leicester, and particularly *The Six O'Clock Show*, played a significant – indeed pioneering – role in the evolution of Asian broadcasting in the United Kingdom.

Notes

1. The British Nationality Act 1948 was an Act of the Parliament of the United Kingdom that created the status of 'Citizen of the United Kingdom and Colonies' (CUKC) as the national citizenship of the United Kingdom and its colonies.
2. Before the Commonwealth Immigrants Act 1962 was passed, citizens of British Commonwealth countries had extensive rights to migrate to the UK.
3. Report of the BBC's Asian Programmes Advisory Committee: M2/37/1 – 1965 to 1968, p. 1.
4. Report of the BBC's Asian Programmes Advisory Committee: M2/37/1 – 1965 to 1968, p. 1.
5. Report of the BBC's Asian Programmes Advisory Committee: M2/37/1 – 1965 to 1968.
6. Summary of BBC Local Radio Programmes for immigrants: RWMM/AAC HQ Unit – 1972, p. 2.
7. Summary of BBC Local Radio Programmes for immigrants: RWMM/AAC HQ Unit – 1972, p. 4.

References

Anwar, M. (1978) *Who Tunes in to What: A Report on Ethnic Minority Broadcasting* (London: Commission for Racial Equality).

Arnold, G. (2012) *Migration: Changing the World* (London: Pluto).

Ballard, R. (2003) The South Asian presence in Britain and Its Transnational Connections. In B. Parekh, G. Sing and S. Vertovec (eds) *Culture and Economy in the Indian Diaspora* (London: Routledge), 197–222.

Bhachu, P. (1985) *Twice Migrants: East African Sikh Settlers in Britain* (London: Tavistock).

Briggs, A. (1995) *The History of Broadcasting in the United Kingdom, Vol. 5: Competition* (Oxford: Oxford University Press).

British Nationality Act (1948) HMSO 03.22.06.

Broadcasting Research Unit (1985) *The Audience for Community Radio in London* (London: Broadcasting Research Unit).

Buda, J. K. (1986) 'The Asian Community in Great Britain', *Otsuma Review*, No. 19, 95–103.

Chaudhuri, K. N. (1990) *Asia Before Europe: Economy and Civilisation of the Indian Ocean from the Rise of Islam to 1750* (Cambridge: CUP Archive).

Cottle, S. (1998) 'Making Ethnic Minority Programmes Inside the BBC: Professional Pragmatics and Cultural Containment', *Media, Culture & Society*, Vol. 20, No. 2, 295–317.

Cottle, S. (2000) *Ethnic Minorities and the Media: Changing Cultural Boundaries* (New York: McGraw-Hill International).

Graham, C. (1991) 'BBC Radio Leicester's Programmes for Asian People', *Annual Review of BBC Broadcasting Research Findings*, No. 17, 69–73.

Lewis, P. and Booth, J. (1989) *The Invisible Medium: Public, Commercial and Community Radio* (Basingstoke: Macmillan Education).

Linfoot, M. (2011) A History of BBC Local Radio in England: c1960–1980, University of Westminster, Doctoral dissertation.

Malik, S. (2002) *Representing Black Britain: Black and Asian Images on Television* (London: Sage).

Parekh, B. (ed.) (1997) *Rethinking Multiculturalism* (Basingstoke: Palgrave Macmillan).

Parekh, B. (1997) 'South Asians in Britain', *History Today*, Vol. 47, No. 9, 65–68.

Peach, C. (2006) 'South Asian Migration and Settlement in Great Britain, 1951–2001', *Contemporary South Asia*, Vol. 15, No. 2, 133–146.

Shaw, S. (1987) 'Radio Listening amongst the Asian Community in Leicester', *Annual Review of BBC Broadcasting Research Findings*, No. 13, 109–118.

Spencer, I. (2002) *British Immigration Policy since 1939: The Making of Multi-racial Britain* (London: Routledge).

Stoller, T. (2010) *Sounds of Your Life: The History of Independent Radio in the UK* (New Barnet: John Libbey).

Vertovec, S. (1994) 'Multicultural, Multi-Asian, Multi-Muslim Leicester: Dimensions of Social Complexity, Ethnic Organization and Local Government Interface', *Innovation: The European Journal of Social Science Research*, Vol. 7, No. 3, 259–276.

Interviews with author

Interview in January 2015 with Michael Barton (Former manager of BBC Radio Sheffield, and Controller BBC Local Radio).

Interview in December 2013 with Owen Bentley (Former manager of BBC Radio Leicester).

Interview in September 2014 with Don Kotak (Owner and founder of Leicester's Asian radio station, Sabras Radio).

Interview in September 2014 with Vijay Sharma (Former head of BBC Asian Network).

Archives

Report of the BBC's Asian Programmes Advisory Committee: M2/37/1, 1965 to 1968.

Summary of BBC Local Radio Programmes for immigrants: RWMM/AAC HQ Unit – 1972.

10
The Teliesyn Co-operative: National Broadcasting, Production Organisation and TV Aesthetics

Dafydd Sills-Jones

Introduction

The Cardiff-based independent film and television production company, Teliesyn, came into being during the cultural ferment of the early 1980s. The 1982 launch of S4C and Channel 4 signalled both a rare victory for left-leaning and radical voices at the time of a political shift to a neo-liberal right, and the introduction of a free-market model into UK broadcasting for the first time (see Goodwin, 1998; Thomas, 2001: 82–88; Darlow, 2004). Founded in 1981, Teliesyn was placed, therefore, at a number of interesting intersections; between the entrepreneurial and cooperative, between populist and avant-garde, between the Welsh and English languages, between established and emerging media production cultures, and between regional and national broadcasting.

From the outset, and throughout its 'first phase' (1981–1989), Teliesyn successfully challenged the traditional production processes and aesthetics of TV by deploying a horizontal, cooperative company structure in which television's usual arrangement of hierarchically separated production roles was modified, and by introducing aesthetic modifications to mainstream television discourse. By doing this, Teliesyn opened up a new cultural space between the BBC/ITV duopoly and independent film and video. This space challenged not only notions of production hierarchy and aesthetics, but also of 'regional' and 'national' in terms of broadcasting identity.

Due to changes in the broadcasting ecology of Wales in the 1990s, the traditional hierarchical nature of TV production began to reassert itself as global trends began to emerge in UK television production. Despite these growing pressures, Teliesyn resisted, throughout its 'second phase' (1990–2002), and stayed true to its particular organisational and aesthetic character. Even as it wound up its operation in 2002, it did so at the crest of an award-winning wave, leaving a rich legacy of distinctive programming, and of programme makers who are still active today. As such, Teliesyn provides a rich case study of how a geographically specific set of conditions can lead to the evolution of a specific production approach and aesthetic.

Teliesyn's 'first phase' (1981–1989)

S4C was launched on the evening of 1 November 1982, the evening before its English counterpart, Channel 4. On a UK level, the fourth channel had been first discussed in 1964, soon after the launch of BBC2, and debates over its positioning and constitution carried on through the 1970s. What emerged, through the filters of successive governments, was a remit to innovate and to give broadcasting space for new voices. What followed on Channel 4 was an unprecedented period of experimentation in terms of broadcast TV, resulting in programmes such as *The Friday Alternative* (Channel 4, 1982–1983) and *The Eleventh Hour* (Channel 4, 1982–1988), and the contributions of regional workshops such as Amber, and The Black Audio Film Collective – bodies of work that still stand out as fresh, critical televisual voices from the left.

S4C had a remit, constitution, and political background different to Channel 4. Whilst Channel 4 had emerged through an alchemy of radical politics and Thatcherite entrepreneurialism, S4C had emerged from a politically engaged nationalist struggle, on England's doorstep, in the midst of the Northern Irish 'troubles'. Whilst Channel 4 was dedicated to providing innovative programming from new voices, S4C was charged with supplying a Welsh version of all the existing television channels, and their spread of genres, in Welsh, in an attenuated schedule. This meant that a new television production capacity had to be built, especially with expertise in 'quality' genres such as documentary and drama. Due to the high production costs and high production values of these genres, they were thought to be beyond S4C's capabilities at this early stage (Williams, 2010). Proving this to be unfounded was essential for the early S4C, as the channel was subject to an initial three year trial period (Price, 2013).

At its inception, and from the perspective of programme production capacity, S4C needed medium-sized companies to complement the duopolistic production houses and 'one-man-band' boutique companies. From the perspective of the brand-new broadcaster looking to establish its mixed schedules quickly, such companies were ideal if they came with duopoly 'track records' and specialised in genres within which S4C had yet to prove themselves. Euryn Ogwen Williams, S4C's first head of programmes, saw Teliesyn's cooperative structure as a means of guaranteeing S4C a steady supply of high-quality documentary and drama output, produced by a medium-sized production company that could provide, by taking advantage of economies of scale, a sustainable base for the development of a nascent commercial broadcasting industry. For Williams, the main danger for a new independent sector in Wales was the replication of the duopoly structures at this new national level:

> I think it was a problem at the start, and a problem now, that an independent producer no matter how small aspired to the models of the BBC and HTV, without realising the advantage of their size was that they were different. (Williams, 2010)

However, far from notions of industrial development, for its members the most important aspect of Teliesyn's organisational culture was its cooperative basis, which had grown from dissatisfaction with duopoly hierarchies, a response heavily inflected by a regional tradition of collectivist political organisation.[1] Teliesyn's was an opportunity to participate in the redefinition of public broadcasting and to move away from the elitism of the BBC, on one hand, and the consumerism of ITV on the other, described by Thomas as

> distaste for the huge profits made by the ITV companies, the 'license to print money' idea. Having expressed antipathy towards all that, most of us or all of us were unhappy BBC members, but we also didn't mean we were attracted to the ITV model. It was like saying there is a third way! We can do it differently. (Thomas 2011)

By broadcasting a combination of Channel 4's radical material (albeit funded indirectly by advertising) and the BBC programming provided to it for free, along with its own home-produced advert-bearing programming, S4C could have appeared to be a dangerous dilution of public-broadcasting values.[2] This was, perhaps, reinforced by the combination of S4C's more conservative nation-building project and the entrepreneurialism of the new independent production sector. But, initially, Colin Thomas saw Teliesyn's mission, and more generally that of the new Welsh independent sector, quite differently, taking broadcasting to the left of the duopoly, rather than a *de facto* privatisation:

> Roy Lockett [erstwhile ACTT Dept. Secretary General] had this phrase; he called us 'Thatcher's Trojan ponies'. At the time, it didn't feel like it, we were breaking up a fossilised hierarchy... All these people with ideas that were getting nowhere inside the BBC or ITV suddenly got their chance. (Thomas 2011)

This specific mix of elements – of Teliesyn's radical aspirations and the pragmatic business of a quasi-commercial and decidedly 'national' S4C – was reflected in Teliesyn's organisation structure. Its constitution meant that each member potentially had an equal say on any company decision, including the pitching of programme ideas to broadcasters. Each member had a single vote in cooperative meetings. Potentially, the vote of a senior 'producer' could count for no more than a vote by an inexperienced 'technician'. The ideal behind this democratic structure was a less exploitative and more creative process borne out of discussion and of knowledge-sharing. Initially, this was unmediated, but soon a board of executives was formed and a manager appointed to execute the decisions of the cooperative, and to propose new measures. Despite the extensive departure from the broadcasting norm, this structure never completely abandoned broadcasting professionalism in the manner of regional film and video workshops, underpinned by the Independent Filmmakers Association (IFA) and Channel 4.

This did not mean that Teliesyn members had to give up their freelance status, as many members worked elsewhere for long periods, the most noticeable example being Colin Thomas' absence from Teliesyn production between 1982 and 1985 whilst making *The Dragon Has Two Tongues* in-house at the Welsh local ITV company, HTV, for Channel 4. Freelancers who were Teliesyn members were tied by what founding member and cameraman Ray Orton called 'loyalty' to the cooperative, but also by the opportunity to put 'an extra element' into the work at Teliesyn, rather than it being a question of 'an extra level of effort'. This gave freelancers a rare 'sense of ownership' over the programmes they worked on (Orton, 2010). Crucially, Teliesyn members could swap production roles, a very difficult feat given the technological and union restrictions of the time, enabling editors to direct, sound recordists to produce and even camera operators to be art directors. In addition, due to a cross-section of roles represented by members, Teliesyn was able to put whole productions together, and were also able to retain editorial control over all elements within the discursive boundaries of the cooperative, in a type of corporate 'vertical integration' (Staniforth, 2011). The integrated nature of the company could, in turn, help in the development of programme projects and the capture of commissions.

This structure did produce a central tension between a more anarchistic (in Colin Ward's sense) structure of authority, and a 'management function' that regulated the company's relationship with the marketplace. While the tension did lead to relational problems within the company during its history, it was also seen as a hallmark of the company's aesthetic approach. Colin Thomas considered this tension to be necessary to the company's operation (Thomas, 2011), and the notion of a creative tension was echoed by Euryn Ogwen Williams, who observed from the side-lines: 'There was an "edge" with Teliesyn... I thought it was a part of the company that there was a rigour attached to the creative process' (Williams, 2010).

What was crucial here was a strong belief amongst Teliesyn members and its key commissioners that its cooperative structure and its divergence from the duopoly were aligned with an aesthetic mission. At the same time as S4C and Channel 4 were looking for programmes the distinctiveness of which would justify their individual remits, Teliesyn members were in search of a new platform in order that their talents and voices could develop as they wished. Each of Teliesyn's founding individuals had a slightly different understanding of this aesthetic mission. Colin Thomas had left the BBC in 1978 in protest at editorial interference from BBC management during the making of a documentary on the Northern Irish 'troubles' (Thomas, 2010), and for him Teliesyn was a space that could accommodate a broader political aesthetic. Another founder, Paul Turner, was a victim of the sharp divide between technical and editorial functions in the BBC. Turner had languished as an editor at the BBC for some years, unable to progress to being a director due to political prejudice and aesthetic stagnation within the BBC (Turner, 2010). Other members were moving for the first time into television from the worlds of theatre, independent film and education. This multiplicity of motivations, allied with the company's democratic structure, lent eclecticism to its output during the 1980s, which included award-winning documentaries, original drama, dramatic literary adaptation and drama-documentaries.

However, the majority of the work made during the early period was broadly within the aesthetic mainstream. This reflects the fact that, whilst Teliesyn shared the Channel 4/ACTT workshop attitude towards horizontal management structures and profit-sharing, Teliesyn was founded before these film collectives and workshops were created under the Channel 4/ACTT agreement of 1982 (Hobson, 2007). In addition, in contrast to English workshops such as Amber or Birmingham Film and Video Workshop, which had their roots in the community arts and counterculture movements of the 1970s (Franklin and Smith, 2013), Teliesyn was created from the outset as a commercial broadcast media company whose members were often trading on duopoly track records, rather than being in opposition to the broadcast system. Within this mainstream aesthetic, however, Teliesyn innovated aesthetically by introducing treatments and topics previously unknown to TV audiences, especially in Wales. This was either because certain types of programmes, such as drama serials, were for the first time being made in the Welsh language, or because they projected material with a Welsh character but in the English language, into a new national broadcasting space.

This was achieved through a variety of means. The first series was a strong strand of adaptations of Welsh literary classics, *Tales From Wales/ Arswyd y Byd* (Teliesyn for S4C and BBC Wales 1982), which brought together works written originally in both English and Welsh into a series that was made back-to-back in both languages and were shown on both S4C and BBC Wales. The practice of back-to-back productions was important in importing hitherto undreamt levels of production value and stardom into Welsh language film and television production, whilst also giving Welsh actors and writers access to wider audiences. Other productions placed Welsh voices, albeit in the English language, into a 'national' network TV space, such as *Cracking Up* (Channel 4, 1989–1990). While the visual screen language was not experimental, this was a manifestation of the new cultural space made possible by Channel 4, in which 'minority' UK voices were to be heard, and by the new national space that S4C had made possible and which Teliesyn fully exploited. As the 1980s progressed, the sophistication of the productions increased, as did the reach of the programmes with international co-production with countries such as Australia (*Derfydd Aur/Realms of Gold*, S4C and Channel 9/ABC co-production, 1989) being a staple of Teliesyn's financing. This again placed Teliesyn in a category very different to the film collectives with which they shared their ideology.

Teliesyn did also innovate with film language and television form – innovation that was to be seen most clearly in programmes that dealt with historical subjects and played with a hybrid of drama and documentary approaches. Building on the success of *The Dragon Has Two Tongues*, made by Colin Thomas outside the cooperative, Teliesyn embarked on a series of programmes with the historian Gwyn Alf Williams. These programmes used an array of innovative filmic techniques to critique and destabilise orthodox television history. One example had an 'authoritative' presenter such as Gwyn Alf Williams sharing the frame with historical characters played by actors: for example, Tim Roth as the cartoonist James Gillray in *Cracking Up: Freeborn Englishman* (Teliesyn, for Channel 4, 1989). At crucial points of historical debate within the programme narrative there would be a break with the usual convention as presenter and character conversed and disagreed over matters of historical record and interpretation. By using such techniques these programmes did not depart drastically from an aesthetic mainstream, but brought a wholly new historico-political voice into the new national broadcasting spaces of S4C and Channel 4.

Second phase, 1990–2002

In the first phase (1982–1989), whilst also being a cooperative, Teliesyn had been a very successful commercial entity, its turnover growing from £35,000 to £3,500,000 (Staniforth, 2011). In 1989, following the departures of Paul Turner and Richard Pawelko to begin their own production companies and Richard Staniforth to pursue a career in film, Teliesyn entered its 'second phase'. This phase coincided with a tumultuous period in UK broadcasting. The 1990 Broadcasting Act had begun the long decline of regional ITV, and had generated a change of ethos at both Channel 4, which became responsible for selling its own advertising, and at the BBC, where budget cuts and 'producer choice'[3] took effect. During this period there occurred a general shift from an ethos of public service in an age of post-war consensus and spectrum scarcity, to a more neo-liberal, marketised and audit-oriented broadcasting ethos, set in the context of a broadcasting 'age of availability' (Ellis, 2000: 61–73). In such an age, the broadcaster's public-service commitment was slowly replaced by a diffuse sense of 'consumer sovereignty' (O'Malley and Jones, 2009).

During this period, audience maximisation became a growing priority for broadcasters, and this imperative was passed on to independent production companies. In turn, independent production companies modified their programme development and programme strategies (TRC, 2002). A more-mobile labour market meant a quicker turnaround in terms of staff (Paterson, 2001). In retrospect, it is clear that this was also a time in which the 1980s anarchic diversity of independent production gave way to a more commercially driven, consolidated and transnational independent broadcast media sector, the most powerful members of which gradually moved to a position from which they could dictate terms to broadcasters over programming and the schedule itself (Mediatique, 2005).

The shift was mirrored in Wales, although modified to some extent by the presence of S4C. The 1992 ITV license auction caused financial problems for HTV Wales and led to the shedding of many jobs (Nisse, 1992). The independent sector across the UK matured during the 1990s, creating an increasingly competitive market for programme ideas, which made the work of programme development more time-consuming as the decade continued (TRC, 2002). At the BBC's national network level during much of the 1990s there was a dearth of opportunities to represent Wales outside its borders (Geraint, 2008). Channel 4's requirement to sell its own advertising from 1993 onwards presaged a distancing between both channels, and Channel 4's retreat from commissioning independents in Wales (Evans, 2012; Pritchard, 2010; Thomas, 2011). Leading on from the consolidation of ITV's structure during the 1990s there was a gradual decline in budgets and regional hours available to independents at HTV. The effect on BBC Wales/Cymru of the budget cuts that came along with the BBC's internal market policy of 'producer choice', was a drastic cutting of budgets and staff (Davies, 2006). In the second half of the 1990s, S4C faced a similar situation of dwindling budgets in reaction to the introduction of digital broadcasting. In particular, the practice of idea 'bundling' (S4C, 2001: 7)[4] led to major changes in commissioning and financing at S4C (Evans, 2009; Simmonds, 2011).

There were several significant changes of management within Teliesyn's main client channels, which affected Teliesyn's workflow and income. Teliesyn found it harder to gain commissions from Channel 4, particularly after the channel's education commissioning editor, Gwyn Pritchard, left in 1992 to become the head of Welsh-language programmes for the BBC in Cardiff (Pritchard, 2010). Teliesyn was now no longer considered 'large' in comparison to the other independents in Wales it had previously competed with (Williams, 2010). In 1995, one of its main members and leading voices died: the historian Gwyn Alf Williams (Stephens, 1995).

Attempts were made by Teliesyn to adapt to the changing market circumstances by being more attentive to the tastes of individual commissioning editors, and by increasing the number of ideas sent in to commissioners (Thomas, 2011), a precursor of what was to become standard practice for UK indies towards the end of the 1990s and onwards (Zoellner, 2009). A larger proportion of the company took on producer and development roles, as evidenced by both the increased amount of work involved in winning commissions through mechanisms such as S4C's bundling system, and in the related adoption of a 'producer's bonus' for bringing in new work (Graham, 2012). The cooperative also lost promising new members, who left to start their own companies as the casualisation of broadcasting became more entrenched (BFI, 1999; Paterson, 2001), and led to a more competitive and potentially lucrative independent sector (Lee, 2008: 252).

Another result was a challenge to Teliesyn's traditions of horizontal management. Even towards the end of the 1990s, idea-generation was still a communal, hierarchically horizontal process at Teliesyn, but there was pressure to shift emphasis from idea-generation to idea-promotion, including the growing need to court editing commissioners. Mergers between Teliesyn and other companies were mooted during this period in order to enlarge the company's ability to invest in future programme development (Evans, 2012). The gradual result of the changing broadcasting environment was fewer network commissions, with more reliance on HTV and S4C, which in turn meant smaller budgets. This crisis in management and organisation was never fully resolved, and between 1997 and 2002 Teliesyn continued to operate successfully, but at a much lower level of output, before voluntarily winding up in 2002.

However, in terms of Teliesyn's aesthetic development, the story is not so bleak. Whilst Teliesyn found itself increasingly unable to win commissions from the UK network broadcasters, its ethos and track record with those broadcasters in the 1980s were influential in securing substantial programme commissions from the what might be considered by a cosmopolitan eye as 'regional' broadcasters: HTV, BBC Wales and S4C (Thomas, 2010). In S4C's case, by the early 1990s S4C and its independent sector had clearly matured, partly due to S4C's financial share in Channel 4's unexpected commercial success in the 1980s and the brokering of favourable long-standing production deals between S4C and key suppliers HTV and BBC Wales (Williams, 2010).

During the 1980s the initial lack of Welsh-speaking broadcasting professionals – including screen actors, writers and especially technicians – had been radically overturned, obviating the need in S4C's early years for non-Welsh speaking crews on Welsh language productions (Price, 2013). Channel 4's retreat from its earlier 'partnership' with S4C, and HTV's gradual decline added to the increasing identification of S4C as the main national Welsh broadcasting platform.[5] The 1990s, therefore, was something of a 'golden age' for S4C, trading on its strengthened indie production capacity, its established audiences and a growing programme making tradition in Welsh speaking areas. This golden age was reflected in Teliesyn's continued development of programme form and content, a development that was specific to its geographical rooting in Wales. This development pursued two paths already outlined here: namely, the use of largely mainstream documentary and drama aesthetics to introduce previously hidden subject matter to a Welsh audience and, second, the use of sophisticated, hybridised drama-documentary forms to interrogate orthodox historical narratives.

The first strand was driven by an influx, during the early 1990s, of powerful women into senior management and production roles. Amongst those joining were: Michele Ryan, from the workshop sector; Angela Graham and Bethan Eames, from the in-house production capacity of HTV; the actress Eiry Palfrey; and the entrepreneur Carmel Gahan.[6] The new recruits were attracted by the organisational ethos and professional reputation laid out in the 1980s and, to some extent, they saw their careers as part of a feminist mission.[7]

These individuals' momentum drove Teliesyn to produce a ground-breaking body of work on the history of women in Wales, and on contemporary Wales through a feminist lens: series such as *Codi Clawr Hanes* (S4C, 1990–1996) and *Living Proof* (HTV, 1991–1993), and standalone programmes such as *Milena Jesenka: The Art of Standing Still* (Channel 4, 1993), *Tu ôl i'r Bais* (S4C, 1994) and *Men!* (BBC Wales, 1995). In addition, the Marxist historical perspective of Gwyn Alf Williams continued to feature in series such as *Hughesovska and the New Russia* (S4C and BBC2, 1991) and *Excalibur/Caledfwlch* (BBC Wales/S4C, 1995).

Formally, the experimentation continued in series such as *Cracking Up* (Channel 4, 1989), as a number of drama-doc hybrid and participative programmes were pioneered. *Branwen* (RTE/S4C, 1994) was an example of how documentary and drama codes and conventions were freely exchanged. On one level, *Branwen* was a screen adaptation of Gareth Miles's play, *Dyrnod Branwen*, itself a contemporary reworking of an ancient story from the Mabinogi. However, driven by what its producer, Angela Graham, refers to as Teliesyn's 'ethos of aiming high', it was shot on location in Northern Ireland at a fragile time in the 'troubles', and it mixed amateur and professional actors as well as incorporating Welsh, Gaelic and English speech (Graham, 2012). The film drew parallels between the ancient myth and the contemporary political situation and, by doing so, looked at Northern Ireland from a Welsh perspective, rather than through the usual journalistic binaries of Loyalist and Republican.

Another example was one of the films directed by Ceri Sherlock for Teliesyn, *Atgof* (S4C, 1998). The title both means 'a memory' and references a poem of the same name that won the National Eisteddfod's Crown in 1924, gaining notoriety for depicting a same-sex relationship. Clearly referencing Isaac Julien's *Looking for Langston* (Channel 4, 1989) in its evocative mute-shot black and white super-16mm footage, *Atgof* used the poem, unpublished diaries and autobiographical literary works to tell the story of an ill-fated homosexual relationship between two Welsh literary figures in the early 1920s. The sophistication of the production also lies in the way in which its graphic sex scenes engendered a contemporary homophobic press response; linking the negative reception of the poem in 1924 to the notionally more 'liberal' Wales of 1998.

The decision to wind up Teliesyn was taken only months after one of its most successful dramas was broadcast: *Eldra* (Teliesyn for S4C, 2002). *Eldra* continued the cooperative's tradition of using mainstream forms to tell stories from different angles and focussed on the life of Welsh Romany travellers, an important constituent of life in North Wales in the 1930s, but one that was always on the margins of industrial society. *Eldra*'s ostensible themes of social justice, and its undercurrent of pagan and environmentalist sympathies, were typical of the cooperative's character and ahead of their time. *Eldra* won five awards at BAFTA Cymru in 2001, was awarded Best Feature Film at the Moondance Festival in 2003, and was the official British nomination for the foreign language Oscar in 2002. Despite this, due to a lack of work in the forthcoming year, and members needing to take other work offered, Teliesyn closed; their final engagement, a farewell party at Cardiff's Coal Exchange:

> In a sense the co-operative ethos was very much there at the end; as a co-operative we could hold our heads up high and say we had survived this long despite everybody saying that co-operatives couldn't survive in this competitive world, and that we had stayed true to our ethos, and we had collectively chosen when we should close, and party! (Ryan, 2011)

Conclusion

Teliesyn's case history shows how the specific industrial, political, national and linguistic conditions in a specific geographical location led to a specific approach. The aesthetic of most television output is necessarily derived from a combination of authorial expressive aspiration and the technological and political–economic limitations of broadcasting institutions. In this case study, the relationship between Teliesyn and a new national broadcaster, S4C, was crucial. It is in the difference between S4C and Teliesyn's aims and aspirations, as well as their commonality through a new national broadcasting platform, that brought about an organisational and aesthetic variation from the norm.

Teliesyn spanned several 'gaps' between elements that had not previously been bridged, including the still-present tensions along Wales' political and linguistic fault-lines, what Teliesyn member Gwyn Alf Williams sometimes called 'the shadow line' (Williams, 1991). By bridging thus, Teliesyn was able to be both commercially successful and aesthetically challenging, continuing to do so long past the point at which its counterparts from the early 1980s had ceased to operate.

Notes

1. Both Teliesyn founders Colin Thomas and Paul Turner had been active in the BBC union, and in wider left-leaning politics before Teliesyn's establishment (Thomas, 2010; Turner, 2010).
2. The formula by which S4C was initially funded through advertising revenue was complex: 17% of all UK TV advertising revenue – TV advertising on ITV, Channel 4 and S4C – went to Channel 4, and S4C received 20% of that portion, equating to around 3.4% of the total advertising revenue (Williams, 2010).
3. For more detail on the BBC's 'Producer Choice' initiative, see Born (2002).
4. Bundling was the process by which independent production companies were required to offer programme ideas to S4C in 'bundles' rather than one by one. Bundles would then be commissioned partially on the economies of scale that could be made across them. It was widely felt that this process disadvantaged smaller companies and those that specialised in 'one-off' and 'quality TV' productions, such as Teliesyn.
5. This identification caused concern amongst non-Welsh speaking Welsh audiences and broadcasting commentators, up until and past the point at which Channel 4 was fully available in Wales (see Talfan Davies, 2009).
6. Teliesyn had always stood as a beacon for gender equality in a male-dominated industry. Jill Thornley and Maxine Brown were both early members, and Mary Simmonds joined from the BBC in 1986, rising through the ranks to become a senior producer.
7. For more on the role of women in Welsh broadcasting at the time, see Ryan (2000).

References

BFI (1999) *Television Industry Tracking Study: Third Report* (London: BFI).

Born, G. (2002) 'Reflexivity and Ambivalence: Culture, Creativity and Government in the BBC Cultural Values', *Cultural Values*, Vol. 6, No. 1–2, 65–90.

Darlow, M. (2004) *Independents Struggle* (London: Quartet).

Davies, R. (2006) Interview with author, London.

Ellis, J. (2000) *Seeing Things: Television in the Age of Uncertainty* (London: I. B. Tauris).

Evans, D. (2012) Author's interview with ex-Teliesyn member.

Franklin and Smith (2013) 'Interview Dossier', *Historical Journal of Film, Radio and Television*, Vol. 33, No. 3, 454–474.

Geraint, J. (2008) '"For Wales, See England": Network Television from "the Nations", 1996–2006', *Cyfrwng: Media Wales Journal*, Vol. 5, 39–53.

Goodwin, P. (1998) *Television under the Tories: Broadcasting Policy 1979–1997* (London: BFI).

Graham, A. (2012) Author's interview with ex-Teliesyn member.

Lee, D. J. (2008) 'Precarious Creativity: Working Lives in the British Independent Television Production Industry', Goldsmiths, University of London, Unpublished PhD thesis.

Mediatique (2005) *From the Cottage to the City: The Evolution of the UK Independent Production Sector* (London: Mediatique).

Nisse, J. (1992) Franchise Costs Force HTV to Slash Budget, *The Independent*, Saturday, 26 September (Accessed 11 July 2014).

O'Malley, T. and Jones, J. (2009) *The Peacock Committee and UK Broadcasting Policy* (London: Palgrave Macmillan).

Orton, R. (2010) Author's interview with ex-Teliesyn member.

Paterson, R. (2001) 'Work Histories in Television', *Media Culture Society*, Vol. 23, No. 4 (July), 495–520.

Price, E. (2013) 'A Cultural Exchange: S4C, Channel 4 and Film', *Historical Journal of Film, Radio and Television*, Vol. 33, No. 3, 418–433.

Pritchard, G. (2010) Author's interview with ex-commissioning editor at Channel 4 and BBC.

Ryan, M. (2000) A Woman's Place: Women and Film in Wales. In S. Blandford (ed.) *Wales on Screen* (Bridgened: Seren Books).

Ryan, M. (2009) Author's interview with ex-Teliesyn member.

S4C (2001) *Economy and Culture: S4C in Wales – Present and future impacts* (Cardiff: S4C).

Simmonds, M. (2011) Author's interview with ex-Teliesyn member.

Staniforth, R. (2011) Author's interview with ex-Teliesyn member.

Stephens, M. (1995) 'OBITUARY: Gwyn A. Williams', *The Independent*, Saturday, 18 November.

Talfan Davies, G. (ed.) (2009) *English Is a Welsh Language: Television's Crisis in Wales* (Cardiff: Institute of Welsh Affairs).

Thomas, C. (2001) 'The Other Side of the Fence', *Planet*, Vol. 157 (February–March, 2003), 82–88.

Thomas, C. (2011) Author's interview with ex-Teliesyn member.

TRC (2002) *Risky Business: Inside the Indies* (Glasgow: The Research Centre for Television and Interactivity).

Williams, E. O. (2010) Author's interview with ex-head of programmes at S4C.

Williams, G. A. (1991) *When Was Wales? A History of the Welsh* (London: Penguin).

Zoellner, A. (2009) 'Professional Ideology and Programme Conventions: Documentary Development in Independent British Television Production', *Mass Communication and Society*, Vol. 12, No. 4, 503–536.

Part IV

Borders, Devolution and Contested Histories

11
Sam Hanna Bell and the Ideology of Place

Hugh Chignell

There can be few radio programmes that more completely express the idea of place than the features and documentaries of Sam Hanna Bell.[1] Working at BBC Northern Ireland from 1945 to 1969 (and then in his retirement until the late 1980s), Bell not only pioneered the craft of radio features making, especially in his use of the words of 'ordinary people', but also produced programmes that powerfully evoked a highly specific sense of place and history. In the most troubled and divided part of the United Kingdom, however, any claims about history, place and culture are bound to contain political messages, no matter how unintended, and Bell's characterisation of 'Ulster' carried heavy ideological baggage. His radio output expressed a sense of Ulster as an historical and cultural entity rooted in centuries of history, and a sense of the unchanging geography of Northern Ireland, a view that was inevitably of more comfort to the Protestant majority than the Catholic minority.

Both of Bell's parents were from Northern Ireland, although he was born in Scotland (in 1909) and raised in a Presbyterian[2] family. In 1918, following the death of his father, Bell and his family moved to the farm of his maternal grandmother in County Down, Northern Ireland. There is no doubt that his subsequent upbringing on the farm had a profound effect on his later work:

> During the few years of childhood that I spent there I saw a pattern of rural life that had existed for three hundred years vanish under the impact of the motor bus and the tractor. (Hanna Bell, quoted in McMahon, 1999: 8)

Bell's family moved to Belfast in the early 1920s; he left school at the age of 14 to earn his living in a variety of jobs, not very well paid, while living the life of the autodidact and aspiring writer. By the start of the war, Bell was an established member of the Belfast literary scene based at the iconic non-sectarian cultural institution, the Linen Hall Library, which allowed both Protestants and Catholics to join. Other members of the group were W. R. Rodgers and John Boyd, both of whom were to make, like Bell himself, the transition to the BBC. The literary journal, *Lagan*, was published in 1943 with Bell an important contributor and, in the same year, his first book, *Summer Loanen and Stories*, was published. *Lagan* was founded on a liberal and non-sectarian commitment to express the 'life and speech of the province' (McMahon, 1999: 28), and this philosophy would be deeply imbedded in Bell's approach to broadcasting. Bell's early writing was characteristic of what was to come. Sophia Hillan King, discussing Bell's first two short stories, wrote: 'Both draw on a deeply felt sense of place and on a knowledge of the importance of place and tradition in shaping the mind for good or ill' (1999: 4).

BBC Northern Ireland (BBC N.I.) began broadcasting on 15 September 1924 to a population divided into a Protestant two-thirds and a Catholic one-third; most of the latter were expressly opposed to the very existence of Northern Ireland as a political entity divided from the South[3] (Cathcart, 1984: 1). In 1936 the BBC's Director of Regional Relations, Charles Siepmann, wrote a report on BBC Northern Ireland that vividly portrayed the social divisions of the time: 'the bitterness of religious antagonism between Protestants and Catholics invades the life of the community at every point', adding that the Northern Irish government was a 'loyalist dictatorship' (quoted in Cathcart, 1984: 3). The strongly pro-Unionist[4] station director, George Marshall, made sure that BBC Northern Ireland broadcast in the interests of the Protestant majority (Cathcart, 1984: 112). This bias included a ban on reporting anything about Southern Ireland ('Éire' from 1937); indeed when the evening news carried the results of the Gaelic games in 1946 this caused a furore in the Protestant community. In his convincing discussion of BBC regionalism pre-1953, Thomas Hajkowski described how BBC N.I. helped maintain a British identity, by providing programmes about Britain and British events, but also helped to construct an 'Ulster' identity, the preferred Unionist term for Northern Ireland (2010: 210).

This inauspicious environment at BBC N.I. was to be the context of Sam Hanna Bell's new career as a radio features producer. In 1945, the celebrated Northern Irish poet and radio producer, Louis MacNeice, was looking for new writers and producers in the province. He found both Bell and W. R. Rodgers, taking the latter eventually back to the BBC

Features Department in London. An important aspect of Bell's appointment was that he was not answerable to the often partisan and illiberal minds in Belfast, but to MacNeice himself in London. Another stroke of good fortune for Bell was the departure of Marshall and the appointment, in 1948, of the committed BBC regionalist, Andrew Stewart, as controller, Northern Ireland. And so the scene was set for this self-proclaimed 'Ulsterman' to write and produce radio features and documentaries for the next forty years, most of which expressed his powerful sense of Ulster as a cultural, historical and geographical entity.

The post-war BBC was committed to a policy of regional broadcasting following the more centralised wartime output. This policy was influenced partly by Siepmann's pre-war report on the regions and the commitment of people like Andrew Stewart, who had moved to Belfast after a spell as programme director for Scotland. Regionalism was further supported by the 1951 Beveridge Report on broadcasting, which recommended devolution. The view that energised regions would add to BBC output was supported by D. G. Bridson, the influential features producer who thought that, because the regions were 'comparatively free from administrative interference', this would facilitate improvements in quality (quoted in Cranston, 1996: 38). Siepmann himself had identified radio features as the most promising aspect of production in Northern Ireland and, in 1945, the Features Department reopened in Belfast with Sam Hanna Bell a key member of the team.

Before examining examples of Bell's programme making it is instructive to look at his writing and, in particular, his best-known novel, *December Bride* (1951), set in the early 1900s on a farm near the shore of Strangford Lough.[5] A mother and her 30-year-old daughter, Sarah, come to live on the farm, and the novel is the story of Sarah and her relationships with the two farmer's sons and eventual marriage to one of them. But, as Bell's biographer Sean McMahon explains, 'the most striking thing about the book is the realisation of place and community' (1999: 75). For Bell the place in question was not the Protestant and Unionist province of Northern Ireland but something ages older. *December Bride* includes reminders to the reader of 'earlier people' who inhabited the shores of the lough. Behind the farm is the 'rath' or fort, a term based on the Gaelic *ráth*; a bald man is called Moiley (also from the Gaelic *maol*, meaning smooth or bald). The old Gaelic words are joined by words from Scottish dialect to suggest a fusion of ancient and more recent influences in the culture of rural Ulster. For Bell, the farmers were dominated by the 'primal force behind all their lives': the land, the country year and its changing moods and insistent demands

(McMahon, 1999: 79). The strength of Bell's writing in *December Bride* is displayed most vividly when describing those primal forces:

> At noon for an hour, an unearthly pearly light fell on the walls and fields, a light that pressed on the head and hurt the brain, and those who had to be out did so with averted heads, hurrying quickly from doorway to doorway. Then the baffled sun drew away and the countryside slid back again into dripping icy darkness. (Bell, quoted in McMahon, 1999: 79)

Bell's radio output was characterised by this depiction of rural culture in particular as something rooted in a more ancient and more 'Irish' past. This celebration of local culture, but with ancient roots, would allow Bell to 'circumvent divisive religious and sectarian issues' (Franklin, 2009: 136). By constantly drawing attention to a shared past, Bell avoided more recent and, indeed, worsening social divisions.

The method of capturing the voices of the people changed significantly in the post-war period. At first it was necessary to bring programme contributors to the BBC studios in Belfast and, given the fairly blatant pro-Unionist bias of the BBC, this was far harder for Catholics than Protestants. Then, soon after 1945, the cumbersome mobile recording unit was introduced, which at least got producers, including and especially Bell, on the road. The recording unit, which Bell drove around in a sturdy Humber car, served to help democratise BBC output. As Bell said, 'Up to this time the working class voice had never been heard in Broadcasting House, Belfast' (quoted in Loughrey, 1996: 69). The recordings were hardly spontaneous, but they were a huge improvement on what had gone before.

> Sam Bell went to Queen's Island and to every glen in the Sperrins with his recording machine. By contemporary broadcasting standards, that material was rigidly scripted and stilted but in its time it was wonderfully innovative and enriching. (Loughrey, 1996: 70)

Tape recorders arrived at the BBC in the early 1950s and these of course were an invaluable aid in the task of capturing working class voices. As Ieuan Franklin has pointed out, in doing this Bell joined the pioneering work of other early radio interviewers, such as Denis Mitchell and Charles Parker, inspired by the search for authentic working class speech (Franklin, 2009: 114).

The reality of Bell's first productions is rather less inspiring than might be expected from such a talented and influential figure. Bell had clear aspirations to gather 'the voices of men and women describing their daily work, their recreations, their hopes and troubles' (Cathcart, 1984: 154). Series like *Country Magazine* (1949–1954), *Within Our Province* (1949–1953) and *Country Profile* (1949–1953) all featured the voices of the people but may have suffered from a folksy nostalgia:

> The new era was heralded by a schedule packed with nostalgia for a pre-war lyricism; for an imagined Northern Ireland not for the real one. (Cranston, 1996: 40)

Motivated by his concern about the loss of a rural culture, including the language of country people and the occupations they followed, and their superstitions and customs, Bell embarked on an almost desperate attempt to record a dying way of life. *Country Magazine* used the magazine format to incorporate news, gossip, song, agricultural tips and, above all, the voices of 'ordinary people' (McMahon, 1999: 49). *Within Our Province* included stories about apple growing, rope making, housing, and tuberculosis, while *Country Profile* featured rural occupations – the dress maker, the country solicitor. The suggestion in all of these early series was of a largely rural population rooted in their often-isolated communities, engaged in traditional occupations and governed not so much by the church or chapel but by the more ancient rhythms of the weather and the land.

A rather more serious, even anthropological, development in Bell's programme making was in the production of 'Fairy Faith' (March to April 1952). Responding to the criticism that the BBC was more interested in the folklore and music of the South, Andrew Stewart tasked the folklorist, Michael J. Murphy, and Sam Hanna Bell to go in search of the 'heroic tales and myths of Ulster' (Cathcart, 1984: 155). Unable to find what Stewart wanted, Bell and Murphy instead offered to make a series of programmes on that well-known aspect of Irish culture, belief in the 'wee folk' or fairies. A series resulted, described as 'the most important work in Irish Folklore in modern times', according to folklorist and professor of folklore, Seamus Delargy (quoted in Cathcart, 1984: 155). Bell was motivated in much of his radio writing and production by a commitment to capturing a vanishing and mysterious rural culture, and the tales of fiddle-playing, horse-riding and milk-spoiling fairies perfectly captured that sense of an enchanted world. It is tempting to observe that fairies were hardly symbols of Protestant Unionism and, indeed, were a reminder of a shared culture with that other land of fairies and leprechauns, Southern Ireland.

Sam Hanna Bell's radio career can usefully be divided into his work as a jobbing series producer, putting in long hours on the road to satisfy the constant demand for the tales of local people, and his work as the writer and producer of individual programmes. It is in the latter that Bell's originality and powerful expression of Ulster as a cultural and geographical entity can be heard. To mark BBC Northern Ireland's 25th anniversary, Bell wrote and produced what is probably his most famous radio feature, 'This is Northern Ireland: An Ulster Journey', first broadcast on 26 October 1949 and re-broadcast on the BBC Home service and the General Overseas Service. Although the only available recording outside Northern Ireland in the BBC Sound Archive is of very poor quality, the full script has been published in *A Salute from the Banderol: The Selected Writings of Sam Hanna Bell* (Hanna Bell, F., 2009), and this source is the basis for the analysis that follows.[6] The programme is in many ways a classic radio feature in the tradition established by D. G. Bridson, Louis MacNeice and others, although without the use of verse as the main narrative vehicle. Music, drama, poetry and actuality are used throughout, and Franklin is right that the programme marks an 'interstitial' point in features production (2009: 122) because of the combination of the scripted narration of a classic feature with the voices of 'ordinary people', including the fishing-boat skipper, the brickworks manager, the farmer and the shirtmaker.

The feature begins with an important statement of intention:

1ST NARRATOR: In this journey the symbols of our map will not represent bridge, waterway and road, but occupation, speech and custom. Its contours will not show the heights and hollows of rock on rock, but the overflowing and mingling of tradition.

Ladies and Gentlemen, *This is Northern Ireland*.

2ND NARRATOR: This is our map. Here, see, is the scalloped Border that binds our Province. Half of it over mountains, loughs and farmland: half under cliffs, over strands, through the sludge of busy ports. Along the coast of Down, under the feet of Armagh, Tyrone and Fermanagh, over the seaward heads of Derry and Antrim, until it meets and clasps in the city of Belfast. (Quoted in Hanna Bell, F., 2009: 9)

These striking words deserve some analysis. The map the listener will encounter is a cultural and social one in which traditions mingle and overflow. So the emphasis will be on how the past shapes the present, an abiding theme in Bell's radio and other work (and especially *December Bride*). But there is also a geographical map, which includes the romantic features of mountain and lough and the six named counties of Ulster. These are described as 'clasped' together and so separated from the rest of the island of Ireland. In reality this is a curious gloss on history and geography because the 1920 partition of six counties was not traditional or ancient at all. The historic entity of Ulster consisted of Northern Ireland, but also the counties of Cavan, Donegal and Monaghan which, following partition, existed in Southern Ireland. Bell's 'clasped' province had none of the historic lineage he suggests; it was a political fix dating back a mere 30 years.

Running throughout 'This is Northern Ireland' is the constant affirmation of the ancient character of Ulster. So 'it was the Norsemen who gave Strangford Lough its modern name' and 'at the Slaney river, near the mouth of the lough, St Patrick landed on his return to Ireland, 1,500 years ago' and perhaps most graphically:

> Great mountainsides peopled by the sheep, the hare and hoody crow. Yet every ridge and boulder and mist-filled hollow has a name, for men and women lived and worked here a thousand years. (Quoted in Hanna Bell, F., 2009: 18)

Another striking characteristic of the programme, and indeed of much of Bell's radio output, is attention to language and dialect. The old language is of course bound up with the history of the ancient places. Bell calls the mountains of Mourne, 'the kingdom of Mourne':

> In it are all the ancient appurtenances of a kingdom. A rhythm of speech, a mythology, a pattern of living laid down on its granite sides. (Quoted in Hanna Bell, F., 2009: 14)

Language is strongly associated with history but also with place, and here Bell allows his more liberal anti-Unionism to show, a genuine warmth towards those who live beyond the borders of Ulster:

> As the texture of the land changes from richness to sparseness, so, as it travels South, speech changes from dryness and an economy of words to the cadence and idiom of an older tongue, till talk and

greeting and story mingle and merge into the voices of Louth and Southern Ireland. (Quoted in Hanna Bell, F., 2009: 14)

Similarly, when mentioning the sectarian divide, he comments that 'it may be only the thickness of a page of Indian paper that divides us'. Thomas Hajkowski's judgement of 'This is Northern Ireland' is partly correct:

> Bell's implicit argument in *This is Northern Ireland* is that the people of Northern Ireland have more in common with each other than with Catholics or Protestants in Eire, by virtue of their shared Ulsterness. (2010: 219)

The emphasis on shared culture, history and geography is indeed non-sectarian despite the Protestant connotations of 'Ulster', but this is hardly a Unionist text. There is no sense at all of Britishness, and the constant references to ancient ways would surely have suggested an Ireland before religious division: before partition? In 'This is Northern Ireland' there are some decidedly mixed messages about Ulster as a unique, historic place – messages that seem to reflect confusion within the Protestant community. One of the fascinations of this canonic feature is the expression of this confusion, of Ulster as having both a shared Irishness with the South but also being fundamentally different from the South in its 'clasped' autonomy.

Made almost exactly a year later, 'Raithlin Island', written and produced by Bell, was broadcast on 6 October 1950. As a radio programme it is remarkably different from the classic artificiality of 'This is Northern Ireland'. The programme is about a small island between Ireland and Scotland, steeped in history and culturally distinct; perfect material for Sam Hanna Bell, and his approach could be described as revolutionary for the time. The foundation of the programme is not the script, as in the traditional feature, but the (apparently unscripted) voices of the inhabitants of the island interviewed by the presenter, Graham Roberts. This is something far closer to a radio documentary, a more journal-istic approach but one that, like 'This is Northern Ireland', creates a powerful sense of place. We hear a farmer interviewed and then a man talking about a 'sweat room'; we hear a woman publican, the sound of men talking, and then one of them tells a story. A lobster fisherman complains he has only caught eight lobsters, and then we hear the voice of the district nurse. The interviews are linked together by Bell's typi-cally lyrical, scripted commentary: 'I saw a rock like a gigantic wedding cake'; 'the road rambles through a bracelet of tiny loughs'; and we hear details of the island's history (the 'hill of screams' where women saw their menfolk slaughtered by the Campbells), culminating in the eccentricity of model yachting, a very popular pastime on Raithlin Island.

Much of Bell's subsequent work as a radio producer and writer employed the techniques and form of 'Raithlin Island' while further developing his intense interest in a dying Ulster traditional culture. 'Memories of Belfast Shipyard Workers' (25 January 1953) included the voices of workers describing the hierarchies and symbolic clothing of men in the early twentieth century. The shipyard was full of men in different hats, which indicated their trade and seniority, a badge of office. Some men wore frock coats, but joiners wore laundered white aprons. A riveter wore a black silk scarf and moleskin trousers. These traditions were dying out, but through the memories of workers Bell evoked an image of urban Belfast with a rich and colourful working-man's culture.

Similarly, 'Hired and Bound' (3 March 1954) included stories of the old fairs of Northern Ireland, where 'farm servants' were hired. Alongside the recorded sounds of a fair (sheep, a man singing), Bell is heard interviewing a number of people about their experiences and memories. As has already been suggested, Bell's work could often be nostalgic, an undoubted weakness in his programmes, but 'Hired and Bound' is a good example of a more realistic and at times grim view of old rural Northern Ireland. One speaker described the farm servant system as 'a second edition to slavery', and there is an emphasis on the extreme poverty and harsh conditions of the workers. Workers were contracted for a period of time and it was almost impossible to leave before the end. The fairs were also remarkably rich in terms of the variety of traders and performers: acrobats, a man with a bear, fortune tellers and foot doctors were all present. The crowds who attended frequently dressed up for the occasion, wearing suits or shawls, and there was much singing and dancing. There were also fights at the hiring fairs, and the dealers often carried sticks to defend themselves.

Sam Hanna Bell's work as a producer of other writers' scripts also allowed him to explore Northern Irish culture and a sense of place. A brilliant example of this is 'The Return Room', written in verse by W. R. Rodgers (23 December 1955). This feature describes Rodgers's Belfast childhood, and the stylised poetic narrative is strongly reminiscent of the work of his friend, Dylan Thomas. The feature combines dramatic performance with music and sound effects, but it is mainly verse narrative. Belfast is described as a city pulsating with characters

(Uncle Jacob, Mr Jelly Belly and Mrs Bitter Cup) around whom children skip and sing. The Belfast street is the programme's focal point and the sounds of the street are described: a street preacher forecasts doom; 'ragamuffins' sing and beg; and we hear Mr Ezekiel Knight, the undertaker – 'a funeral in our street was a state occasion'. Religion is also a central theme in 'The Return Room' but the references (from a Protestant perspective) are affectionate and largely humorous: 'we ignored Good Friday as being too close to Rome'; Sunday was 'the longest day of week, every minute had mildew on it'; and 'in the street, Mrs Mulligan talking to her 12 children' and discovering that one had stolen a sixpence, tells them to 'get down on your knees and pray'. Some of the sharpest writing, however, is reserved for the Protestants; Rodgers refers to his mother's 'sad little Presbyterian mouth', and the children sing with 'their bitter old Puritan tongues'. In Rodgers's account of mid-twentieth-century Belfast, a sense of religious divide is present but simply adds to the colour and gaiety of a child's world. As producer, Bell would have relished the task of evoking Belfast as a culturally diverse and richly textured urban space.

It would be a serious mistake to denigrate Sam Hanna Bell's representation and celebration of Ulster as simply part of a Protestant, Unionist ideology, and that is certainly not suggested here. By mapping the geography, history and culture of Ulster, Bell is certainly demarcating the North from the South, a critically important component of Unionist ideology, but Bell's Ulster is also vividly different from the rest of Britain. Martin McLoone, in his discussion of the early BBC N.I., has written of the 'degree of confusion over what it was the unionists (...) wanted in terms of more acceptable representations of their Ulster identity' (1996: 27). On the one hand there was a desire to acknowledge Ulster as an alternative form of 'Irishness', different to that promoted by the South, but 'On the other hand, there was also a desire for the Britishness of Ulster to be recognised as no different to the Britishness of London' (1996: 27). Those who wanted Ulster to look as much like London as possible would have been deeply disappointed by Bell's hyper-regional account of Northern Ireland as a unique cultural and historical entity, but one which was frequently coloured by Gaelic history, customs and words; not to mention Gaelic belief in the 'wee folk'.

Hanna Bell's legacy is of considerable interest to radio scholars, as he moved with some speed through the different forms of post-war factual broadcasting; from the early magazine programmes to the more artificial classic radio features and then to the more relaxed interview-based documentaries. But his significance is far greater than that, as he is now remembered principally as a novelist and, especially, as the author of *December Bride*. Driving Hanna Bell's literary and broadcasting career was his love of the land and its dying culture – a culture in which he saw the hope of peace for his troubled home. Hence, his powerful evocation of Ulster as a unique and ancient place: a well-intentioned, if at times naïve, representation of Northern Ireland.

Notes

1. The term 'features' is here used to describe a creative style of factual programme, which might include music, verse and drama as well as recorded sound and the voices of interviewees.
2. Presbyterianism is a Scottish form of Protestantism influenced by Calvinism.
3. Ireland was partitioned in 1920, creating the Irish Free State, a predominantly Catholic south and west of Ireland and a Protestant dominated north.
4. The Protestant majority in Northern Ireland was 'Unionist', favouring union with the rest of Britain.
5. This is the anglicised spelling of the Scots/Irish Gaelic word 'loch', meaning lake.
6. It should be noted that the study of radio programmes based on transcripts lacks an appreciation of their specifically sonic quality; this is particularly true of radio features with their often diverse range of sounds.

References

Cathcart, R. (1984) *The Most Contrary Region: The BBC in Northern Ireland 1924–1984* (Belfast: The Blackstaff Press).

Cranston, D. (1996) From Portland Stone to the Rive Foyle: The Decentralisation and Democratising of BBC radio. In M. McLoone (ed.) *Broadcasting in a Divided Community: Seventy years of the BBC in Northern Ireland* (Belfast: Queen's University Belfast).

Franklin, I. (2009) Folkways and Airwaves: Oral History, Community and Vernacular Radio, Bournemouth University, Unpublished PhD thesis.

Hajkowski, T. (2010) *The BBC and National Identity in Britain, 1923–53* (Manchester: Manchester University Press).

Hanna Bell, F. (ed.) (2009) *A Salute from the Banderol: The Selected Writings of Sam Hanna Bell* (Belfast: The Blackstaff Press).

Hanna Bell, S. (1951) *December Bride* (London: Dobson).

Hillan King, S. (1999) 'A Salute from the Banderol' Sam Hanna Bell's Contribution to Ulster's Cultural Life. *Writing Ulster* No. 6, Northern Narratives, 1–11, www.jstor.org/stable/30022133 (Accessed 5 August 2014).

Loughrey, P. (1996) Culture and Identity: The BBC's Role in Northern Ireland. In M. McLoone (ed.) *Broadcasting in a Divided Community: Seventy Yearsof the BBC in Northern Ireland* (Belfast: Queen's University Belfast).

McLoone, M. (1996) The Construction of a Partitionist Mentality: Early Broadcasting in Ireland. In M. McLoone (ed.) *Broadcasting in a Divided Community: Seventy Years of the BBC in Northern Ireland* (Belfast: Queen's University Belfast).

McMahon, S. (1999) *Sam Hanna Bell: A Biography* (Belfast: The Blackstaff Press).

12
Resisting Redefinition: The Portrayal of Northern Irish Identity in Ulster Television's Schools Output, 1970–1977

Ken Griffin

Introduction

The teaching of subjects such as history and geography in Ireland has been closely associated with the concepts of religious and national identity since the island was conquered by the Tudors in the sixteenth century. Despite Ireland's close proximity to the British mainland, the English crown's position remained insecure due to intermittent outbreaks of Irish separatism and concerns about the loyalty of its native population, who were reluctant to convert from Catholicism to Anglicanism. As a result, reinforcing the crown's position through cultural assimilation emerged as a key preoccupation of English policy in Ireland until the twentieth century.

Education was a cornerstone of this strategy as the government aimed to force Catholic children into Protestant schools so they received an education 'guaranteed to train them up to be loyal Protestant subjects' (McManus, 2002: 16). This was reflected by the preponderance of measures concerning schools within the Penal Laws, statutes restricting the rights of Irish Catholics that were introduced from the late seventeenth century. These included prohibitions on Catholics sending their children abroad for schooling, on establishing Catholic schools in Ireland, and on Catholics working as teachers (Coolahan, 1981: 9). Even after these measures were repealed a century later, Ireland's new education structures retained the core aim of fostering British identity. Although secondary schools were independently run, the state regulated and funded the island's primary school system. The resultant curriculum and associated textbooks 'contained very little material relating to a distinctively Irish environment' (Coolahan, 1981: 21). During this period, the state oversaw a sharp decline in Irish-language usage through its refusal to include the language within the Irish school curriculum, and its insistence that all children be taught exclusively in English. By the time the Irish language was allowed into the curriculum in 1904, it had been relegated to minority status (21).

The fate of Irish arguably shaped educational policy on both sides of the Irish border after the island was partitioned in 1921. The new Irish Free State sought to reverse the cultural legacy of the British education system and focused heavily on reviving the language. By 1934, infant schools had to operate entirely in Irish, and the language had become a compulsory subject for older students. Many aspects of the state's primary-school curriculum had been pared back to maximise the amount of time spent on Irish instruction. Meanwhile, Northern Ireland's new Unionist government pursued cultural assimilation with renewed vigour, extending its oversight to secondary schools and discouraging the teaching of Irish history and local geography.

By the 1960s, the undesirable consequences of such policies were evident on both parts of the island. The Republic of Ireland had become progressively more isolationist while a dangerous decline in community relations had occurred in Northern Ireland. While the Irish government took corrective action, its Northern counterpart refused to alter its approach to education, bringing about a situation in which liberal educators felt compelled to introduce reforms through the backdoor. Although teacher-training colleges were major drivers of reform, schools television series produced by historian and geographer Dr Rex Cathcart for Ulster Television (UTV), Northern Ireland's ITV franchise, also made an important contribution. Cathcart's role in the reform movement has previously been obscured by the unavailability of these programmes, only one of which was retained in UTV's archive. The remainder were wiped soon after their final broadcasts. In 2012, however, a sizeable cache of Cathcart's schools programmes were found among uncatalogued films and domestic videotapes held by UTV and his estate. These discoveries mean that it is now possible to explore Cathcart's contribution to schools television.

Division within Northern Irish schools

Cathcart's programmes sought to challenge a schools system and curriculum moulded by the Unionist Party, which had governed Northern

Ireland since 1921. Upon taking office, the government soon tightened its grip on education through the introduction of a two-tier system of controlled and voluntary schools. Controlled schools were governed by the state and fully state-funded. They catered exclusively for Protestant students due to legal provisions that indirectly banned Catholic religious education in such schools. The government later introduced a legal guarantee ensuring that only Protestant teachers could work in controlled schools (Murray, 1983: 137). Catholic students were taught in voluntary schools which remained independent of the state and only received state funding for heating and lighting (Murray, 1983: 136). The Catholic hierarchy aimed to ensure that such schools preserved 'full continuity with the religious life of the home' (Conway, 1970: 12) and only employed Catholic teachers.

The existence of parallel school systems delineated by religion soon led to an ever-widening divergence in subject choices and teaching approaches. One particularly contentious topic was Irish history, the teaching of which was 'virtually regarded as a seditious activity' by the government (Cathcart, 1979: 5). Northern Ireland's Ministry for Education sought to promote the region's identity as part of the United Kingdom and discouraged any references within the classroom to long-standing historic and cultural ties between Northern Ireland and the rest of the island. It vetted all history textbooks prior to use in schools, showing a strong preference for those which 'placed an emphasis on British and modern European history and had their Irish history compressed into one or two dull and almost meaningless chapters' (Magee, 1970: 19). While Irish history technically remained on the history syllabus, its presence was so marginal that students could get a top mark in the Northern Irish GCE history exam 'without having heard of either Ireland or Ulster' (Darby, 1974: 42).

While controlled schools suppressed Irish history in accordance with the government's wishes, some voluntary schools reacted by either rejecting government's preferred textbooks or teaching the subject as an extracurricular activity using materials imported from across the border (Magee, 1970:19). Such lessons were highly politicised. In 1969, republican MP Bernadette Devlin recalled how her headmistress used history lessons to teach her pupils that 'everything English was bad'. Meanwhile, republican activist Eamon McCann later discussed how his teacher would make his pupils tear out 'passages of fiction' in the Irish history chapters of their state-approved textbooks (Cairns, 1987: 129).

The result was that Protestant and Catholic schoolchildren developed divergent beliefs about the history of their region, affecting their sense of identity and their later interactions with the other community. By 1971, the divisions were so stark that Robinson (1971: 385) found that Catholic pupils in Derry now identified their city as part of the Irish Republic while their Protestant peers viewed it as part of Northern Ireland. Meanwhile, most Protestant children were unaware of the city's origins as a sixth-century monastic settlement, compared with over 40% of the Catholic pupils surveyed. Robinson's findings were not unique, and Cairns (1987: 131) indicates that a similar study in a small town revealed similar divergences in perception.

The origins of Cathcart's series

Cathcart first arrived in Northern Ireland in December 1967, a time when community relations in the region were transitioning from dysfunctional to violent. His appointment as the Independent Television Authority's officer for Northern Ireland, handling the day-to-day regulation of UTV, reflected the deteriorating situation. At that time, the ITA was fielding an increasing volume of complaints from both communities about perceived biases in the station's output. Cathcart's personal background meant that he was one of the few individuals capable of retaining the trust of both sides. While Cathcart was an Irish nationalist from Dublin, he was also a Protestant who had experienced religious discrimination in the Republic. Although his background was primarily in education, he had played a key role in the development of schools television in the Republic as the chairman of Telefís Éireann's advisory committee on education.[1] In this capacity, he had emerged as a capable producer and had devised a successful adult-education series, *Irish Landscape* (1968–1970).[2]

He soon found that schools television was far less advanced in Northern Ireland. Although UTV had launched the region's first local series, *The Young Citizens' Club* (1965–1967), it had shown little subsequent interest in its schools output. Upon his arrival in Belfast, Cathcart found that UTV had ceased to employ an educational officer and that its managing director had vowed that the station would never make another schools series.[3] Meanwhile, the BBC's first Northern Irish schools television series, *Ulster in Focus* (1967–2002), was an undemanding miscellany of short films, which could range from a study of Belfast children's games[4] to the life of a sheep farmer.[5] As a result, Cathcart soon found himself considering potential opportunities for a new schools series. He was naturally drawn to the debate surrounding Irish history teaching in Northern Irish schools. He had also become concerned about how the region's primary school curriculum focused almost exclusively on British history and geography, alienating children from their immediate surroundings. He noted that its approach demanded a high level of abstract thought from pupils who had 'scarcely reached the stage when they can appreciate what is abstract or foreign to their experience' (Cathcart, 1979: 15).

At that time, the Northern Ireland government remained instinctively hostile to any hint of reform (Fischer, 2011: 245), particularly when it involved Irish history, which it viewed as 'a means of introducing nationalist propaganda into schools' (Cathcart, 1979: 8). Unbeknownst to Cathcart and his peers, the Northern Ireland cabinet would soon even resolve to sabotage the region's soon-to-be established independent Schools' Examination Council. The Unionist Party viewed the examination system as a key means of suppressing Irish separatism and was unwilling to surrender direct control of it. As a result, government ministers devised a plan to maintain the status quo by only appointing Catholic council members from a secret list of trusted 'Roman Catholic people who might be considered for appointment to boards, etc., within the public service'.[6]

Despite the government's deep-seated opposition to reform, Cathcart apparently spotted a loophole in the regulations governing UK schools broadcasting, which meant that producers were not tied to any official curriculum (St John Brooks, 1971: 86). He was not the first to exploit this situation, and elements within BBC Northern Ireland had been promoting Irish history since 1965 through the radio schools series, *Today and Yesterday in Northern Ireland* (whose early programmes often featured the tales and voice of Sam Hanna Bell) and *Two Centuries of Irish History* (Hawthorne, 1996: 56, 61). Cathcart, however, was the first to bring Irish history and geography to schools television, and the first to overtly challenge the Unionist government's attempts to redefine Northern Ireland as a British region.

Let's Look at Ulster

Cathcart's first Northern Irish series, *Let's Look at Ulster*, ran for 30 episodes produced between 1970 and 1977. It focused broadly on the region's historical and industrial development, mixing episodes on specific industries with in-depth case studies on the growth of major settlements. Each transmission run consisted of ten episodes and was typically composed of a mix of repeats and newly made episodes. The first series, consisting of 19 episodes filmed between June 1969 and March 1975, was aimed at 10- to 13-year olds. A second series, consisting of 11 episodes produced in 1976–1977, featured a revised format aimed at 8- to 11-year olds. Following recent archival discoveries, ten episodes from each of the first and second series are now known to exist.

The series stemmed from an approach made to Cathcart by the Northern Irish Head Teachers' Association, seeking the ITA's support in its attempts to convince UTV to make another local schools series. The association wanted the station to produce a series about environmental studies, a new subject in Northern Irish schools which had posed difficulties, as it was an 'eclectic discipline … where the traditional distinctions between the subjects are blurred' (St John Brookes, 1971: 39). Cathcart was immediately attracted to its proposal due to environmental studies' strong focus on educating children about their surroundings. He later admitted that he saw it as a means of providing 'schools with a series which was effectively an introduction to *Irish*[7] history and *Irish* geography' (1979a: 7).

Cathcart not only backed the proposal but resolved to produce the series himself due to his concern that environment studies could further propagate sectarianism in Northern Ireland if taught inappropriately (1979: 16). He quickly developed the basic concept, assisted by UTV director Andrew Crockart, which Cathcart presented to the station's managing director, Brum Henderson, in early 1969. Henderson was an old acquaintance from Cathcart's student days at Trinity College Dublin. Given UTV's previous opposition to a new schools series, Cathcart was surprised to find that Henderson 'loved the thought [of Cathcart making a schools series] because they had been at Trinity together'.[8] Cathcart subsequently persuaded the ITA to overlook the inherent conflict of interest involved, probably by arguing that UTV was too small to make a schools series without Cathcart's assistance (St John Brooks, 1971: 38). The authority's only stipulation was that Cathcart could not be paid or credited for his work on the series.[9]

In its initial incarnation *Let's Look at Ulster* promoted Cathcart's own view of Ulster and its cultural heritage. He conceptualised Ulster in terms of the ancient Gaelic province, comprising the six counties of Northern Ireland plus Cavan, Donegal and Monaghan, which were now within the Republic. All nine had strong commercial and cultural links, which the Northern Ireland government had sought to break since partition. The government's goal was to reduce the concept of Ulster to the six-county unit under its control and transform the Irish border into a permanent bulwark between British 'civilisation' and Irish Republican 'barbarism at the gate' (Ruane and Todd, 1996, cited in McCall, 2011: 208). In the region's schools, the border was regularly utilised as a potent symbol of Northern Irish separatism from the remainder of Ireland. The poet Seamus Heaney once recalled how the large map of 'Ulster' that hung on his classroom wall emphasised the border as 'a thick red selvedge all the way from Lough Foyle to Carlingford Lough. That vestigially bloody marking halted the eye travelling south and west' (1983: 7). Heaney observed that this cartographical device was calculated to divorce Ulster from its history as a Gaelic province: 'Ulster shrinks to a six-county region, its hero is not Cuchulainn but Carson' (1983: 6). He also noted how the map subliminally portrayed Britain as more welcoming: 'travelling east...small black steamships lured the eye across the blue wash of St. George's Channel' (1983: 7).

The first series of *Let's Look at Ulster* represented a sustained challenge to Unionist attempts to reinforce the border. The series consistently represented the border as a permeable internal divide within the nine-county region. Unlike other Northern Irish educational resources, the series depicted the boundary in an episodic and casual manner. Maps of cross-border phenomena, such as a chart of Ulster's nineteenth-century railway system, featured in 'Carrying Goods' (1970), omitted the border. The series' general approach was best encapsulated, though, by the large model of Ireland that formed the backdrop to the studio scenes for the four episodes produced in 1973. The government's bulwark, generally portrayed elsewhere as a solid line with exacting precision, was depicted on the model in a stylised and geographically imprecise manner as a broken dotted line, implying that crossing it was far from the physical and ideological impossibility suggested by the maps in the region's classrooms (see Figure 11).

The series also implicitly critiqued Unionist characterisations of what lay beyond the border, characterisations that had grown increasingly extreme since the 'troubles' began in 1968. In March 1972, for example, a senior Unionist MP, Albert Anderson, told the Northern Ireland parliament that he supported the permanent closure of the Irish border on the grounds of regional security if such a prospect were feasible. Anderson singled out Donegal as representing a particular threat to 'Ulster', describing it as 'a part of Eire [Ireland] which is bitterly opposed to us. Every day the people of that area are giving all the aid and succour they can to the gunmen and bombers'.[10] By contrast, the county featured prominently throughout *Let's Look at Ulster*, which emphasised its extremely strong links to the North-West corner of Northern Ireland. Indeed, a significant portion of the series' third episode, 'Power'(1970), was based in the county and focused on how Donegal farmers were maintaining the old Ulster tradition of peat harvesting.

Figure 11 John McCavert introduces 'Belfast', a 1973 episode of *Let's Look at Ulster*

Let's Look at Ulster did not just challenge Unionism's drive for regional redefinition: Cathcart also attempted to tackle Republican attempts to monopolise Irish identity through the appropriation of previously shared cultural forms such as traditional music. The latter process had proven extraordinarily successful during the 1960s. At the start of that decade, UTV's most popular programme was the traditional music series *With a Fiddle and a Flute* (1961–1964). Less than a decade later, though, Cathcart's ITA duties included handling dozens of complaints and threats from Unionists about such programmes.[11] He subsequently sought to remove some of the political baggage now associated with such music by featuring it prominently throughout *Let's Look at Ulster*. The importance of this gesture to Cathcart was such that he commissioned a series of unique recordings from leading Northern Irish folk singer, David Hammond.[12] These topped and tailed most episodes, including a 1970 episode about the Unionist strong-hold of Ballymena.

Meanwhile, Cathcart instigated a competition to encourage schools to conduct their own local studies projects based on the material contained in the series, and he devoted the final episode of each transmission run to such projects. The studies featured were selected on a competitive basis with the winners invited to produce segments within the episode about their particular project, aided by the series' production team. The children were allowed to script, narrate and appear within these segments (UTV, 1974: 19). Cathcart appears to have viewed the competition as a powerful means of delivering the series' objectives, and he persisted with the specials despite the production headaches they created. Each special had to be put together in less than six weeks from judging to recording, placing the production team under considerable time pressures. The initial 1970 special nearly had to be broadcast live,[13] while the 1975 edition was only completed on the night before transmission.[14]

This Island About Us

Despite its gently subversive edge, *Let's Look at Ulster* was so well received within Northern Irish schools that UTV soon found itself fielding requests from local teachers' groups for a second local schools series. While many of groups sought a series promoting better community relations, the station opted for the safer option of commissioning another environmental studies series conceived by Cathcart. *This Island About Us* ran between January 1972 and March 1976 and was aimed at 10- to 13-year olds. Each transmission run consisted of ten episodes, which typically mixed repeats with newly updated episodes. A total of 16 episodes were produced in all. For many years, the series' content was obscure, as the master videotapes for every episode were erased and reused in the late 1970s. Fortunately, 11 episodes along with a sizeable chunk from a 12th were recovered in 2012. These episodes reveal that the series differed somewhat in focus from *Let's Look at Ulster*. While its predecessor concentrated on human geography, *This Island About Us* was concerned with Ireland's physical landscape.

Possibly emboldened by the positive response to *Let's Look at Ulster*, Cathcart mounted an overt challenge to Unionist attempts to redefine Ulster as a British region. Throughout the series, Northern Ireland was consistently positioned within an all-Ireland geographical and historical framework, which ignored its political status as part of the United Kingdom. In the teachers' booklet for the series, Cathcart argued:

The geographer treats the island as a whole, for its political division into Northern Ireland and the Republic of Ireland does not coincide with any geographical features known to him. (UTV 1971: 3)

The centrality of this all-Ireland approach within the series was made explicit within seconds of the start of the first episode by the appearance of the series logo (depicted in Figure 12), which was based on a borderless map of Ireland.

The logo's appearance was followed by a spoken commentary asserting the universality of a unique Irish identity to all individuals living on that island:

The sea surrounds Ireland and makes it an island. We are all – those of us who have been born here – island men and island women. Our ancestors whether they came recently or in the distant past all originally came from over the sea and when they settled here the sea acted as a barrier to cut them off. In this island, they lived their own lives and developed their own customs.

Figure 12   The *This Island About Us* logo as seen in the first episode of the series

During the series, Cathcart appeared to be attempting to use geography to reawaken a broad sense of Irish identity among the Unionist population, who had become alienated from their physical environment through their focus on their British origins. Major Northern Irish geographical features, such as the Giant's Causeway, were repeatedly referred to as 'Irish', a tendency which became established as early as the second episode, 'Mountains' (1972). Although Cathcart could argue that these locations were Irish by virtue of their geographic position, such references skirted the boundaries of political commentary as the Republic officially referred to itself as 'Ireland' and had, via its constitution, placed a territorial claim on Northern Ireland. Meanwhile, the series treated the border itself as though it were non-existent: the occasional cross-border excursions of *Let's Look at Ulster* were expanded so that entire editions of *This Island About Us* were largely based in the Republic, such as an episode on Viking Dublin.

While *This Island About Us* contained much to provoke Unionist ire, the series was extremely well received by teachers. After its initial screening, UTV received an unusually high amount of response cards from schools about the series, most of which were positive. Of those schools which gave the series an overall rating, 64% judged the series to be either 'very good' or 'good'. Only 8% felt it was 'poor' and none thought the series was 'worthless'. A report compiled by Cathcart for the ITA suggested that this positive response was linked to the lack, in Northern Irish schools, of teaching materials that addressed Irish geography. He quoted a typical response from one primary school teacher who stated that *This Island About Us* had proved to be 'invaluable containing a wealth of information unobtainable from textbooks and reference libraries [and] the children not only learned a [illegible] lot about their own country – but also enjoyed the programmes'.[15]

The difficulties of division

By his own admission, Cathcart sometimes struggled to produce shared accounts of Northern Ireland's history and development for *Let's Look at Ulster* and *This Island About Us* due to the region's legacy of sectarian strife, wealth displacement and ghettoisation. These problems almost derailed the production of the first series of *Let's Look at Ulster*. Cathcart had intended to devote two episodes in each run to detailed case studies charting the development of specific Northern Irish towns. Ballymena, a staunchly Unionist settlement, was the first to be tackled in this manner. Because of segregated settlement patterns, the town defied all attempts by Cathcart to write a script that contained a cross-community balance. The final script inevitably focused 'on one tradition: the town was shown to have been developed by settlers, [in the words of the programme] "men with agricultural backgrounds, ardent Presbyterians, hard-headed and thrifty"'. In the end, Cathcart was forced to adopt a crude balance that involved featuring one Unionist town and one Nationalist town per transmission run (1979a: 5).

The conflicting identities of the region's two communities also forced Cathcart to make a number of editorial compromises, which weakened the series. He realised at an early stage that 'a head-on assault on the issues that divide us would only alienate large sections of one or other of the communities' (Cathcart, 1979a: 6). With little consensus on much of the region's history, he judged that a situation could emerge wherein 'part of the potential audience is so offended that it switches off or doesn't even bother to switch on' (Cathcart, 1979a: 6). As a result, the two series did not cover the region's political history, even though their coverage of industrial and social developments stretched into the 1960s. Key historic events, such as the Battle of the Boyne, the Siege of Derry, and the partition of Ireland were never even referenced.

The most significant compromises concerned *Let's Look at Ulster*'s handling of Northern Ireland's second-largest city, Derry, which had become a microcosm of the wider struggles surrounding identity in the region. The two communities could not even agree on its name: Nationalists called it Derry while Unionists referred to it as Londonderry. The use of either name was viewed as adopting a political stance. This conflict ensured that the city had a marginal presence within *Let's Look at Ulster* despite its size and importance. Derry was not even the subject of a town study until March 1975. The resultant programme was a fudge that sought to satisfy all sides by utilising both settlement names in an inconsistent manner, while omitting contentious episodes from the settlement's history, including the Siege of Derry, an event commemorated annually in the city. Meanwhile, to accommodate the two conflicting accounts of its origins, both seventh-century monks and seventeenth-century planters were credited as the city's founders. The omissions left various unanswered questions about the city's past, including the issue of why and when its famous walls were built.

In spite of editorial compromises, the series provided a convincing argument for Cathcart's contention that 'through history the communities have shared a common struggle to wrest their livelihoods from the soil and that the manifestations of the struggle in tools, customs and modes of living were very similar' (Cathcart, 1979a: 6). *This Island About Us* was particularly strong in this respect, often revealing how developments in Northern Ireland could be best contextualised through reference to events elsewhere on the island. One notable example was the episode, 'Inland Towns' (1972), in which a shortened and revised version of *Let's Look at Ulster*'s study of Ballymena was successfully combined with material about the founding of towns in the Republic.

Cathcart's impact and later output

It is beyond the scope of this chapter to quantify the precise contribution made by Cathcart's series to the rehabilitation of Irish history and geography within Northern Irish schools in the 1970s. Past accounts of this phenomenon (such as Fischer, 2011) have tended to emphasise developments within the region's teacher-training colleges at that time. One issue with such narratives is that the influence of such institutions would have been largely limited to new entrants into the teaching profession. Meanwhile, there is some evidence to suggest that Cathcart's output had a broader reach, particularly within the primary school system. *Let's Look at Ulster* and its local studies competition triggered such an upsurge in fieldwork in these schools that UTV felt moved to document the series's impact in a booklet, *The Story of a Success*, in 1974. As referred to previously, *This Island About Us* successfully introduced geographical material, omitted from the official syllabus, into the classroom. Cathcart's peers clearly held his work in high regard, and he was appointed professor of education at the New University of Ulster in 1973. He subsequently joined Queen's University in 1977.

For his part, Cathcart suggested that the key turning point in the rehabilitation of Irish history and geography was the suspension of the Northern Ireland parliament and the imposition of direct rule from London in March 1972 (1979: 9). This measure immediately released the schools system from the Unionist Party's grip, meaning that educational bodies could operate without direct local political interference. The region's new British administrators broke with the past and pursued a policy of independent appointments. The local Schools' Examination Council promptly 'released the study of Irish history from its total subordination to British history' by improving its prominence in state examinations (Cathcart, 1979: 9)

By 1976, Cathcart clearly sensed that the battle for reform had been won and his subsequent productions showed a shift in emphasis. During that year, he was commissioned by UTV to remake *Let's Look at Ulster* in colour, which stemmed from the fact that, due to the limited number of new episodes produced for each run, only black and white versions existed for most episodes. The station also decided to cancel *This Island About Us*, which had proven, in hindsight, too similar in content to its predecessor to successfully coexist as a standalone entity. Instead of simply remaking the original series, though, Cathcart opted to refashion *Let's Look at Ulster* into a programme that was 'less detailed, less factual and less historical' (Cathcart, 1977: 3) than before.

The series abruptly ceased to engage with identity politics, a development symbolised by the uncontested appearance of the Irish border on all maps featured in the new episodes. Although folk music still featured heavily, its function had been reduced to a production device utilised to provide a 'lighter, affective dimension' to the series (Cathcart, 1977: 3). In fairness, there remained a political subtext: Cathcart sought to promote environmentalism, a topic in which he had become increasingly interested, and to show children that 'man is in the process of destroying his own world' (Cathcart, 1979a: 6). On one level, though, the new-look *Let's Look at Ulster* still reflected Cathcart's hope that the divide between the region's two communities and their identities could be bridged. In 1979, he suggested that its focus on environmentalism partly stemmed from his belief that the fight against pollution was a common cause, one which 'ought to unite our communities' because of how it threatens both equally (1979a: 6).

The new episodes – which debuted between January and March 1977 – suffered, however, from the lack of the urgent political imperative provided by questions of identity, which development seems to have led to a corresponding decline in Cathcart's interest in his schools output. In April 1977 he proposed a new, non-schools series to UTV: *The Face of Ulster*, a seven-part adult education series that aimed to make the region's geography 'comprehensible to every man'.[16] He also ceased revising *Let's Look at Ulster* after overseeing a straightforward remounting of the first new episode, 'Our Market Town', for a repeat run in September 1977. The series subsequently remained unaltered until it ceased to be repeated in 1981, a situation expedited by the abrupt discontinuation of its popular local studies contest.

Cathcart diverted his energies to his work at Queen's University and to bringing *The Face of Ulster* to fruition. It eventually emerged in 1981 as *Ulster Landscapes*, a prestigious ten-part series which featured extensive location filming. It was to be Cathcart's final series for UTV, as he concentrated on his academic output until his death in 1994. The final episode was a fitting swansong: a special introductory episode filmed after the series was purchased for national broadcast by the newly established Channel 4. The programme was unique within Cathcart's output, as the producer himself went before the camera and took on the responsibility of presenting the concept of Ulster as a nine-county entity to the wider UK television audience.

Notes

1. Committee on Educational Broadcasting, *The Irish Times*, 24 June 1964:1.
2. The Face of Ulster or Ulster Landscapes, Programme Proposal to UTV from Rex Cathcart, 14 April 1977.
3. *ITA Regional Officer's Report*, December 1967.
4. An Irishman's Diary, *The Irish Times*, 27 May 1972:11.
5. In St Peter's Square, *The Irish Times*, 20 October 1975:10.
6. *Northern Irish Cabinet Minutes*, 6 November 1969, PRONI File No: CAB 4/1490
7. Emphasis taken from original text.
8. Untransmitted interview footage with Andrew Crockart filmed for *Your TV – 50 Years of UTV* (2009).
9. Interview with Cathcart's widow, Prof. Rosalind Pritchard, 8 November 2012.
10. *Northern Irish House of Commons Parliamentary Debates*, 1972, Vol. 84, 1501–1502.
11. *ITA Regional Officers Report*, March/April 1970.
12. Interview with Prof. Rosalind Pritchard, 8 November 2012.
13. Interview with Prof. Rosalind Pritchard, 8 November 2012.
14. Script for *Let's Look at Ulster* No. 10, UTV Production No: 41.397, Recorded 17 March 1975.
15. ITA Schools Committee. *Ulster Television Limited*, 16 June 1972, SC Paper 17(72).
16. The Face of Ulster or Ulster Landscapes, Programme proposal to UTV from Rex Cathcart, 14 April 1977.

References

Cathcart, R. (1972) 'Educational Television and Environmental Studies', *The Northern Teacher*, Vol. 10, No. 4, 3–8.
Cathcart, R. (1977) *Let's Look at Ulster: Teacher's Booklet* (Belfast: Ulster Television).
Cathcart, R. (1979) *Teaching Irish History – The Wiles Week Open Lecture 1978* (Belfast: Queen's University).
Cathcart, R. (1979a) *The Educational Role of Regional Broadcasting in Ulster* (Belfast: Queen's University).
Cathcart, R. (1984) *Most Contrary Region: B.B.C. in Northern Ireland, 1924–84* (Belfast: Blackstaff Press).
Conway, W. (1970) *Catholic Schools* (Dublin: Catholic Communications Institute of Ireland).

Coolahan, J. (1981) *Irish Education: Its History and Structure* (Dublin: Institute of Public Administration).

Darby, J. (1974) 'History in the Schools', *Community Forum*, Vol. 4, No. 2, 37–42.

Fischer, K. (2011) 'University Historians and Their Role in the Development of a "Shared" History in Northern Ireland Schools, 1960s–1980s: An Illustration of the Ambiguous Social Function of Historians', *History of Education*, Vol. 40, No. 22, 241–253.

Hawthorne, J. (1996) Above Suspicion or Controversy?: The Development of the BBC's Irish History Programme for Schools in Northern Ireland. In M. McLoone (ed.) *Broadcasting in a Divided Community* (Belfast: Queen's University), 51–65.

Heaney, S. (1983) *Among Schoolchildren* (Belfast: John Malone Memorial Committee).

McCall, C. (2011) 'Culture and the Irish Border: Spaces for Conflict Transformation', *Cooperation and Conflict*, Vol. 46, No. 2, 201–221.

McManus, A. (2002) *The Irish Hedge School and Its Books, 1695–1831* (Dublin: Four Courts Press).

Murray, D. (1983) Schools and Conflict. In J. Darby (ed.) *Northern Ireland: The Background to the Conflict* (Belfast: Appletree Press), 136–150.

Robinson, A. (1971) 'Education and Sectarian Conflict in Northern Ireland', *New Era*, Vol. 52, No.1, 384–388.

UTV (1974) *The Story of a Success* (Belfast: Ulster Television).

UTV (1971) *This Island About Us* (Belfast: Ulster Television).

St John-Brooks, C. (1971) *The History and Development of Educational Broadcasting in Ireland* (Coleraine, Londonderry: New University of Ulster).

13

'Nothing Similar in England': The Scottish Film Council, the Scottish Education Department and the Utility of 'Educational Film' to Scotland

Mandy Powell

National institutions, local networks, policy arenas and cultural distinctiveness

Media present and media past in Scotland has been characterised by asymmetrical relations of power in the nexus of the UK policymaking arena (Schlesinger, 2008; Blain, 2009). Following the 1998 devolution settlement, political oversight of media and communications remained with Westminster, but oversight of culture devolved to the Scottish Parliament. This chapter situates itself in the period between the 1930s and 1990s, the period of administrative devolution in Scotland. It will argue that cultural precipitants for political devolution developed in the conjunctions and disjunctions between film and education policy in the 1930s and then again between media and education policy in the 1970s. On both occasions, the argument for an administrative solution to the Scottish problem was felt to be the 'least revolutionary' option (Mitchell, 1989). By 1998, however, political devolution was conceded, possibly on the same grounds.

Scholarly work producing knowledge about feature and documentary film in Scotland[1] evolved through the twentieth century, using what have become familiar disciplinary concepts (Grieveson and Wasson, 2008).[2] Historical institutional accounts of broadcasting in Scotland (McDowell, 1992; Sweeney, 2008) offer insight into Scottish institutional policymaking and the struggle for representation in the UK arena, but the early history of the Scottish Film Council (SFC), Scottish Screen's predecessor, remains relatively under-explored. Constituted as both a cultural and an educational institution, the SFC operated at the crossroads of a number of interesting policy conjunctions. This included the Scottish Education Department, a devolved power since 1707, the autonomy of which was subject to negotiation with the Privy Council until 1939 and with the Scottish Office thereafter until 1998, and the British Film Institute (BFI), also subject to the Privy Council in the early days of its formation.

This chapter will consider the usefulness of the relationship between the Scottish Film Council and the Scottish Education Department (SED) in the argument for and efficacy of devolution. There has been little sustained analysis of the corpus of educational film in Scotland. Possibly more banal (Billig, 1995) than other filmic markers of Scottish distinctiveness, 21,308 educational films had been borrowed from Scotland's 'regional' film library, the Scottish Central Film Library (SCFL), by 1941[3]. This chapter suggests that the work performed by educational film had a double utility in that it made visible a cultural particularity upon which contracts for devolved powers in both film and education arenas were negotiated by policy makers and upon which the continued legitimacy of Scottish institutions relied. The history of the Scottish Film Council, and arguably Scottish cinema, is inextricably bound to the history of Scottish education and the history of devolution in Scotland. Everyday devolutionary practices, situated in the politics of cultural difference in the nexus of continuously shifting spaces and places of power, created an infrastructure that would scaffold a precarious filmmaking community in the address of 'the Scottish problem' (Mitchell, 1989).

The SFC was formally constituted in Glasgow in 1934.[4] Established in the year following the formation of the British Film Institute (BFI), the identity of the SFC as a national institution, rather than a regional film office, was navigated from the outset with the help of the Association of Directors of Education in Scotland (ADES), an influential group of Scottish educationists (McPherson and Raab, 1988). ADES was a professional body representing the newly organised local education authorities. Before ADES emerged in 1920, the administration of Scottish education by the London-based Scotch Education Department was operationalised by the schools inspectorate (HMI) (Humes, 2000, 1986). ADES offered a potentially democratic element to the governance of Scottish education and together with HMI provided powerful central stewardship.

The Scottish Educational Film Association (SEFA) was the second key local intermediary. Comprising 5,000 teacher members from across Scotland (Barclay, 1993), SEFA encouraged the teaching workforce to engage with film in all its emergent forms. SEFA's advocacy positioned film as 'useful' (Acland and Wasson, 2011; Hediger and Vondereau, 2009) in and for Scotland and, therefore, as a public good.

Problem Scotland: devolution, devolution, devolution

Successive political, economic and cultural policy failures to address Scottish particularity frames Scotland as a problem space. In the late nineteenth and early twentieth centuries the 'problem' was primarily considered in terms of proximity. Difficult to administer at such a distance, the Scottish Office was reorganised and relocated to Edinburgh, which was regarded as the 'least revolutionary' of the alternatives – including home rule or 'complete absorption and anglicisation' (Mitchell, 1989). Mass unemployment in the 1930s was regarded as a distinctive Scottish problem stemming from an over-reliance in West-Central Scotland on a narrow industrial sector. The failure of Whitehall to implement at the time the Scottish Office's recommendation to diversify regional industrial production until the 1960s and focus, instead, on alleviating unemployment through social expenditure was suggestive of a bigger problem (Campbell, 1979). Political devolution had been under discussion since at least the 1920s, but the merger between the National Party of Scotland (formed in 1928), and the Scottish Party – formed in 1932 – establishing in 1934 the Scottish National Party, led to a solution widely described as 'administrative devolution' (Cameron, 2010; Mitchell, 2009).

Political oversight of Scottish culture was not devolved to the Scottish Parliament until the 1998 settlement. However, Gardiner (2004) roots the emergence of a rationale for cultural devolution in the distinctiveness of Scottish education and its promotion of civic identity. The concept of democratic intellectualism was deployed by Walter Elliot in 1932, a secretary of state for Scotland who, in 1938, appointed the first Films of Scotland Committee, to describe Scottish education as a heritage wherein 'discipline is rigidly and ruthlessly enforced but where criticism and attack are unflinching, continuous and salt with a bitter and jealous humour. It is a heritage wherein intellect, speech and, above all, argument are the passports to the highest eminence in the land' (Elliot, 1932: 64). Elliot was highly critical of 'merely utilitarian education' and advocated a technical education that should show 'industrial capacity has an intellectual side'. It was in this context that the constitution of the Scottish Film Council was negotiated.

One month before the Scottish Independence Referendum in 2014, James Robertson, author of *The Testament of Gideon Mack* (2006), *And The Land Lay Still* (2011) and *The News Where You Are* (2014), described his struggle to construct a narrative history of devolution in Scotland. Imagined by him initially as a phenomenon rooted in the 1950s, Robertson was surprised to locate his starting point in the 1920s. For James Mitchell (2009), the modern concept of devolution emerged in the late nineteenth century, driven by 'a growing body of Scots [who] felt that Scottish distinctiveness was being ignored' (19). Mitchell describes devolution at this time as an administrative solution to a political problem that had

> both a symbolic and a substantive function. Symbolically, it represented recognition by government at the centre that Scotland was different. Substantively, it developed a considerable range of responsibilities. (17)

The capacity of this new office of central government came under increasing scrutiny as the twentieth century evolved. Its efficacy was challenged publicly in 1979 when the first devolution referendum was held. The UK government moved to constrain the outcome of that referendum and, despite a result narrowly in favour of political devolution: 51.6% voted yes and 48.8% voted no – it failed to meet the requirement for 40% of the electorate. Eighteen years later, the 1998 devolution referendum result was 74.3% and 25.7% respectively (Hutchison, 2001).

Media, education and the public sphere

John Reith and John Grierson explicitly articulated a purposive relationship between media, education and the public sphere in their visions for radio broadcasting and documentary film respectively. However, Grierson's claim to have organised an 'educational revolution' (1990) in the process is questionable. The social purpose of publicly funded broadcasting in Britain is declared through its three principles: to educate, inform and entertain. Sufficient definitional vagueness facilitates an arguably useful classificatory blurring that relegates education to a service role on the periphery of disciplinary interest. Film and media theory in Britain has yet to evidence the educational work film and broadcasting performs, yet its aesthetic and production culture have been condemned to the wastelands of instrumentality and propaganda, respectively. By contrast, Maija Runcis and Bengt Sandin's (2010) study of educational broadcasting in Sweden takes a multidisciplinary approach and offers a compelling rationale for the value of such work. Concluding that educational broadcasting provides a 'forum for negotiation for a number of interested parties' (172), the book's title, *Neither Fish Nor Fowl*, captures the dilemma well.

Very little research has been undertaken in the United Kingdom regarding the classification of 'educational film' or its utility. Scholarly work on the corpus of industrial film in Europe (Hediger and Vondereau, 2009) and the cultural utility of 'other' cinema (Acland and Wasson, 2011) analyses the everyday work of film culture and argues that the strategic weakness of form refocuses the analysis on the job of work film was made to do. Zoe Druick's (2008, 2011) work on education and film in The League of Nations and UNESCO draws a similar conclusion. When writing about 'non-canonised' film (Elsaesser, 2009: 26), the idea of focusing 'on a specific location, a professional association, or even a national or state initiative' (22) in the context of this edited collection on regional media aesthetics is helpful. Elsaesser's case for a broader research agenda that incorporates film history in media archaeology is also pertinent in this context.

In her work on industrial film, Yvonne Zimmerman discusses the fruitfulness of analysing industrial film as 'a media practice that focuses on its function as utility film' (2009: 102). She quotes the head of Condor Documentaries in the 1980s, who claimed: 'What Hollywood is to America, the corporate film is to Switzerland' (102). The Scottish Film Council's historical association with the Scottish Education Department and the work of the Scottish Educational Film Association (SEFA) was marginalised by film and media scholars in the 1970s. Such judgments have elided the political, social and cultural work educational film performed in and for Scotland.

The constitution of the SFC in 1934 was an event that both consolidated and institutionalised the use and production of educational film in Scotland. In the politics of what has been termed a 'renaissance' of Scottish film culture (Petrie, 2000) and in the media education moment of the 1980s, the history of the SFC in general and Scottish educational film in particular were constructed as problematic. In *Scotland the Movie* (1996), former director of the SFC, David Bruce, described the relationship between Scottish Cinema and Scottish education as 'politically grey' and 'complex' (136). Bruce's compendium of film in Scotland was published in 1996, a year before the second devolution referendum in 1997 and the recasting of the SFC as Scottish Screen (SED, 1988). More than a decade later, in a chapter on the early history of film in *The Media in Scotland* (Blain et al., 2008), Bruce identifies a number of influences informing this period until fiction film became 'the main mode of Scottish Cinema'. Bruce made mention of documentary production, but no trace of educational film is evident. All reference to the production of educational film in Scotland had faded from 'grey' to invisible. However, if analysis of the work of educational film is scant in Scottish film histories, accounts of its contribution in histories of Scottish education are equally difficult to find.

Glasgow puts educational film to work

In the 1930s Glasgow Corporation's education officials were particularly successful in promoting the use of film, both inside and outside the classroom (Lebas, 2011). The development of a systematised service in Scotland created the space for Glasgow Corporation to raise its profile. Some of the Corporation's teachers and founding members of the Film Society of Glasgow (1929) and the newly appointed director of education for Glasgow (R. M. Allardyce), founded the Scottish Educational Cinema Society (SECS) in 1930.[5] The Chair of the Corporation's Education Committee, Charles Cleland, was SECS Honorary President. Charles Cleland had held a number of elected positions within the Corporation since 1891. He was also a member of the Commission on Educational and Cultural Films set up by the British Institute for Adult Education. Its report, *The Film in National Life* (Gott, 1932) was the impetus for establishing the British Film Institute in 1933. Cleland later became a Governor and acting chair of the BFI. Both Allardyce and Cleland were committed to the use of film for civic purposes. Importantly, Allardyce had considerable influence on the Scottish Education Department in the inter-war years, not least because 'In a country the size of Scotland, you cannot afford to ignore one fifth, which is Glasgow' (McPherson and Raab, 1988, 449).

The dual membership of committees across administrative jurisdictions enabled officials to practice navigating the line between forging a distinctive Scottish particularity at local level and the concern of the Scottish Office to maintain British uniformity. Scottish education's distinctiveness, according to Robert Anderson (2003) and David McCrone (2003), is a marker of national identity robustly defended against assimilation with England. Lindsay Paterson (1997) argues that this process of 'negotiating' autonomy from the UK required the practice of 'pragmatic nationalism', whereby devolved powers were conditional on the basis of sufficient but not excessive difference.

The *Glasgow Herald* reported the Corporation's early experiments with the 'teaching film'.[6] The availability of educational film up to this point had been limited to what was being produced in the United States and did not meet the needs of Scottish classrooms. Described as a 'didactic instrument' the educative or 'teaching' film, also termed 'scholastic',[7] had a different purpose to the looser category of educational film.[8] The teaching film was required to 'avoid cheap humour', use repetition, slow motion and 'continuous shots' (*Glasgow Herald*, 1931). By contrast, educational film, or the 'background film' (educative film foregrounded pedagogy) was 'material, narrative, scenic or descriptive' and held to be particularly valuable for 'cinema children' who 'showed greater understanding of the work done than those who had to rely only on other means'.[9] The work educational film performed for literacy development therefore linked explicitly with 'equal opportunities' (SFC and SEFA, 1940).[10] At that time, local education authorities were in the process of constructing a contemporary model of education that would be fit for an industrial twentieth century. The support of the emerging middle-classes for the provision of a universal public education system that widened access and increased participation was vital. The use of new film technologies and texts in Scotland's classrooms, therefore, was important to the myth of Scotland's 'democratic intellectualism' and, thus, a distinction that would frame Scottish education as different from that on offer elsewhere in the UK. Non-fiction film in general and educational film in particular, therefore, was put to work in pursuit of this objective.

The east coast rival to the Educational Cinema Society was formed in Edinburgh in 1933 (Barclay, 1993). The Scottish Educational Sight and Sound Association (SESSA) needed to position itself differently, and declared an interest in both sound and visual technologies in education. The west coast cousin had tried to persuade them to form an east coast branch of the Educational Cinema Society rather than form a separate organisation. There were substantive areas of disagreement between these two associations, however.[11] The Glasgow-based Educational Cinema Society opposed the use of sound film in the classroom on both technological and aesthetic grounds. For SECS, cinema was an emergent form, the potential of which may have been compromised by sound. Sound projectors were also more expensive and less accessible. The Edinburgh-based Sight and Sound Association, on the other hand, were opposed to the Educational Cinema Society's involvement in the making of educational films. SESSA were concerned that SECS members were paying more attention to making films than they were paying to the pedagogy of film. According to SESSA, making films was the province of the film trade alone. A tension between film-maker and educationist emerged in Edinburgh that was not apparent in Glasgow. The film critic, Forsyth Hardy, an associate and biographer of Grierson, was an influential member of the Edinburgh Film Guild and may have contributed to this tension. The first Films of Scotland Committee did not convene until 1938, and Hardy referred to this early period as 'the battle over control of educational film development'.[12]

In public discourse, while the 'teaching film' did the work of legitimising the use of film in the classroom, education researchers in Scotland were also interested in children's popular cultural tastes and preferences and the use of the 'background film' and the 'entertainment film'. Both Edinburgh and Glasgow city councils undertook research into children, young people and the cinema.[13] The Director of Education in Edinburgh, J. D. Frizzell, was also an influential figure in the administration of Scottish education. Allardyce had the ear of the Scottish Education Department, but Frizzell led the Association of Directors of Education. The Edinburgh study was part of a wider programme of social enquiry looking at children's attendance at the cinema in the United Kingdom (Smith, 2005).

The Glasgow study, on the other hand, underway at the same time, and described by the *Glasgow Herald* as 'An Aid to Backward Children',[14] focused on the potential of film for progressing learning. Other research, such as the Middlesex Experiment (Richards, 2010), had established the case for general interest or background films, but the Glasgow experiment was keen to understand 'the effect of using film regularly as an integral part of the teacher's stock-in-trade'.[15] The Edinburgh study legitimised children's popular cultural tastes and preferences, whilst the Glasgow study legitimised the pedagogy of film. School cinemas also screened popular 'entertainment' films for children; the first school in Glasgow to install a cinema was in 1931 in the Gorbals, an area with acute socio-economic challenges.[16] Teachers accompanying children to commercial cinemas for matinee performances during the school day were also encouraged, as was attendance at the matinee programmes on Saturdays.

A new industry: the construction of (just enough) difference

Following the emergence of the British Film Institute in 1933, the directors of education in Glasgow and Edinburgh, together with Charles Cleland, who would bring his experience of the BFI negotiations to bear, organised a conference of 'educational bodies, film societies and other organisations interested in the film in Scotland'.[17] For the educationists in particular, it was the 'heterogeneous combination of film societies',[18] rather than the trade, who gave the greatest concern. The invitations to sit on the initial organising committee, issued by the educationists, betray unease about the activities of the film societies in Scotland. The aim of the conference was to form a Scottish National Film Council. Cooperation between those interested in the educational, cultural, artistic, industrial and commercial possibilities of film was deemed preferable to the fracturing of Scottish interest. Agreement between the parties involved was struck on the basis that partnership with the Institute was financially desirable, but the extent of the Institute's cultural and educational influence in Scotland would need to be constrained. The main advantage of partnership arrangements with the Institute was 'to share in the more tangible of its assets which would be derived from English sources'[19] (although in the event, those assets were more imagined than real). What emerges subsequently is a Scottish National Film Council that, like Scottish education, was administratively devolved. The overriding desire for Scottish national autonomy brought the different interest groups together, acting as a galvanising force in a way not evident in the formation of the BFI. Establishing the Scottish Film Council as distinctive secured its administrative autonomy from the British Film Institute and enhanced the distinctiveness of Scottish education. The interests of the statutory sector were secured when the west coast Educational Cinema Society and the east coast Educational Sight and Sound Association merged to form a new professional association: the Scottish Educational Film Association (SEFA).

By 1938, SEFA had 5,000 members, calculated by Trevor Griffiths (2013) to constitute 18% of the teaching workforce. More significantly for policy discourse there was no equivalent English association. SEFA established an experimental filmmaking group that used colour filters, exposure meters and animation.[20] Teachers who did not have the time (or inclination) to make films themselves submitted treatments/scenarios for the filmmaking group to produce.[21] SEFA organised study circles, film weekends and summer schools, and held projector demonstrations in schools in Glasgow, where 1,000 teachers were reported to have attended, in just one week, for instruction in the use of projectors. ADES requested that SEFA's Film School be acknowledged as a qualification credential (Barclay, 1993).

In 1938, SEFA had also organised 32 matinees in 41 theatres for a total audience of 80,000 and put together age-appropriate programmes to help guide cinema programmers. SEFA had also instituted the Film Reviewing Scheme,[22] and it was noted that 'arrangements in England were to be brought into line'.[23] This involved 70 study groups and 1,000 teachers who developed a grading system for educational films. In 1938, Edinburgh's Director of Education became president of SEFA. In 1940, the Scottish Film Council and the Scottish Educational Film Association jointly authored a *Report by the Advisory Committee on the General Principles Governing the Production of Educational Films (With Lists of Subjects For Films)* published by the University of London Press Ltd.

By 1944, the director of education in Edinburgh asserted: 'the time is past when for realism one must go to the documentary and for drama to the popular film. Both schools of filmmaking are now reacting on one another'.[24] SEFA declared the cinema to be a respectable social activity at the same time as advocating its use for educational purposes in the classroom. Its members organised exhibitions and demonstrations of film technology and raised the profile of film amongst this new professional class, as well as the profile of the SFC in its early years.

Films of Scotland versus Educational Films of Scotland: Hardy wins the battle (and the SFC gets a bloody nose)

Importantly, SEFA was responsible for the significant improvement in the Scottish Council's finances, not least upon the opening of the Scottish Central Film Library in Glasgow in 1939. Russell Borland, a founding member of the Educational Cinema Society and the SFC's first employee, had encouraged amateur production groups to make local films that would not be viable commercially. Many of these were then made available through the Central Film Library.

Since its formation in 1934, this period of the Council's history illustrates the extent to which the interests of both the department and the Council had become inextricably linked. The National Committee for Visual Aids in Education was set up as a UK body in 1946. For Scotland, the option of seeking Scottish representation on the UK body was not sufficiently attractive because 'on questions of film production there is likely to be a divergence of view between Scotland and England, and experience suggests that the views of a Scottish minority might have little chance of materially influencing policy' (SED, 1950). The view that Scotland had made significant advances, and that SEFA was already doing the work proposed for the UK body, prompted the Scottish Education Department to fund the establishment of a Joint Production Committee (JPC) to be administered by the SFC and SEFA. In 1962 this would become Educational Films of Scotland (EFS).[25]

The JPC would 'deal with the production of films that might be sponsored by the government' (Barclay, 1993). Its creation as a source of government funding for the production of Scottish film was reported in the *Daily Record* in 1950; 'Quietly, without fuss, a minor Scottish film industry is under way with the production of short documentaries and interest films for school children'.[26] Meantime, films circulated by the Central Film Library during the war had worn out, and projectors were in short supply. The Library had been self-supporting from 1939 until 1949, but could not supply the increased demand following the war. The reputation of Scotland in the field had developed nationally and, with the establishment of the Edinburgh International Festival in 1947, it began to develop further afield. Keen to protect its jealously guarded asset, the Scottish Education Department continued to fund the Library's operational costs. By 1948 the department had agreed to provide the funding for 'additional assistance' to the work of the Library, enabling it to purchase new stock from British production companies and to oversee the work of the JPC.

However, in 1947, the Council lost Borland, its then director, to Gaumont British Instructional Films, and the search for his replacement was on. Concerns from the filmmaking community about the Council's relationship with the statutory sector re-emerged. Forsyth Hardy re-stated his objection to the dominance of educational film in the Council's activity. Such a policy had, according to the film society movement, been hijacked by the drive to produce and distribute educational film in Scotland. In light of the forthcoming Radcliffe Report, a change of emphasis was required. Eventually, this would result in increased funding for the Council by the Institute, and Hardy became the director of the re-convened Films of Scotland Committee from 1954 to 1974.

Although the council had effectively been operating as an educational institution until this point, it had not been constituted as such. Two significant and shared assets, the Central Film Library and the JPC, represented the vested interests of SEFA and the Film Council. Frizell, still director of education in Edinburgh and with considerable influence in the department, had positions in the Council, in SEFA, in SCFL and the JPC. The work of educational film had brought Scottish educational and cultural particularity to new audiences and represented a significant asset in the context of its constitutional relationship within the UK. In the same way, therefore, as Frizell managed the setting up of the Council in 1934, he managed the negotiation of the Council's transition to charitable status in 1950. The Film Library was appointed as the official agent for the distribution of films to Scottish schools, the operating costs to be met by the department, but as an asset and as a title, the Film Library was transferred to the Council. Frizell's influence continued to be key to the survival of both the Scottish Film Council's autonomy from the British Film Institute and the Scottish Education Department's international reputation until his retirement in 1961.

The emergence of the new culture and technology of film created a productive coalition of interest amongst educationists, the film trade and the new local government structures emerging in urban Scotland in the 1930s. Those alliances in pursuit of social change were particularly empowering in the cities of Glasgow and Edinburgh and enabled a fledgling national film agency to support the trade by facilitating the development of product, technology and audiences at a local level. The work educational film performed in the first half of the twentieth century in Scotland constituted film and cinema as public good and public service. Imagined by the British Film Institute (BFI) as a regional office to 'fill any vital gaps',[27] at the Scottish Film Council's (SFC) eighth Annual General Meeting in 1941, Oliver Bell, the director of the British Film Institute (BFI), claimed that 'in Scotland far more than in England the film was playing an ever increasing and useful part in the life of the community'.[28]

Between 1950 and 1974, however, the SFC struggled to channel the distinctiveness and utility of either Scottish film culture or Scottish education into a significant contribution towards changing technological, cultural, economic and political landscapes in the United Kingdom and Europe.[29] In 1974, the SFC was reconstituted under the umbrella of a new Scottish institution: the Scottish Council for Educational Technology (SCET). For Ronnie Macluskie, the director of the SFC and the Scottish Central Film Library (SCFL), this offered a number of new opportunities to address arguably more pressing concerns, but the development was viewed with disdain by the Scottish film-making community.

Throughout the 1970s in Scotland, questions of representation and accountability were emerging in political, economic, administrative and cultural domains. Such questions exposed the failure of administrative devolution to address the constitutional problematic of a 'stateless nation' (McCrone, 1992), particularly during a period of profound societal change. At this time, Scotland's institutions were failing to put its particularity to work *for* Scotland, and its license to devolved powers was thus put at risk.

Betwixt and between: the spaces and places for practising everyday distinctiveness

This chapter has not attempted to combine spatial and temporal signifiers to distil a national essence.[30] Instead, it has explored how analytical history (Tosh, 2006) makes more visible the process of negotiating everyday distinctiveness in the flows of power between nations, regions and cities through space and time. Scholars in the political and social sciences point to the manifest acceleration of support for political devolution in Scotland as an increasingly more viable solution to local economic, social and cultural issues than its administrative predecessor could provide.[31] The term itself did acquire more substantive conceptual value as the decade unfolded. However, a binocular lens that explicitly links media and education policy across the twentieth century in Scotland affords a better understanding of devolution as a cultural practice enacted in the politics of space and place.

The decision to separate media and communications from culture in the second 1998 devolution referendum settlement may not have been a wise decision in a constitutive moment (Hampton, 2005). The potential for social and political change lies in the distinctiveness of cultural practices enacted in the everyday conjunctions and disjunctions forged between spaces and places, and between jurisdictions, national institutions, local networks and policy arenas in a converged media environment. At the time of writing, the first 2014 independence referendum in Scotland returned a majority in support of the continuation of political devolution. Whether that will be judged to have been the 'least revolutionary' option remains to be seen, but as a solution to the problem of Scotland, its time may have been called.

Notes

1. For a polemical critique of representations of Scotland on screen, see McArthur, C. (ed.) (1982) *Scotch Reels: Scotland in Cinema & Television*. London: BFI and the debates that followed. Also see McIntyre, S. (1984, 1985) in *Screen*, vols 25:1 and 26:1 respectively. For a historical overview of film and television in Scotland, see Petrie, D. (2000) *Screening Scotland. An Extensive Research Guide to*

Scottish Cinema, and Murray, J. (2005) *That Thinking Feeling: A Research Guide to Scottish Cinema 1938–2004*. Edinburgh/Glasgow: Edinburgh College of Art/Scottish Screen. For documentary, a historical overview can be found in Blain, N. (1990) *A Scotland as Good as Any Other? Documentary Film 1937–82*, in Dick, E. (ed.) *From Limelight to Satellite: A Scottish Film Book*. Scottish Film Council and British Film Institute. An account of the formation of the Films of Scotland Committee is given in Butt, R. (1996) 'The Films of Scotland Documentaries: Cultural Formations and Institutional Constraints', *Media Education Journal*, No. 20, 25–28. Detailed analysis of the work of the Films of Scotland Committee can be found in Butt, R. (1996) 'History, Ethnography and the Nation' (see bibliography). Accounts of two particular documentary film makers can be found in McBain, J. and Cowle, K. (1997) *With an Eye to the Future: Donald Alexander and Budge Cooper – Documentary Film Makers*. Glasgow: Scottish Screen.

2. For work on 'becoming' an academic discipline see Goodson, I. (1981) 'Becoming an Academic Subject: Patterns of Explanation and Evolution', *British Journal of Sociology of Education*, Vol. 2, No. 2, 163–180.

3. SEFA. Educational Film Bulletin, June 1943. SSA: 1/5/223. National Library of Scotland.

4. SFC. Minutes of First General Meeting of the Scottish Film Council. September 1934. SSA: 1/5/250. National Library of Scotland.

5. *Glasgow Herald*. Films for the Schoolroom: New Scottish Society's Aims, 18 May 1931, p9c. Glasgow: Mitchell Library.

6. The Film in the Classroom, Glasgow Corporation Education Department, 1933. SSA 1/1/237.

7. SFC. Minutes of First General Meeting of the Scottish Film Council. September 1934. SSA: 1/5/250.

8. '"Educational" for the purposes of such a library [SCFL] should be interpreted in the broadest sense, and to some it would seem that one of the principal functions of the Scottish Central Library should be to build up a collection of films which illustrate the life and work and spirit of Scotland itself'. The Cinema And The Teacher: A Year's Progress. Norman Wilson. Source unknown. c1940. SSA. The difference between 'educative' and 'educational' broadcasting was described in the 1966 BBC report *Educational Television and Radio in Britain: A New Phase in Education*.

9. Glasgow Corporation Report 1931–1932. Mitchell Library.

10. See work in New Literacy Studies emerging in the 1990s in the United Kingdom for a more contemporary frame.

11. SESSA. File of correspondence. SSA: 1/10/28. National Library of Scotland.

12. H. Forsyth Hardy. Letter to R. B. Macluskie, 14 July 1976. SSA: 1 February 1995. National Library of Scotland.

13. Glasgow Corporation Education Department. *The Film in the Classroom*. 1933. Glasgow: The Corporation of Glasgow Education Department. Mackie, J. (1933) *The Edinburgh Cinema Enquiry*. Edinburgh: The Edinburgh Cinema Enquiry Committee.

14. *Glasgow Herald*. 'An Aid To Backward Children: Educational Value Proved', 16 December 1931, p7b. Glasgow: Mitchell Library.

15. *The Film in the Classroom*, Glasgow Corporation Education Department, 1933. SSA 1/1/237. National Library of Scotland.

16. *Glasgow Herald*. 'Glasgow School's Lead: Films for Educational Purposes', 28 May 1931, p7d. Glasgow: Mitchell Library.
17. *The Scotsman*. 'Scots Film Council: To Be Integral Part of British Institute: Autonomy Safeguard', June 1934. SSA: 1/1/237. National Library of Scotland.
18. Allardyce, R. M. Letter to East Lothian County Council, 22 June 1934. SSA: 1/1/237. National Library of Scotland.
19. *The Scotsman*. 'Scots Film Council: To Be Integral Part of British Institute: Autonomy Safeguard', June 1934. SSA: 1/1/237. National Library of Scotland.
20. SEFA. *Handbook of the Scottish Educational Film Association 1937–1938*. SSA: 1/5/162. National Library of Scotland.
21. SEFA. Minutes of the Scottish Educational Cinema Society. Glasgow Branch. April 1935 to April 1936. SSA: 1/5/8. National Library of Scotland.
22. SFC. Minutes of the Seventh Meeting. 4 September 1935. SSA:1/1/250. National Library of Scotland.
23. SFC. Minutes of the Education Panel. 31 January 1936. SSA: 1/1/247. National Library of Scotland.
24. Frizell, J. B. The Cinema As a Social Force. SSA: 1/5/155-160. National Library of Scotland.
25. Educational Films of Scotland would provide much needed work for Scottish film production crews, for example, Bill Forsyth in 1964.
26. *Daily Record*. 'The Schools Will Be in Luck', 15 December 1950, p4. SSA: 1/1/60. National Library of Scotland.
27. The Scotsman. 'Scots Film Council: To Be Integral Part of British Institute: Autonomy Safeguard', June 1934. SSA: 1/1/237. National Library of Scotland.
28. SFC. Minutes of the Eighth Annual General Meeting, 29 October 1941. SSA: 1/1/251. National Library of Scotland.
29. See Powell, M. (2010) 'The Origins and Development of Media Education in Scotland'. Stirling: University of Stirling, Unpublished PhD.
30. Scholars point to a shift away from a concern with the essence of national representations. See Neely, S. (2005) 'Scotland, Heritage and Devolving British Cinema', *Screen*, 46(2), 241–245 and Neely, S. (2008) Contemporary Scottish Cinema. In N. Blain and D. Hutchison (eds) *The Media in Scotland*. Edinburgh: Edinburgh University Press.
31. See Cameron (2010), Mitchell (2009), Paterson, L. (1994) *The Autonomy of Modern Scotland*. Edinburgh: Edinburgh University Press; Midwinter, Keating and Mitchell (1991) *Politics and Public Policy in Scotland*. London: MacMillan; and Kellas, J. G. (1975) *The Scottish Political System: Second Edition*. Cambridge: Cambridge University Press. Also see Bechhofer, F. and McCrone, D. (eds) (2009) *National Identity, Nationalism and Constitutional Change*. London: Palgrave Macmillan; and McCrone (1992), in McCrone, Kendrick and Straw (eds) (1989) *The Making of Scotland: Nation, Culture and Social Change*. Edinburgh: Edinburgh University Press.

References

Acland, C. and Wasson, H. (2011) *Useful Cinema* (London: Duke University Press).

Anderson, R. (2003) The History of Scottish Education. In T. G. K. Bryce and W. M. Humes (eds) *Scottish Education: Second Edition, Post-Devolution* (Edinburgh: Edinburgh University Press).

Archer, J. (2014) 'Commentary: Unlocking Potential, Embracing Ambition', *Cultural Trends*, Vol. 23, No. 3, 193–196.

Barclay, J. B. (1993) *The Film in Scottish Schools* (Edinburgh: Private Publication).

Billig, M. (1995) *Banal Nationalism* (London: Sage).

Blain, N. (2009) The Scottish Dimension in Film and Television. In K. Veitch (ed.) *Scottish Life and Society: Transport and Communications. A Compendium of Scottish Ethnology*, Volume 8 (Edinburgh: Birlin) (Imprint: John Donald in association with the European Ethnological Research Centre), 768–792.

Blain, N. and Hutchison, D. (eds) (2008) *The Media in Scotland* (Edinburgh: Edinburgh University Press).

Bolas, T. (2009) *Screen Education: From Film Appreciation to Media Studies* (Bristol: Intellect).

Bruce, D. (1996) *Scotland the Movie* (Edinburgh: Polygon).

Bruce, D. (2008) The History of Film and Cinema. In N. Blain and D. Hutchison (eds) *The Media in Scotland* (Edinburgh: Edinburgh University Press), 71–86.

Butt, R. (1996) 'History, Ethnography and the Nation: The Films of Scotland Documentaries', Edinburgh, Queen Margaret University, Unpublished PhD thesis.

Butt, R. (1997) Critique of the Film: Wealth of a Nation. In J. McBain and K. Cowle (eds) *'With an Eye to the Future': Donald Alexander and Budge Cooper – Documentary Film Makers* (Glasgow: Scottish Screen), 17–22.

Cameron, E. A. (2010) *Impaled Upon a Thistle: Scotland since 1880* (Edinburgh: Edinburgh University Press).

Campbell, R. H. (1979) 'The Scottish Office and the Special Areas in the 1930s', *The Historical Journal*, Vol. 22, No. 1, 167–183.

Druick, Z. (2011) UNESCO, Film and Education: Mediating Postwar Paradigms of Communication. In C. Acland and H. Wasson (eds) *Useful Cinema* (London: Duke University Press), 81–102.

Elliot, W. (1932) 'The Scottish Heritage in Politics' in His Grace the Duke of Atholl et al., *A Scotsman's Heritage* (London: Alexander MacLehose & Co.), 53–65.

Elsaesser, T. (2009) The Place of Non-Fiction Film in Contemporary Media. In V. Hediger and P. Vondereau (eds) *Films That Work: Industrial Film and the Productivity of Media* (Amsterdam: Amsterdam University Press), 19–34.

Gardiner, M. (2004) *The Cultural Roots of British Devolution* (Edinburgh: Edinburgh University Press).

Glasgow Herald (1931) Glasgow Schools Lead: Films for Educational Purposes, 28 May 1931, 7d.

Gott, B. S. (1932) *The Film in National Life: Report of an Enquiry Conducted by the Commission on Educational and Cultural Films into the Service Which the Cinematograph May Render to Education and Social Progress* (London: George Allen & Unwin Ltd).

Grierson, J. (1990) Eyes of Democracy. Occasional Papers No. 3 (University of Stirling: The John Grierson Archive).

Grieveson, L. and Wasson, H. (eds) (2008) *Inventing Film Studies* (London: Duke University Press).

Griffiths, T. (2013) *The Cinema and Cinema-Going in Scotland, 1896–1950* (Edinburgh: Edinburgh University Press).

Hampton, M. (2005) 'Review Essay: Media Studies and the Mainstreaming of Media History', *Media History*, Vol. 11, No. 3, 239–246.

Hediger, V. and Vondereau, P. (eds) (2009) *Films That Work: Industrial Film and the Productivity of Media* (Amsterdam: Amsterdam University Press).

Humes, W. (1986) *The Leadership Class in Scottish Education* (Edinburgh: John Donald Publishers Ltd).

Humes, W. (2000) State: The Governance of Scottish Education 1872–2000. In H. Holmes (ed.) *Scottish Life and Society: Education. A Compendium of Scottish Ethnology*, Volume 11 (East Lothian: Tuckwell Press), 84–105.

Hunter, A. (1990) Bill Forsyth: The Imperfect Anarchist. In E. Dick (ed.) *From Limelight to Satellite: A Scottish Film Book* (London: Scottish Film Council and British Film Institute), 151–162.

Hutchison, I. G. C. (2001) *Scottish Politics in the Twentieth Century* (Basingstoke: Palgrave Macmillan).

Lebas, E. (2011) *Forgotten Futures: British Municipal Cinema 1920–1980* (London: Black Dog Publishing).

McCrone, D. (1992) *Understanding Scotland: The Sociology of a Nation* (London: Routledge).

McCrone, D. (2003) Culture, Nationalism and Scottish Education: Homogeneity and Diversity. In T. G. K. Bryce and W. M. Humes (eds) *Scottish Education: Second Edition, Post-Devolution* (Edinburgh: Edinburgh University Press), 239–249.

McDowell, W. H. (1992) *The History of BBC Broadcasting in Scotland 1923–1983* (Edinburgh: Edinburgh University Press).

McPherson, A. and Raab, C. (1988) *Governing Education: A Sociology of Policy since 1945* (Edinburgh: Edinburgh University Press).

Miller, W. (1985) Politics in the Scottish City 1832–1982. In G. Gordon (ed.) *Perspectives of the Scottish City* (Aberdeen: Aberdeen University Press), 180–211.

Mitchell, J. (2009) *Devolution in the UK* (Manchester: Manchester University Press).

Mitchell, J. (1989) 'The Gilmour Report on Scottish Central Administration', *Juridical Review*, Vol. 34, No. 2, 173–188.

Murray, J. (2011) *Studies in the History and Culture of Scotland. Volume 4: Discomfort and Joy: The Cinema of Bill Forsyth* (Bern: Peter Lang AG).

Paterson, L. (1997) Policy-making in Scottish Education: A Case of Pragmatic Nationalism. In M. Clark and P. Munn (eds) *Education in Scotland: From Pre-schools to Secondary* (London: Routledge), 138–155.

Petrie, D. (2000) *Screening Scotland* (London: BFI Publishing).

Richards, J. (2010) *The Age of The Dream Palace: Cinema and Society in 1930s Britain* (London: IB Tauris).

Robertson, J. (2006) *The Testament of Gideon Mack* (London: Penguin).

Robertson, J. (2011) *And the Land Lay Still* (London: Penguin).

Robertson, J. (2014) *The News Where You Are*, https://www.youtube.com/watch?v=ZhL57cjN8xY.

Robertson, R. (1992) *Globalisation: Social Theory and Global Culture* (London: Sage).

Runcis, M. and Sandin, B. (2010) *Neither Fish Nor Fowl: Educational Broadcasting in Sweden 1930–2000* (Lund: Nordic Academic Press).

Schlesinger, P. (2008) Communications Policy. In N. Blain and D. Hutchison (eds) *The Media in Scotland* (Edinburgh: Edinburgh University Press), 35–51.

SED (1950) *Visual and Aural Aids: A Report of the Advisory Council on Education in Scotland* (Edinburgh: HMSO).

SED (1988) *Scottish Film Council: Report of Policy Review and Implementation Plan* (Edinburgh: Scottish Education Department).

SFC and SEFA (1940) *Report by the Advisory Committee on the General Principles Governing the Production of Educational Films (With Lists of Subjects for Films)* (London: University of London Press Ltd).

Smith, S. J. (2005) *Children, Cinema and Censorship: From Dracula to the Dead End Kids* (London: I. B. Tauris).

Sweeney, M. (2008) Broadcasting: From Birth to Devolution...and Beyond. In N. Blain and D. Hutchison (eds) *The Media in Scotland* (Edinburgh: Edinburgh University Press), 87–103.

Tosh, J. (2006) *The Pursuit of History: Aims, Methods and New Directions in the Study of Modern History*. Fourth Edition with Sean Lang (Harlow: Pearson Longman).

Zimmerman, Y. (2009) 'What Hollywood Is to America, the Corporate Film Is to Switzerland': Remarks on Industrial Film as Utility Film. In V. Hediger and P. Vondereau (eds) *Films That Work: Industrial Film and the Productivity of Media* (Amsterdam: Amsterdam University Press), 101–117.

14
Impossible Unity? Representing Internal Diversity in Post-Devolution Wales

Simon Gwyn Roberts

The gradual transformation of British politics through the processes of devolution has been a 'work in progress' since Scotland and Wales voted in favour in the 1997 referenda (in the case of Wales, for the creation of an assembly with devolved powers). Yet these major constitutional changes have not been matched by a realignment of the UK media (Cushion, Lewis and Groves, 2009). In this context, the particular deficiencies of the Welsh media have become increasingly politically relevant in recent years, with their shortcomings (in terms of informing the public about devolved politics) regularly highlighted by politicians, academics and journalists. A 2014 BBC poll, for example, found that fewer than half of Welsh respondents knew the NHS was devolved, which Thomas (2014) suggests results from a Welsh media landscape in which 'huge numbers of people' get their news from London-based newspapers. The contrast with Scotland is marked: while Scottish devolution provided a pretext for London-based national newspapers to reduce news content from all three devolved nations, it simultaneously provided a catalyst for the further development of an independent media policy in Scotland itself. In interviews, London journalists argued that, since Scotland had its own parliament, it had its 'own news' and its own newspapers to carry it (Denver, 2002). More recently, Macwhirter (2014) rued the financial decline of the Scottish newspaper industry, suggesting that this makes it harder for the Scottish media to perform their traditional role as 'cultural curators' and a forum for informed debate. However, sentiments like this merely highlight the more acute media deficiency in Wales, because the Welsh media are considerably more fragmented than their Scottish equivalent, with no real tradition of a Welsh national press to draw on, and the majority of newspaper readers dependent on London-based publications. Around 1,760,000 people (from a total population of 3 million) read newspapers with 'virtually no Welsh content' (Davies, 2008).

In this context, it is perhaps not surprising that the *internal* complexities of Welsh culture and identity are inadequately treated and represented by the media in the widest sense. This chapter concerns itself not with the much-debated democratic deficit faced in a post-devolution Wales poorly served by the news media, although that deficit remains a relevant political context for a related accusation: that the media *within* Wales has failed to accurately represent areas historically marginalised by the dominant national narrative of the newly devolved entity. In this context the fragmented political and cultural geography of Wales is particularly notable, because commercial imperatives have led to a reductive portrayal of the internal diversity in Welsh culture and politics.

This chapter takes a holistic approach to the media's representation and construction of politically and culturally marginalised areas of Wales, focusing on the ways in which the local print media and televised drama have attempted to represent marginality in one Welsh county, Flintshire. It will assess the form and content of media portrayal and reflect on the implications for cultural identity and civic engagement. The chapter focuses exclusively on representation post-devolution. Indeed, the marginalisation of the county is encapsulated by the fact that any holistic treatment of media representation is necessarily limited to the local print media and to a single series of televised drama, because, at least in the contemporary sense, there have been very few attempts to represent or discuss Flintshire as a coherent geographical or cultural unit. The impact and reception of the representation of the area in the only contemporary televised drama to be set in the county are assessed in parallel with the local print media – with the chapter attempting to situate the post-devolution representational strategy of Flintshire newspapers in a wider historical context.

Although dated and arguably somewhat simplistic, Denis Balsom's 'Three Wales Model' (1985) remains the best-known attempt to encapsulate the cultural and political fragmentation of the nation. Balsom argued that Welsh voting patterns, alongside related issues of media use, cultural allegiance and language, could best be illustrated by dividing the country into three broad units: the 'Welsh Wales' of the South Wales valleys (Welsh-identifying, Labour-voting, but predominantly English-speaking); the Welsh-speaking, 'culturally' Welsh 'Fro Gymraeg' of the North-West and West; and 'British Wales' (parts of Pembrokeshire and areas adjacent to the English border). The 'British Wales' tag remains relevant post-devolution as shorthand for the problems of encouraging a sense of Welsh identity, and democratic participation in those areas of the country in which voters have historically prioritised their British identity. It acts as a useful point of departure, despite the fact that it masks nuances that this article will attempt to draw out by discussing the micro-region that perhaps best represents the archetype of 'British Wales'. Flintshire, in the north-eastern corner of Wales, exhibits the cultural and political features of 'British Wales', particularly the county's urbanised and industrialised eastern fringe along the English border. The area's marginalisation from the rest of Wales is rooted in its geographical location, particularly its proximity to the border and the large urban areas of north-west England.

That border has always been less defined than its Scottish equivalent. Indeed, the north-eastern fringes of Wales are characterised by a notable physical banality: instead of mountains or uninhabited moorland, the Anglo-Welsh border here is suburban and semi-industrial in character, passing through housing estates and industrial complexes on the edge of the English border town of Chester. Yet despite this ill-defined geographic and cultural context, which mitigates against simple 'storytelling' and lacks a strong and coherent identity narrative, the reality of devolution forces engagement, with the border now more politically significant than at any time in modern history. Although predating UK devolution, Bhabha's 'continuous narrative of national progress' (1990: 1) has a particular resonance in the Welsh context given the nascent status of the devolution project, particularly in relation to what he calls the ambivalent margin of the nation space, which may contest claims to cultural supremacy. Shields (1991: 3) argues that the marginal status of peripheral areas often arises from being seen to represent 'the other pole to a great cultural centre'. In the case of Flintshire and other areas along the Welsh border, the 'great cultural centre' is best viewed as plural: the two stereotypical narratives of post- and pre-devolution Wales are industrial South Wales (Balsom's 'Welsh Wales') and rural, Welsh-speaking west and north-west Wales (Balsom's 'Fro Gymraeg'). These have long been the dominant national images of Wales, for both internal and external consumption, and devolution merely heightened a tendency for the media to accentuate them.

Nairn (2005: 138) highlighted this from his (Scottish) perspective when he argued that the 'post-imperial return' of Wales has, in contrast to Scotland, resembled much more closely the typical ethno-linguistic trajectory of repressed nationhood, where cultural mobilisation is directed towards nation building. Therefore, the powerful imagery of 'Welsh Wales' and 'Y Fro Gymraeg' come to represent Welshness through their strong sense of identity, in much the same way as the North of England's landscape and culture balances the imagery of the pastoral 'South' as the two most immediately recognisable English identities. Rawnsley (2000: 3) argues that the North of England is a reified landscape that encapsulates various rhetorical interpretations of the past and the present. No other region, he says, has such an intensified 'sense of place'. Flintshire, of course, also borders the North of England: a third reified 'pole' that further acts to emphasise its own liminality.

In this sense, the geographic marginality of Flintshire is paralleled by its peripheral social status, placed on the edge of what Shields (1991) describes as 'cultural systems of space' in which places are ranked relative to each other. This ranking, or perceived worth, is of critical importance in terms of media definition, particularly if one sees devolution as an ongoing project of nation building, in which notions of identity construction are crucial drivers. Nairn's (2005) 'ethno-linguistic trajectory' is therefore given shape by a cultural mobilisation that most obviously expresses itself through media construction and representation. Writing two decades before devolution, Welsh historian G. A. Williams (1979: 192) seemed to anticipate the work of Benedict Anderson (1983) when attempting to articulate the Welsh experience of identity definition: 'Nations are not born, they are made. Nations do not grow like a tree, they are manufactured'. Indeed, in the context of Welsh devolution – a work in progress – Anderson's work, which sees the print media as central to processes of identity construction, assumes a renewed significance. Phillips (2005) points to the role these new media-driven narratives and histories have in the creation, and recreation, of national identity – particularly in the Welsh context. Where two strong narratives compete for legitimacy as the nations of the United Kingdom attempt to assert themselves post-devolution, the news media have an obvious, defining role. They constitute the arena in which the processes of devolution are transmitted to the voting public – but areas marginalised by these processes are then inevitably compromised in terms of representation and, subsequently, political engagement.

In a broader context, Bhabha (1990: 1) referenced the 'impossible unity of the nation as a symbolic force' despite attempts by nationalist discourses to produce the idea of the nation as a continuous narrative of national progress. In a post-devolution environment, that 'continuous narrative' assumes a particular significance in the wider media. Yet, Chris Williams has argued (2005) that a post-devolution Wales that does not take proper account of the ambiguities and complexities that render the national project problematic will generate a future embraced by only a minority of its citizens. An approach that emphasises the plurality of cultures, and the multiplicity of landscapes with which those cultures are associated, are clearly preferable given the social and cultural fragmentation of Wales. Such a position rejects a unitary view of culture as the product of an elite, but asserts the value of popular culture (wherever that originates and whatever it represents), both in its own terms and as an implicit challenge to dominant values (Jackson, 1989: 1). Celebrations of that 'popular culture' are common in the contemporary Welsh media, but revolve around the two dominant narratives and, when applied to Flintshire, present an uncomfortable challenge to the evolving sense of Welsh nationhood, as the prevailing 'culture' often owes more to adjacent areas of urban north-west England. As Jackson points out (1989: 3), in the wider British context dominant cultural institutions exert a subtle and pervasive influence on the lives of many thousands of people, establishing a 'preferred reading' of local and national circumstances. In Wales, such processes are inherently media-based and have been shaped by assumptions about the relationship between TV, linguistic decline and nation building, which were 'the bedrock on which debates about TV in Wales rested in the 1960s and 1970s...shared by the critics of the BBC and ITV as well as their defenders' (Barlow et al., 2005: 147).

These assumptions became (and remain) an 'unshakeable dogma' (Barlow et al., 2005) in Welsh cultural life, with television occupying an unusually central position in Welsh politics and culture as a result. Any reading of Welsh media representation therefore must take television as its point of departure. In such a context, it is perhaps unsurprising that intensively Anglicised regions of Wales have been marginalised by a media keen to halt linguistic decline and to engage in 'nation building'. In terms of Welsh-language televised drama, for example, the wider region of north-east Wales has been almost entirely ignored by both Welsh- and English-language productions in favour of the two dominant national narratives of Balsom's 'Welsh Wales' and 'Fro Gymraeg'. McElroy (2008: 247) has outlined the ways in which Welsh-language television subsequently developed its 'conversation' with the Welsh-speaking community of Wales, 'in the process sometimes closing down the routes to belonging among others in Wales'. For Gruffydd Jones (2007: 203), the absence of contemporary television drama set in the north-east means that a 'whole repertoire of linguistic dialects are hardly ever heard' on Welsh language television: 'The images of the north of Wales are almost exclusively those of the western part

(Fro Gymraeg) and the reality of life in the industrialised towns in the north-east or in the rich farmland of its inland vales including the experience of living on the border with England are rarely examined' (Gruffydd Jones, 2007: 204).

Representing marginality: TV in Flintshire

The single exception to this rather dismal rule was the production of *Mostyn Fflint n'aye* in 2004. This, the first contemporary Welsh language drama to be set in north-east Wales, was made by a Cardiff company for the Welsh-language channel S4C and traded in what some saw as stereotypical depictions of Flintshire as a kind of pseudo-Liverpudlian backwater. The series featured a range of rather crude storylines revolving around the anti-hero of the title, 'a washed-up cabaret singer who's been thrown out by his wife'. It played with notions of the vulgarity of the coastal resorts and towns of the area, and emphasised this by featuring cameos from 'end-of-the-pier' comedy acts (dated, yet distinctively northern English) like Cannon and Ball. For example, the first episode saw Mostyn buying an adult magazine before visiting his old home to give his son a Christmas present. Subsequently, 'things go horribly wrong' when the vicar steals the magazine and Mostyn sees his estranged wife out with her new boyfriend. Episode two continues in the same vein, as Mostyn's wife attempts to start up a new life with her lover after 'confessing all to her husband' (*Radio Times*, 2004).

A novelty in the history of Welsh broadcasting, the series arguably presented an opportunity to rework established notions about this Anglicised and marginalised region of Wales. It was written by playwright Siôn Eirian, who was responsible for several high-profile and critically acclaimed Welsh language films and series in the 1990s, notably *Gadael Lenin* (1994) and *A Mind to Kill* (1994–2004). Eirian was part of a small group of writers and actors who formed Theatr Bara Caws in the 1970s: this was a deliberate attempt to broaden the appeal of Welsh drama away from the Welsh-speaking elite. The concept was to take Welsh-language theatre into different communities. Although not a Theatr Bara Caws production, *Mostyn Fflint* is best viewed in that context; a deliberate attempt to represent the unrepresented, meaning that a certain reliance on stereotypes is perhaps inevitable and even desirable. Anthony Cohen (1987: 7) has argued that 'group stories' are often used to further the symbolic construction of community by differentiating insiders from outsiders who do not share the knowledge of such stereotypical imagery. For Cohen, a knowing audience's membership in a 'community of belief' is thus confirmed. In *Mostyn Fflint n'aye*, this opportunity was arguably missed, although the guiding principle was indeed a comedic interpretation of the region's distinctiveness. The title of the series makes clear reference to its regional rationale, combining two industrial, working-class towns on the Dee estuary (simultaneously providing the lead character with his name), with a local distinctively *Anglo*-Welsh dialect term (roughly equating to the contemporary English 'innit'). The series generated a mixed reception among Welsh-speaking viewers. Some were encouraged by the novelty of a series set in Flintshire, although even the positive viewpoints tended to be equivocal and often critical of a perceived reductive portrayal of the wider region. This comment, for example, appeared on a Welsh-language Web forum (Maes E.com, 2004) about Welsh-language drama, translated for the purposes of this chapter:

> It's about time the people of the north-east got some recognition in the Welsh media. But I have an issue with fair recognition. Is it OK for the series to be filmed in Cardiff, a place very different to Flintshire, without creating jobs in the area [the northeast]. This seems a pity. And I wonder why Denbighshire [also in northeast Wales], where the language is very strong, is never covered by Welsh TV – what about the people of the Vale of Clwyd? I'm sure it's because it's easier to put on a Cofi [Caernarfon] or Gwynedd [that is, Balsom's 'Fro Gymraeg'] accent rather than a Vale of Clwyd [north-east] one. (Maes E.com, 2004)

Other contributors argued that 'it's nice to see a production about Flintshire from S4C…. about fooking time!' The expletive, deliberately rendered in a comic northern English accent, is another reflection of Flintshire's reputation and 'space myth' in the rest of Wales (as with the Anglo-Welsh 'n'aye' expression of the title and the cameos from northern English comedians). Others emphasised the 'regional' angle, pointing out its similarity with the long-running BBC comedy, *Last of the Summer Wine*, set in Yorkshire, whilst emphasising that *Mostyn Fflint* was a considerably more vulgar take on regional identity. Interestingly, several contributors took a positive view of the 'toilet humour' and regional slang, arguing that it illustrated the richness of contemporary Welsh as an organic, living language: 'It's nice to hear the language of the border dealing with a 'lovable loser' who drinks too much and buys porn' (Maes E.com, 2004). In general, however, *Mostyn Fflint n'aye* was not received particularly well by the Welsh-speaking audience, and it is notable that it did not run to a second series: 'Please say you're joking...I wish S4C wouldn't waste money producing programmes like this' (Maes E.com, 2004). Others were cynical about the motives and 'tokenism' of a series professing to depict north-east Wales (although it should be noted that their accusations were statistically inaccurate) suggesting that it largely dealt in the reproduction of stereotypes: 'The way to get your script commissioned by S4C is to write about, and use the accent of, areas where less than 3% of the population speak Welsh...I take it that S4C want to "extend their appeal" even though everyone in Flintshire watches Channel 4' (Maes E.com, 2004).

The reasons for, and origins of, such reductive representations are not hard to discern. Barlow, Mitchell and O'Malley (2005: 148) point to the fear, among Welsh-language campaigners in the 1960s, of the impact of TV, 'seeing beneath its dominant Englishness a real threat to identity'. They suggest that the 'unshakeable dogma' that emerged in the politicised climate of the 1960s was that Wales had a distinct culture and as such should have a distinctive TV service. This attracted the attention of high-profile figures from across the political spectrum. TV was specifically linked to linguistic decline and, therefore, there was a clear conception that it should have a role in the promotion of Welsh national identity. McElroy (2008: 233) argues that in the political discourse of contemporary Wales, language, culture and national identity are intertwined to the extent that the establishment of S4C can be viewed as 'born out of political protest', a testament to the capacity of individuals to work in cultural groups to contest their own cultural erosion and develop a media institution specifically to address this. Indeed, in 1980 Gwynfor Evans threatened to go on a hunger strike if the then Conservative government did not establish a Welsh language TV channel. Evans was the former president of the Welsh nationalist party, Plaid Cymru, and his threat attracted a great deal of publicity. A dedicated Welsh-language television channel, S4C, was later established and Welsh-language television has since played an unusually important role in Welsh cultural life. Given this, and its associated and well-documented role in Nairn's (2005) post-devolution 'nation building', it is not surprising that accurate representations of marginalised areas of Wales, especially Anglicised (and largely English-speaking) ones, would not be prioritised. Eirian (the writer of *Mostyn Fflint*) grew up in the Amman Valley in South Wales, and, while this need not preclude accurate representation, Flintshire's marginalisation from the cultural centres of Welsh life is encapsulated by the fact that no production companies are based in the county.

Yet this does present a notable paradox, because the cultural meaning of 'place' is a central concept for anybody working in minority languages, and in this sense it is particularly notable that Welsh-language television fiction cannot claim to reflect the whole of Wales, with the north-east the most obvious 'missing' region (Gruffydd Jones, 2007). This seems a considerable oversight, given that Gruffydd Jones (2007: 208) also observes that televisual Wales is generally constructed as a 'community of communities' and does not follow the same capital-centric tradition of television that is often associated with British and other state broadcasters. Indeed, Welsh-language TV replicates structures found in other Welsh-language institutions – the Eisteddfod, for example – which have a very deliberate decentralist approach (the Eisteddfod is an annual mobile cultural festival that is always staged in different parts of Wales). This cannot be separated from the wider post-devolution political picture if we apply to televisual representation Shields's assertion (1991: 222) that a mechanism of shared myths reinforces a process of spatialising people, placing them as citizens within a community and a nation territory. It is equally pertinent to point out that in Flintshire there has never been an attempt to represent the region through the medium of English television drama: given that only 12.7% of the population can speak Welsh – compared to a Welsh national average of 18.56%, rising to 64.3% in Gwynedd, the heart of Y Fro Cymraeg in north-west Wales (ONS, 2011). Challenges to the legitimacy of devoting so much time and money to a separate Welsh-language TV channel, when there had never been an English-language equivalent, continue to provoke debate in Wales (Barlow et al., 2005: 150). In 2014, for example, BBC Director General Tony Hall said English-language TV in Wales, from all broadcasters, had been 'eroded' for a decade, adding that it should try to improve the way it reflects national life in Wales (BBC, 2014). Indeed, the focus on cultural identity, which characterised the fight for S4C is, for some, linked to the rejection of industrialisation and its culture: 'In this rejection the cultural life of the English-speaking working classes, by far the majority in Welsh society for most of the C20, was sidelined' (Barlow et al., 2005: 150). From the perspective of north-east Wales, however, such a view should be seen in relative terms, as Balsom's 'Welsh Wales' (the industrialised South Wales valleys) has, by comparison, received a great deal of attention in terms of televised drama and the wider media. This lack of representation is particularly important in relation to TV, because the medium (to return to an earlier point) is embedded to an unusual extent in Welsh political and cultural life, partly because of its perceived links with language and associated questions of national identity.

Border narratives in the print media

The primacy of television and televised drama in debates about the Welsh media meant that the print press received less attention until the post-devolution 'democratic deficit' rose to political prominence. The respective priorities given to both forms of media were arguably accentuated by the fact that the local newspaper press is, in theory, more agile in terms of its ability to adapt to, and represent, a changing political paradigm. In a more general critique of the Welsh media's approach to representation, Barlow, Mitchell and O'Malley (2005: 22) argue that the media (in that general sense) fails to adequately represent the diversity of Wales, leading to a sense of cultural deficit. This feeling of cultural deficit is rarely related to intensively Anglicised areas of Wales, like Flintshire, yet it remains pertinent to residents' relationship with the news media in particular. In terms of media representation and portrayal, mainstream newspapers along the Anglo-Welsh border have sometimes engaged with the post-devolution reality, and their constructions of this new paradigm have, at times, encouraged border residents to consider their position and identity in unfamiliar ways. The established tradition of cross-border media along the Anglo-Welsh border superficially suggests a more nuanced and sophisticated attempt to represent and articulate the peculiarities and concerns of the region as it negotiates and adapts to the post-devolution paradigm. Newspapers always reflect, and simultaneously construct, a geographical and cultural reality. The Anglo-Welsh border is often urban in character and in some areas suburbs spill across what, pre-devolution, was merely an 'administrative' boundary. Inevitably, these areas are characterised by a certain ambiguity of identity and, as a partial consequence, newspaper remits and readerships often transcend the border.

An innate conservatism characterises the popular press in the United Kingdom, however. For Conboy (2002: 183), the popular press relies on narratives that invariably draw on established genres and scripts. As a result, when local newspapers such as the *Chester Chronicle* and *Evening Leader* (both with long-established target audiences on both sides of the Anglo-Welsh border) find themselves at the heart of a rapidly evolving political paradigm (i.e., devolution), they remain subtle purveyors of normative assumptions to a mass audience. However, they have a key role in narrating political change regardless of the commercially driven approach they take to constructing and articulating what Conboy calls the 'popular experience' of that change. Despite this, the regional and local press have often been disregarded when studies are made of cultural representation in the United Kingdom. This seems a curious oversight, as Berry (2008: 105) suggests that cultural specificity can be seen as a 'survival strategy' for local newspapers, which are produced to monopolise their market. He argues that the county and region of Gwent, in South-East Wales, is 'nothing more than a figment of imagination and no more than an idea, which is used and exploited by the *South Wales Argus* to maintain a monopolistic position in a fictionalised Gwent region. In order to achieve this, the paper invokes history, tradition, nostalgia, culture and identity from a Gwent perspective and within a Welsh context'. Such a strategy has clear echoes of Hobsbawm's and Ranger's (1993) notion of 'invented traditions'. For Berry, local newspapers build up an image of community partly through market research and partly based on historical judgments concerning culture, identity, mythology and tradition.

Shields (1991: 162) cites the existence of a similar series of 'space-myths' in a rather wider context, adding that such myths characterise media representation in many parts of the world. For the news media in particular, this kind of discourse approaches the status of 'mythology' because they marshal so many place-images that can be appropriated as symbols of specific nationalistic discourse. Shields cites the space-myth of the Canadian 'True North Strong and Free' as an example that attempts to reconcile regional viewpoints. There is, in short, an oppositional spatialisation whereby southerners construe the North as counterbalance to the civilised world of the southern cities yet, simultaneously, the core of their own, personal Canadian identity. For Schama (1996: 9), even the landscapes (like the North American wilderness) that we suppose to be most free of our culture may turn out, on closer inspection, to be its product. Therefore a cultural identity is built from both sides of the equation: defining a dichotomy and then reappropriating elements of that dichotomy. There are wider implications to this kind of dualism: indeed, in the English context the 'North' acts as a similar 'wild' pastoral foil to other, collectively romanticised images of the South (Shields, 1991: 207), another space-myth. Rawnsley (2000: 16) cites Priestley's *English Journey* of 1934, in which he 'takes the reader through a very un-English terrain, with the open countryside around Huddersfield 'nearly as wild and cold as Greenland'. The spaces and places of northern England have been an important tradition in British realist drama (*A Taste of Honey*, 1961; *This Sporting Life*, 1963) as well as long-running series like *Coronation Street* (1960–), and these space-myths find echoes in the North–South rhetoric common in UK newspapers and the wider media. Rawnsley

(2000: 13) points out the 'irony' of the BBC's role in interpreting and projecting the regional distinctiveness of the North of England, given its founding rationale as uniting the United Kingdom through a 'conscious social purpose'.

This representational dualism is intriguing when viewed from the Welsh context. If the two dominant national narratives of 'Welsh Wales' and 'Y Fro Cymraeg' represent a similar dualism in Wales, symbolising the two varieties of stereotypical 'Welshness', the fact that these categories can then be negotiated by Berry's (2008) 'fictionalised Gwent region' (which fits squarely into Balsom's 'British Wales') is notable. It might, therefore, be expected that Flintshire and other areas of the north-east would be portrayed in similar 'mythical' and constructed terms. Yet, this is rarely the case, despite what Berry cites as the commercial advantages to mobilising this kind of distinctive localism, which often deliberately stresses difference from the dominant narrative. A border identity is occasionally referenced and exploited by the local newspapers in Flintshire, but – as with Gwent – the area can only be seen as further marginalised in the sense that it does not occupy part of the national 'imagination' or national narrative. Instead, it is (as the comments relating to *Mostyn Fflint* suggest) often interpreted and represented by the wider media in ways that echo Priestley's 'un-English terrain': a profoundly 'un-Welsh' landscape and culture, characterised by flat fields, suburban housing, small industry, semi-Liverpudlian accents, and football. Schama (1996: 14) suggests that our entire landscape tradition is built from a rich deposit of myths, memories and obsessions. Yet these are hard to discern in the Flintshire borderlands. The tropes of Welsh nationhood are missing, and the opportunity to explore the post-devolution implications of the often-nuanced identity politics of the region, are therefore frequently lost.

This is curious, not just from Berry's (2008) perspective, which stresses the commercial imperative to 'localism', but also when local news media representation is set in a broader historical context. In the late nineteenth century, for example, cross-border newspapers tasked with serving both north-east Wales and the English border town of Chester – for example, the still-extant *Chester Chronicle* – conceived of their role as articulating the views of a distinctive cross-border community. They were aware of journalistic innovations being introduced by London-based newspapers at the time (e.g., sensationalism) and used them to gain a commercial advantage in a highly competitive, and crowded, local newspaper market (Roberts, 2014). At this time, the politicised language used by the leader columns of local newspapers (a recent innovation in the 1860s) chimed with the increased vibrancy and appeal of the local press. Lee (1976) argues that newspapers were seen as agents of social control, partly because of high circulation, but also because of their willingness to attempt to shape opinion. In a climate of political tension, such as Wales experienced during the industrial unrest in the late nineteenth century, it was almost inevitable that local newspapers would take the opportunity to attempt to influence the views of its audience by using new journalistic techniques, which addressed readers directly and personally, often on geographically specific grounds.

An editorial passage from the 11 June 1869 edition of the *Flintshire Observer*, in which the newspaper gives its verdict on the implications of that summer's Mold Riots (which resulted in the deaths of four people) illustrates the willingness of the local press to emphasise localism and its own credentials as the only Flintshire-specific newspaper to express its views on the unrest. This also revealed a wider truth about the commercial relationship between newspapers and their audiences: the importance of clearly identifying the local audience's values, and directly articulating those values via opinion pieces, is commercially successful and has profound political implications.

> Alas! for Flintshire. Hitherto quiet and peaceable. Law and order, if we may make use of a homely phrase, are now 'turned upside down'. The Mold tragedy for the present is over, seven rioters have been committed for trial. The verdict of the jury has been recorded as 'justifiable homicide', the press of England approves of the verdict and Mr Bruce the Hon Sec endorses it. (*Flintshire Observer*, 11 June 1869: 2)

The Conservative-supporting *Chester Chronicle*, also tasked with appealing to a cross-border audience, illustrates a more reactionary representation of the unrest. Its response to the Mold Riots makes the national dimension clear, alongside an implicit link with Irish republicanism, as if in acknowledgement of the potential political consequences of industrial unrest in Wales:

> Unhappily for the good name of the little neighbouring town of Mold and to the disgrace of the Welsh colliers concerned, the proceedings were followed by scenes of almost unparalleled violence and bloodshed. Great as the concession was on the part of the prosecution the Welsh colliers seem to have been infuriated with the thought of two of their comrades being carried to prison. They were blinded by passion.

As the day advanced, rumours of the wildest nature were prevalent, one, to which considerable prominence was given, being that the colliers would march to Flint and attack the prison with picks to release the prisoners. Rather improbably, seeing that they were in safe keeping in Chester gaol and that Chester would be prepared to give the riotous colliers as warm a reception as they did the fenians.

We have to ask who were primarily in fault for these calamities and what will be their probable effect? The answer is one of a painful kind. We are met at the outset with the patent fact that for a considerable time the miners of this half governed district have been in a state, as far as the rule of law is concerned, of semi-civilisation. (*Chester Chronicle*, 5 June 1869, 1)

Victorian newspapers attempted to use their considerable influence to negotiate a newly emerging political dynamic in which issues of national and class-based political identity came to the fore. Moreover, in north-east Wales, these issues were lent more significance by geography, in the sense that the coalfields of Flintshire are much closer to the English border than their counterparts in South Wales and north-west Wales; both newspapers studied were, hence, tasked with negotiating that geographical reality in terms of how they appealed to readers who were far from being a monocultural or monolingual bloc.

Most local newspapers in Flintshire still have a 'cross-border' remit and scope, in that they are tasked with appealing to, and selling to, residents on both sides of the Anglo-Welsh border. Diverse sources of regional and local news are clearly essential to the functioning of a democracy (Franklin, 1998; McNair, 2000) and, given the limitations of the Welsh national media, that function post-devolution is of crucial importance in Flintshire. The specificity of the local press is notable in this context, and potentially provides a source of competitive advantage in a climate of declining circulations. This is not to say that reflecting or celebrating the region's ambiguity is written into the editorial guidelines of any cross-border media operation, merely that the target audience has to be addressed in the context of devolution. Targeting a cross-border audience, though, is now fraught with a new form of journalistic difficulty as a result of the new cultural paradigm in which political changes have forced a reconfiguration of national identities from British to English and Welsh. If borders traditionally are places that facilitate the identification of difference and of congruence, then this particular border's new reality raises interesting questions in terms of how the local and the regional press choose to address their audiences. Because, despite the ill-defined geographical and cultural context, with mixed identities and a complex set of national allegiances, the reality of devolution forces political engagement for the residents in the area. On the Welsh side, residents find themselves subject to an increasing number of distinctive changes enacted by the Assembly government. In the case of the *Leader*, for example, a paper tasked with appealing to a cross-border audience with three different editions (Wrexham and Flintshire in Wales, and Chester in England), an editorial decision has been taken to retain a cross-border feel by blending stories from both sides of the border. In November 2013, for example, the local news split was 44% 'English', 50% Welsh, with the small number of remaining stories 'cross-border' in tone. In general, however, it is hard to avoid concluding that placing an emphasis on the parochial (Conboy's conservatism) may be commercially astute in the sense that doing so is inexpensive and attracts a steady but small audience, but that the local news media simultaneously miss an obvious post-devolution opportunity to articulate broader regional concerns.

Conclusion

For Powell (2007), the idea of 'region' is categorically different from other conceptualisations of place – such as home, community, city, state and nation – in as much as region must refer, not to a specific site but to a larger network of sites. Region is always a relational term, he argues, because a region can never be an isolated space, withdrawn from larger cultural forces and processes: 'When we talk about a region, we are talking not about a stable, boundaried, autonomous place but about a cultural history, the cumulative, generative effect of the interplay among the various, competing definitions of that region' (2007: 5). Despite regionalism traditionally being used to define and isolate networks of places and spaces, Powell suggests that it can provide a rhetorical basis for making claims about how spaces and places are connected to conceptually broader patterns of meaning. For Carter et al. (1993: ix) the logic of modernisation and globalisation frequently led to representations of localised identities being deemed regressive, and to undermining the old allegiances of place and community. But the burgeoning of identity politics and civic forms of nationalism reveals a clear resistance to such universalising strategies (and this may encompass specific attempts to decentralise, such as devolution).

The context of devolution emphasises the media's role in communicating and prioritising cultural narratives and the associated wider issues of representing marginalised regions that fail to conform to the most coherent of those narratives. Devolution is a project, a work in progress and, as a result, the strongest national narratives inevitably dominate media discourse and representation. Nairn (2005) and others suggest a solution by arguing for civic nationalism of the kind that might begin to address the political disconnect experienced in Flintshire, where that disconnect is expressed in a reluctance to engage with devolved politics (only 35.5% of the Alyn and Deeside electorate turned out in the 2007 Assembly elections, although this was a substantial increase on the 25.9% turn-out in 2003). Similarly, the *Parekh Report* (2000) sought to reinvent Britain as a community of communities, as if in acknowledgement of Shields's (1991: 4) argument that places on the margins expose the central role of what he calls 'spatialisation' in cultures and nation states. This, says Shields, is not merely a matter of myth. Rather, each case history highlights the centrality of spatial conceptions and imagery in daily life. These images and stereotypes, an imaginary geography of places and spaces, have social impacts that are (as in the electoral statistics outlined above) empirically specifiable. This often underpins political rhetoric and, for Shields, the collective weight of these 'discourses on space' can be linked with the symbolic creation of a sense of community and with nationalism (Anderson, 1983). The importance of the media's political role in post-devolution nation building is clear in this context, and again emphasises the logic of prioritising dominant, and sometimes idealised, national narratives (e.g., Welsh Wales, Fro Gymraeg) at the expense of more nuanced and compromised narratives (e.g., British Wales, particularly Flintshire).

Media-driven identity construction can take time. Huggins (2000: 137) argues that in much of North-East England, both local and subregional identities had to be constructed almost from scratch, and that the media was central to this. It took some time, he says, for communities to have a clear sense of their own identities, partly because they were new, formed by in-migration to work in new industries. Flintshire, too, experienced significant levels of in-migration to the new steel industry over the course of the early and mid-twentieth century. Yet the Anglo-Welsh border has no tradition of emphasising its marginality or celebrating its ambiguity: in contrast to, for instance, Berwick-upon-Tweed on the Anglo-Scottish border. It would, however, be one possible solution to the post-devolution paradigm in terms of political identities and civic engagement, and would chime with both Parekh's 'community of communities' manifesto and Nairn's call for civic nationalism. And, as this chapter suggests, there have been recent attempts to articulate a nuanced border identity in both the Welsh broadcast media and local newspapers – echoing Berry's (2008) observation that such a representational strategy also has commercial benefits in terms of targeting a geographically and culturally specific audience. Indeed, the question of whether local newspapers or the wider broadcast media can successfully articulate regional interests in the post-devolution climate, as opposed to an endless recycling of fragmented local issues, might come to define their commercial future given the economic pressures such titles are facing in a post-Web world.

References

Anderson, B. (1983) *Imagined Communities* (London: Verso).

Balsom, D. (1985). The Three Wales Model. In J. Osmond (ed.) *The National Question Again: Welsh Political Identity in the 1980s* (Llandysul: Gomer).

Barlow, D., Michell, P. and O'Malley, T. (2005). *The Media in Wales: Voices of a small nation* (Cardiff: University of Wales Press).

BBC (2014) http://www.bbc.co.uk/news/uk-wales-26853353 (Accessed May 2014).

Berry, D. (2008) 'The *South Wales Argus* and Cultural Representations of Gwent', *Journalism Studies*, Vol. 9, No. 1, 105–116.

Bhabha, H. (1990) *Nation and Narration* (New York: Routledge).

Carter, E., Donald, J. and Squires, J. (1993) *Space and Place: Theories of Identity and Location* (London: Lawrence and Wishart).

Cohen, A. (1987) *Whalsay: Symbol Segment and Boundary in a Shetland Island Community* (Manchester: Manchester University Press).

Conboy, M. (2002) *The Press and Popular Culture* (London: Sage).

Cushion, S., Lewis, J. and Groves, C. (2009) 'Reflecting the Four Nations?' *Journalism Studies*, Vol. 10, No. 5, 655–671.

Davies, G. (2008) *Media in Wales: Serving Public Values?* (Cardiff: Institute of Welsh Affairs).

Denver, D. (2002) 'Voting in the 1997 Scottish and Welsh Devolution Referendums: Information, Interests and Opinions', *European Journal of Political Research*, Vol. 41, No. 6, 827–843.

Gruffydd Jones, E. H. (2007). The Territory of Television: S4C and the Representation of the 'Whole of Wales'. In M. Cormack and N. Hourigan (eds) *Minority Language Media: Concepts, Critiques and Case Studies* (Clevedon: Multilingual Matters), 188–212.

Hobsbawm, E. and Ranger, T. (1993). *The Invention of Tradition* (Cambridge: Cambridge University Press).

Huggins, M. (2000). Sport and the Social Construction of Identity in North-East England, 1800–1914. In N. Kirk (ed.) *Northern Identities: Historical Interpretations of 'The North' and 'Northernness'* (Aldershot: Ashgate), 132–162.

Jackson, P. (1989) *Maps of Meaning* (London: Routledge).

Impossible Unity? 247

Lee, A. (1976) *The Origins of the Popular Press, 1855–1914* (London: Croom Helm).

Macwhirter, I. (2014) 'Democracy in the Dark: The Decline of the Scottish Press and How to Keep the Lights On', *The Saltire Society, Saltire Series*, Vol. 5.

Maes E.com (2004) http://maes-e.com/viewtopic.php?f=8&t=8667 (Accessed March 2014).

McElroy, R. (2008) Indigenous Minority-Language Media: S4C, Cultural Identity, and the Welsh-language Televisual Community. In P. Wilson and M. Stewart (eds) *Global Indigenous Media: Cultures, Poetics and Politics* (Durham, NC: Duke University Press), 232–249.

Nairn, T. and James, P. (2005) *Global Matrix: Nationalism, Globalism and State-Terrorism* (London: Pluto Press).

ONS (2011) http://www.ons.gov.uk/ons/rel/census/2011-census/key-statistics-for-unitary-authorities-in-wales (Accessed January 2014).

Parekh, B. (2000) *The Future of Multi-Ethnic Britain* (London: Profile Books).

Phillips, R. (2005) Island Stories and Border Crossings: School History and the Discursive Creation of National Identity in Wales. In J. Aaron and C. Williams (eds) *Postcolonial Wales* (Cardiff: University of Wales Press), 39–54.

Powell, D. R. (2007) *Critical Regionalism: Connecting Politics and Culture in the American Landscape* (Chapel Hill, NC: University of North Carolina Press).

Radio Times (2004) http://www.radiotimes.com/programme/ckmwxv/mostyn-fflint-n-aye/episodeguide/series-1.

Rawnsley, S. (2000) Constructing 'The North': Space and a Sense of Place. In N. Kirk (ed.) *Northern Identities: Historical Interpretations of 'The North' and 'Northernness'* (Aldershot: Ashgate), 3–22.

Roberts, S. G. (2014) '"Half a Loaf Is Better Than None": The Framing of Political and National Identity in Welsh Border Newspapers in the Aftermath of the Mold Riots, 1869', *Journal of Historical Pragmatics*, Vol. 15, No. 2, 187–206.

Schama, S. (1996) *Landscape and Memory* (London: Fontana Press).

Shields, R. (1991) *Places on the Margin: Alternative Geographies of Modernity* (London: Routledge).

Thomas, H. (2014) Measuring Devolution: How Have Media Covered Wales? BBC News, 13 June, http://www.bbc.co.uk/news/uk-wales-27804380 (accessed June 2014).

Williams, C. (2005) Problematizing Wales. In J. Aaron and C. Williams (eds) *Postcolonial Wales* (Cardiff: University of Wales Press).

Williams, G. A. (1979). When Was Wales? In S. Woolf (ed.) *Nationalism in Europe* (London: Routledge).

Index

Printed and bound by CPI Group (UK) Ltd, Croydon, CR0 4YY